LAUGHING AND W
EARLY MODERN ……………

Did Shakespeare's original audiences weep? Equally, while it seems obvious that they must have laughed at plays performed in early modern theatres, can we say anything about what their laughter sounded like, about when it occurred, and about how, culturally, it was interpreted? Related to both of these problems of audience behaviour is that of the stage representation of laughing, and weeping, both actions performed with astonishing frequency in early modern drama. Each action is associated with a complex set of non-verbal noises, gestures, and cultural overtones, and each is linked to audience behaviour through one of the axioms of Renaissance dramatic theory: that weeping and laughter on stage cause, respectively, weeping and laughter in the audience.

This book is a study of laughter and weeping in English theatres, broadly defined, from around 1550 until their closure in 1642. It is concerned both with the representation of these actions on the stage, and with what can be reconstructed about the laughter and weeping of theatrical audiences themselves, arguing that both actions have a peculiar importance in defining the early modern theatrical experience.

Matthew Steggle is Reader in English at Sheffield Hallam University, UK.

General Editor's Preface
Helen Ostovich, McMaster University

Performance assumes a string of creative, analytical, and collaborative acts that, in defiance of theatrical ephemerality, live on through records, manuscripts, and printed books. The monographs and essay collections in this series offer original research which addresses theatre histories and performance histories in the context of the sixteenth and seventeenth century life. Of especial interest are studies in which women's activities are a central feature of discussion as financial or technical supporters (patrons, musicians, dancers, seamstresses, wigmakers, or 'gatherers'), if not authors or performers per se. Welcome too are critiques of early modern drama that not only take into account the production values of the plays, but also speculate on how intellectual advances or popular culture affect the theatre.

The series logo, selected by my colleague Mary V. Silcox, derives from Thomas Combe's duodecimo volume, *The Theater of Fine Devices* (London, 1592), Emblem VI, sig. B. The emblem of four masks has a verse which makes claims for the increasing complexity of early modern experience, a complexity that makes interpretation difficult. Hence the corresponding perhaps uneasy rise in sophistication:

> Masks will be more hereafter in request,
> And grow more deare than they did heretofore.

No longer simply signs of performance 'in play and jest', the mask has become the 'double face' worn 'in earnest' even by 'the best' of people, in order to manipulate or profit from the world around them. The books stamped with this design attempt to understand the complications of performance produced on stage and interpreted by the audience, whose experiences outside the theatre may reflect the emblem's argument:

> Most men do use some colour'd shift
> For to conceal their craftie drift.

Centuries after their first presentations, the possible performance choices and meanings they engender still stir the imaginations of actors, audiences, and readers of early plays. The products of scholarly creativity in this series, I hope, will also stir imaginations to new ways of thinking about performance.

Laughing and Weeping in Early Modern Theatres

MATTHEW STEGGLE
Sheffield Hallam University, UK

Routledge
Taylor & Francis Group

LONDON AND NEW YORK

First published 2007 by Ashgate Publishing

Published 2016 by Routledge
2 Park Square, Milton Park, Abingdon, Oxfordshire OX14 4RN
Third Avenue, New York, NY 10017, USA

First issued in paperback 2016

Routledge is an imprint of the Taylor & Francis Group, an informa business

British Library Cataloguing in Publication Data
Steggle, Matthew
  Laughing and weeping in early modern theatres. – (Studies in performance and early modern drama) 1. English drama – Early modern and Elizabethan, 1500–1600 – History and criticism 2. Laughter in literature 3. Crying in literature
  I. Title
  822.3'09353

Library of Congress Cataloging-in-Publication Data
Steggle, Matthew.
  Laughing and weeping in early modern theatres / by Matthew Steggle.
     p. cm. – (Studies in performance and early modern drama)
  Includes bibliographical references (p.   ).
  ISBN 978-0-7546-5702-6 (alk. paper)
  1. English drama – Early modern and Elizabethan, 1500–1600 – History and criticism.
2. Laughter in literature. 3. Crying in literature. I. Title.

  PR658.L37S74 2007
  822.309'353–dc22

                                                                                2007001196

ISBN 13: 978-1-138-24940-0 (pbk)
ISBN 13: 978-0-7546-5702-6 (hbk)

For Ian Roth

Contents

List of Figures

Abbreviations and Procedures

Unless otherwise stated, early modern printed texts are cited from facsimiles in the database *Early English Books Online*, http://eebo.chadwyck.com. In the case of early modern printed plays, the texts used are referred to in brief form within the chapters, and the reader is directed to the Bibliography for a fuller citation of the text including details such as publisher and place of publication. Shakespeare is cited from the Bevington *Complete Works*, but when the quotation features "ha", "ho", or related interjections, reference is also made to an appropriate early text to confirm the spelling used there. Jonson is cited from the edition of Herford, Simpson and Simpson, abbreviated to H&S. Texts are cited in old-spelling, with contractions silently expanded. In citing early modern plays, two changes are made for the sake of clarity: speech-prefixes are expanded, standardised and capitalised, and stage directions are consistently italicised.

When making quantitative statements, this book makes use of the "English Drama" collection within the Proquest database *Literature On-Line*, http://lion.chadwyck.co.uk, to create a working corpus of English drama, and within that selects only those texts classified by *LION* as first performed between the dates 1550 and 1642. At the time of writing, this corpus consisted of 745 texts. To work solely on the collection of texts used here, users of *LION* must select "individual collections" and then "English drama". Quotations found by searching *LION* have been rechecked against and referenced from an appropriate edition, usually an *EEBO* facsimile. In the case of quantitative statements about stage directions in this corpus, this study relies on the metadata in *LION*'s markup to identify stage directions. The corpus work makes no claims to be comprehensive, but rather to offer a report on a large and indicative sample of early modern drama.

References to the *Oxford Dictionary of National Biography* and to the *Oxford English Dictionary* are, implicitly, to the online editions as they stood in June 2006. References to websites are to those websites as they stood at the same date.

Acknowledgements

This project was completed during a sabbatical funded by the HEFCE Promising Researcher Scheme, and administered by Sheffield Hallam University. I am grateful to both institutions for their support. Thanks also to the staff of the university libraries in which I have worked, in particular those at Sheffield Hallam, Sheffield, Nottingham and Leeds; and to the staff of the British Library.

Thanks are due to scholars who have generously shared their expertise, including Matthew C. Hansen; Matthew Woodcock; Bill Lloyd, for advice on *Greene's Tu Quoque*; Peter Happé, for finding weeping audiences in medieval France; Lucy Munro, for finding laughing audiences at university tragedies; and Tiffany Stern, for sharing her work on *Orlando Furioso*. Emily Yossarian, of Proquest, provided one vital piece of technical help. Part of Chapter 6 is based on a paper written for Martin Butler's seminar "Ben Jonson: New Directions", which took place at the 2006 annual conference of the Shakespeare Association of America, and I am grateful to all those who took part in that seminar for their feedback, especially Martin Butler, Heather James, Ian Munro, Joseph Navitsky, Helen Ostovich and Julie Sanders. I owe especial debts of thanks to colleagues at Sheffield Hallam, including Steve Earnshaw, Ian Baker, Chris Hopkins, Tom Rutter and Annaliese Connolly; to the community of postgraduate students working in Renaissance studies there; and to Lisa Hopkins, whose inspirational work has created that community, and who has been a friend and guide throughout this project. Thanks to my family, and thanks, above all, to Clare, who has put up both with the laughing and with the weeping.

This piece of writing is dedicated to Ian Roth, whose encouragement over many years has meant a lot to me, and I hope that he will judge it with his usual generosity.

Introduction

This book is a study of laughter and weeping in English theatres, broadly defined, from around 1550 until their closure in 1642. It is concerned both with the representation of these actions on the stage, and with what can be reconstructed about the laughter and weeping of theatrical audiences themselves, and it argues that in a study of the former lie some of our best clues to the latter.

In many ways, laughter and weeping are iconically central to our ideas of what drama *does*, and perhaps particularly of what classic drama does. The masks of Comedy and Tragedy, respectively laughing and weeping, have a pedigree which goes back to the classical world, and are emblematic of the supposedly timeless qualities of theatre from Greek tragedy, to the Elizabethans, to the present day. Non-linguistic, or rather at the edge of language, laughter and weeping seem to be transhistorical absolutes which fitly emblematise the idea that drama deals in fundamental, universal human truths. Thus, Elizabeth Barrett Browning praises Shakespeare's "eyes sublime/ With tears and laughter for all time". In a similar, but more audience-centred, formulation, Terence Hawkes offers a sardonic summary of ahistorical constructions of Shakespeare, central to which is the belief that he still "makes us laugh and cry like billy-oh" in the same way as he made his early audiences do.[1]

That phrase "for all time", of course, is open to attack. In particular, as one recent collection of essays has argued, even emotions have cultural histories. In the pre-Cartesian world of the early modern, according to the editors of that collection, passions are not perceived as internal objects or bodily states, so much as complex vehicles which "characterize the macrocosm's shifting interaction with a continuously changing microcosm".[2] And as this study will argue, theatrical laughter and weeping, like the problematic emotions of which they are problematic signs, can also be studied diachronically as a set of changing cultural conventions. Information on the stage performance of tears and laughter can be gained from a wide range of texts, most of all from playtexts themselves, which notate that performance in ways varying from ekphrastic description to variants of the line "ha ha ha". Equally, a wide range of early modern texts bear on the question of audience behaviour, and the norms around audience weeping and laughter. This study will examine those references. Furthermore, it will argue, there is an intimate relationship between, on the one hand, stage laughter and weeping, and, on the other, audience laughter and weeping.

---

1   Terence Hawkes, "Introduction", 10–11, in Hawkes (ed.), *Alternative Shakespeares Volume 2* (London: Routledge, 1996).

2   Gail Kern Paster, Katherine Rowe and Mary Floyd-Wilson (eds), *Reading the Early Modern Passions: Essays in the Cultural History of Emotion* (Philadelphia: University of Pennsylvania Press, 2004), qtn from 18.

Some of the co-ordinates for the project come from the current flourishing of historicised performance studies in all forms. In recent years, much scholarly work has been done reconstructing the early modern theatre in greater detail than before. London's Shakespeare's Globe Theatre is the most obvious flagship of this initiative, but the activity has not been limited to recovering the physical environment of the playhouse. An interest in the cultural environment of early modern theatre can also be seen in recent scholarly attention to the reconstruction of the economics of theatres; of acting styles; of rehearsal practices; of the social composition of theatre audiences; and in a shift towards studies of sets of plays based not on a single common authorship but on the repertories of particular theatrical companies. What Tiffany Stern has termed the "stage-to-page" field within this area has developed a better picture of the relationship between printed text and performance.[3] This study aims to contribute to that field by historicising the equivalent norms around both stage convention and audience behaviour concerning laughing and weeping in the best detail possible.

One cogent reference point for this is recent work in "acoustic approaches" to early modern literature, in the form of studies such as Bruce Smith's *The Acoustic World of Early Modern England*, which aims to interpret early modern drama not just as a verbal but also as an acoustic artefact.[4] Smith is not just interested in the words spoken on the early modern stage, but in the noises made there. Such an approach does not merely pay attention to the obvious sound-makers of the Shakespearean stage – the trumpets, cannons and lutes – but to sound effects produced by everything from the incidental clanking of stage weapons to the rustling of gowns. Smith writes of the early modern theatre:

> Theaters as instruments for the production and reception of sound ask to be thought about in different ways than the theaters as frames for the mounting and viewing of spectacle ... let us inspect the instrument itself before we attempt to inventory the range of sounds, first artificial, then human, that could be played on – and within – the largest, airiest, loudest, subtlest sound-making device fabricated by the culture of early modern England.[5]

---

3   See, for instance, Andrew Gurr, *Playgoing in Shakespeare's London*, 3rd edn (Cambridge: Cambridge University Press, 2004); Tiffany Stern, *Rehearsal from Shakespeare to Sheridan* (Oxford: Clarendon Press, 2000); Tiffany Stern, *Making Shakespeare: From Stage to Page* (London: Routledge, 2005), with fuller bibliography; for an exemplary study of stage practice using corpus-based statistics, see Mariko Ichikawa, *Shakespearean Entrances* (Basingstoke: Palgrave Macmillan, 2002); on repertory-based work, see Lucy Munro, *Children of the Queen's Revels: A Jacobean Theatre Repertory* (Cambridge: Cambridge University Press, 2005).

4   Bruce R. Smith, *The Acoustic World of Early Modern England: Attending to the O-factor* (Chicago: University of Chicago Press, 1999), and subsequent work including, for example, Matthew Steggle (ed.), *Listening to the Early Modern, Early Modern Literary Studies* 7:1/Special Issue 8 (2001), at http://purl.org/emls/07-1/07-1toc.htm; Wes Folkerth, *The Sound of Shakespeare* (London: Routledge, 2002).

5   Smith, *Acoustic World*, 207–8.

If, as Smith argues, early modern drama can indeed be considered in almost symphonic terms, then the various noises made by characters onstage laughing and weeping are, one might say, instruments within that orchestra. The audience, too, have their role as important contributors to the symphony. Andrew Gurr speaks for the general consensus of theatre historians when he argues that the audience was "an active participant" in the early modern theatre, and quotes, for instance, Drayton's *Idea*, Sonnet 47,

> With Showts and Claps at ev'ry little pawse,
> When the proud Round on ev'ry side hath rung,
> Sadly I sit, unmov'd with th' Applause...

as evidence for early modern theatregoers' highly demonstrative responses to the plays they watched and listened to. Indeed, as Drayton's words also suggest, that auditory intervention, which in this case, takes the particular form of "th'applause", is itself perceived as, usually, a cause of further emotional affect in its own right.[6] The noises made by the audience, loud enough in Drayton's poem to make the whole building resonate, are elements within the acoustic environment of the early modern theatre, and are also among the airs that can be played on Smith's sound-making device.

The noises made by the audience? It is easy to imagine audience laughter as an acoustic intervention in the world of the theatre, but harder to imagine an audience making an equivalent sound through the noise of weeping; nor am I proposing that early modern audiences routinely wept as noisily and openly as they are imagined to do, for instance, in the film *Shakespeare in Love* (1998). However, an audience moved towards tears, hushed and attentive, does make an acoustic impact by the depth of its silence. Early modern accounts of laughing and of weeping see them both as a syndrome with degrees of effect, not as an on–off state: so mere smiling or mere "change of countenance" are, in a sense, mild manifestations of laughing or of weeping. Audience weeping, for the purposes of this study, need not always be imagined in terms of audible sobbing, but of an equally audible lack of other noise, a change in the acoustic texture in the theatre.

This book begins, then, with a chapter which reviews early modern constructions of weeping and laughter, looking at the syndrome of actions and sounds associated with each in early modern medical and religious discourse. Then, it moves to the stage itself. Laughter and weeping both occur remarkably often in early modern drama, with a frequency, indeed, which can only effectively be explored using the new generation of electronic corpora. Chapter 2, for instance, traces over 800 occurrences in drama of the period of the phrase "ha ha ha", which, although inserted into dialogue, almost always functions in effect as an implied stage direction – actors do not speak the words "ha ha ha", they perform an action. Chapter 2 offers an

---

6 Gurr, *Playgoing*, 259; Drayton, obviously, is talking particularly about the effect of the applause on him as the writer of the play in question, but the point of the sonnet is that the theatre is an emotionally charged arena.

overview of the different orthographies of laughter used in the drama of the period, and explores the gestural vocabulary that is associated with this strange and specific instruction to the Renaissance actor. As for weeping, it is required in over 100 explicit stage directions from the period; in over 150 implied stage directions of the form "these ... tears"; and in a large number of examples cued by other forms of implicit stage direction. Chapter 3 considers the various components of gesture and noise associated with this frequent stage image, and also observes the status of weeping as an activity on the edge of language. Tears, on the Renaissance stage, are almost utterances, since, as Leucippus says in Beaumont and Fletcher's *Cupid's Revenge*, "you see my teares deliuer / My meaning to you".[7]

Given their sheer frequency, onstage laughter and weeping are clearly worthy of study. But one of the central arguments of this book invests them with particular importance, proposing that, as a rule, stage laughter anticipates and shapes audience laughter, and stage weeping anticipates and shapes audience weeping. Therefore, it will be argued, onstage laughter and weeping can provide not a totally reliable, but a powerful index to the reaction playwrights expected from their early audience. In assessing questions of tone in early modern drama, the presence of onstage laughing or weeping is potentially a useful litmus test. The first step in making such an argument is to collect together evidence around early modern audience laughter and weeping. This is the project of Chapters 4 and 5 of the study.

Types of evidence here include references within plays; references in the paratexts to plays, such as Prefaces and commendatory poems; and "eye-witness" accounts of many types, all complicated and compromised to some extent by the circumstances of their preservation in textual form. Chapters 4 and 5 look to make some sense of these accounts, arguing that a historicised sense of the norms around early modern audience laughter and weeping is particularly desirable given the current move towards performance criticism, in which the reactions of modern audiences are used to construct readings of early modern plays. The historicised accounts offered here may serve as a corrective, and perhaps also as a guide, to such reconstructive archaeology.

In the second part of the book, Chapters 6, 7 and 8 consider particular aspects of early modern theatre in the light of ideas developed in Chapters 1 to 5. Chapter 6 examines in more detail the poetics of Lyly and Jonson, both of whom, famously, express reservations about audience laughter at their comedies. Chapter 7 discusses in detail one of the thorniest questions of recent performance criticism, the phenomenon of "horrid laughter" – is it true that audiences would be expected to laugh during Renaissance tragedies, and can anything be said about what they might laugh at there? Finally, Chapter 8 moves on to the greatest of early modern theatre professionals. It offers a reading of Shakespeare's theatre of sympathy, suggesting ways in which some of Shakespeare's plays use the conventions of laughing and

---

7   Beaumont and Fletcher, *Cupid's Revenge* (1615), f. 4r.

weeping outlined in the earlier chapters within a theatre in which these conventions are of central importance.

Crucial to this project, then, is the widespread Renaissance observation that both outside and inside the theatre, laughter and weeping are contagious. This idea is of course by no means unique to the early modern. A particularly eloquent metaphor is used by the theorist Jean-François Marmontel, describing the theatre of eighteenth-century France:

> Imagine five hundred mirrors sending to one another the light that they reflect, or five hundred echoes of the same sound: this is the image of a public moved by the ridiculous or pathetic. It is there most especially that the example is contagious and powerful. One laughs first at the impression that the risible object makes, one receives in the same way the direct impression that a touching object makes; but what is more, one laughs at laughing, one cries as well at crying; and the effect of these repeated emotions goes very often to the point of convulsive laughter or to suffocating pain. Now, it is especially among the people, those without seats, that this kind of electricity is sudden, strong, and rapid.[8]

Marmontel's imagery speaks to the terms of this project particularly clearly, in that it identifies two stages within a theatrical audience's response: firstly, a response to the stimulus itself, and secondarily, an iterative effect of response to others' responses, whether in the form of laughter or in the form of weeping. Marmontel's concern is mainly with how laughter (or weeping) propagates through a theatre audience, figured in both visual and auditory terms.

Furthermore, the ideas that Marmontel expresses can be parallelled from the early modern. For instance, Sir Kenelm Digby's treatise on the weapon-salve, best known now perhaps for its appearance in Umberto Eco's *Island of the Day Before*, contains a discussion of the mystery of forces acting at a distance. Among these forces, Digby argues, are laughter and weeping, both of which have a mysterious contagious power:

> If one come perchance to converse with persons that are subject to excesse of laughter, one can hardly forbear laughing, although one doth not know the cause why they laugh. If one should enter into a house, where all the World is sad, he becomes melancholy, for as one said, *Si vis me flere dolendum est primum ipsi tibi* [if you wish me to weep, you must grieve first].[9]

---

8   Jean-François Marmontel (1723–99), cited from Dominique Bertrand, "Contagious Laughter and the Burlesque: From the Literal to the Metaphorical", in Claire L. Carlin (ed.), *Imaging Contagion in Early Modern Europe* (London: Palgrave, 2005), 177–94, qtn from 191.

9   Kenelm Digby, *A late discourse made in a solemne assembly of nobles and learned men at Montpellier in France touching the cure of wounds by the powder of sympathy* (London: R. Lownes, 1658), 93. Other examples include Richard Brathwaite, *The English Gentleman* (London: John Haviland, 1630), 129, who cites it to gloss the following argument: "It is above imagination to consider of the rare effects derived from moving or perswasive Rhetoricians, resembling in some sort passionate Actors; Who to move passion, such an order keepe, /

A similarly scientific metaphor of action at a distance is used by the physiognomist John Bulwer in a discussion of facial expressions: laughter, he says, is contagious from person to person "by a kind of magneticall virtue".[10]

Nor is this solely a scientific curiosity, since the Latin tag quoted by Kenelm Digby in his observation above leads us to Horace's *Ars Poetica*, one of the most influential of all classical texts on the subject of poetics, widely studied on school curricula, and written with especial reference to drama and the theatre. In it, Horace uses weeping and laughter as paradigmatic examples of the importance of decorum in writing drama:

> Men's faces, still, with such as laugh, are prone
> To laughter: so they grieve with those that mone:
> If thou wouldst have me weep, bee thou first dround
> Thy selfe in teares, then me thy losse will wound,
> *Peleus*, or *Telephus*.[11]

Whereas Marmontel and Digby are primarily concerned with the phenomenon itself, Horace is interested in how a theatrical writer can exploit it, by, in effect, seeding it: giving the process of echoing an artificial start. For Horace, the art lies not just in displaying what Marmontel calls the "object", the pathetic or ridiculous scene which might create the requisite physiological effects in members of the audience, but also in displaying those effects themselves onstage, by showing characters laughing and weeping, in order to cause the effects to propagate through the audience more powerfully. A generation of playwrights, including Jonson, whose translation is quoted here, took Horace's advice.

To move into the realm of accounts which claim to observe the behaviour of real audiences, several of these (collected and discussed in more detail in Chapter 3) focus on scenes which involve onstage weeping, claiming that they were particularly likely to induce audience weeping. Thus Thomas Stanley writes of Beaumont and Fletcher's *The Maid's Tragedy* that "[W]hen *Aspasia* wept, not any eye / But seem'd to wear the same sad livery".[12] Equally, the infectiousness of laughter is a common theme in Renaissance discussions of audience laughter. A frequent complaint, here illustrated from *Hamlet*, is that onstage laughter is used as a way of inducing audiences to laugh even when the material does not justify it: "Let not your clowns speak more than is set down for them; for there be of them that will themselves laugh,

---

As they feigne teares to make their hearers weepe"; Thomas Rymer, *A Short View of Tragedy* (London: Richard Baldwin, 1693), 4.

10   J[ohn] B[ulwer], *Pathomyotamia, or, A dissection of the significative muscles of the affections of the minde* (London: Humphrey Moseley, 1649), 129.

11   Jonson, *Horace, of the Art of Poetrie*, 142–7, cited from H&S, 8.311; *Ut ridentibus arrident, its flentibus adflent / Humani vultus. Si vis me flere, dolendum est / Primum ipsi tibi: tunc tua me infortunia laedent, /Telephe, vel Peleu.*

12   Beaumont and Fletcher, *Comedies and Tragedies* (1647), b4v.

to set on some quantity of barren spectators to laugh too...".[13] Such complaints are pursued in more detail in Chapter 4, but what is interesting here is that the example shows that the action advised by Horace on the level of literary theory is also part of contemporary stage practice.

A wider context for this idea of the infectiousness of emotions in the early modern theatre is provided by a point made by Paster, Rowe and Floyd-Wilson. According to them, studies of early modern emotion should be cautious of "the current privileging of emotions as inward rather than social phenomena", itself a result of an anachronistic post-Romantic fascination with the solitary self. Instead, the meanings of early modern emotion may be located in a communal context: "a too persistent focus on the passionate *individual* may ... overshadow the early modern investment in emotional expression as either a generic marker of social status or the sentient matter of communal bonds".[14] This too is an idea which is foundational to the current project. As Francis Bacon puts it, using as he does so a strikingly acoustic metaphor, drama

> has been considered by wise men and great philosophers as if it was a plectrum to play men's souls with. And it is certainly very true, and almost a secret of nature, that the minds of men are more receptive to impressions and affections when they are gathered together, more than when they are alone.[15]

As accounts such as those collected above make clear, the theatre is one of the great venues not merely for shared and communal reception, but also for shared and communal displays of emotion.

To an extent, the proposition that the onstage audiences of Shakespeare (or Jonson, or any other Renaissance dramatist) can be read as metaphors for the theatrical audience seems so reasonable that it might be in danger of being overlooked as a critical commonplace. But the implications of it, particularly as regards laughing and weeping, bear further scrutiny. By and large, there is little detailed reception history about the precise reactions of early audiences through the course of any particular Renaissance play. On the basis of what evidence there is, one might propose as a rule of thumb that onstage laughter cues audience laughter, and that onstage weeping indicates scenes at which an early audience might be expected to be moved towards tears.

Clearly, this is more of a statistical tendency than an absolute principle, and there are exceptions to the rule. Exaggerated weeping is occasionally mentioned as one of the comic techniques of the early modern clown, and a group of such examples, implying a distinctive aesthetic of comic weeping, is discussed in Chapter 2. Conversely, there are some occasions on the Renaissance stage which specifically make capital out of a failure of sympathy: a character (generally an evil character)

---

13 Shakespeare, *Hamlet*, 3.2.38–40.

14 Paster, Rowe and Floyd-Wilson (eds), *Reading the Early Modern Passions*, 13.

15 Francis Bacon, *De Augmentis Scientiarum*, cited from Bacon, *Opera* (London: John Havilland, 1623), I.109. My translation.

laughing at the weeping of another character. And Marston's *Jack Drum's Entertainment*, for instance, includes a vignette which deliberately turns on its head the usual expectations:

> *Enter two Pages, the one laughing, the other crying.*
> FIRST PAGE: Why do'st thou crie?
> SECOND PAGE: Why do'st thou laugh?
> FIRST PAGE: I laugh to see thee crie.
> SECOND PAGE: And I crie to see thee laugh.[16]

But the force of this exchange depends precisely on the fact that it is so exact a reversal of the usual modes of operation, not just of the theatre but of human sympathy in general. In the majority of cases, where no such special pleading applies, the more usual expectation should be that onstage laughing and weeping cues audience laughing and weeping. Thus, the several hundred examples of onstage laughter, and the several hundred examples of onstage weeping, are of interest not just for their importance as stage business, nor just for their prominence as elements within the linguistic system of the plays. They offer, potentially, a skeleton outline, across Renaissance drama as a whole, of some of the expected responses of the original audiences.

Thus, the project of this book intersects with two of the grand narratives of early modern cultural history. The first is the idea, perhaps most persuasively articulated by Bakhtin, of whom more later, that the early modern period sees a move from a culture of folk festivity to a more élitist conception of social discrimination rather than social inclusion. Keith Thomas has argued that a growing suspicion of public laughter provides one barometer of that process in action. Another, according to many commentators, is provided by early modern theatre as a whole. Thus Richard Helgerson writes of moments in early modern theatre, such as the departure of Will Kemp from Shakespeare's company in 1599, in terms of a much larger historical shift: "the alienation of the clown from the playwright, of the players' theater from the authors' theater, of the people from the nation and its canonical self-representations."[17] The evidence presented here does not contest the overall sweep of this grand narrative, although, as we shall see in Chapter 1, early modern theories of laughter by no means unanimously share Bakhtin's view of it as anarchic and subversive. However, it does, by and large, speak to the idea that early modern theatre still celebrates community, still celebrates communal displays of emotion, and still celebrates the theatre as a place where (within certain cultural limits) it is

---

16   Marston, *Jack Drum's Entertainment* (1601), B4v; indeed, images of laughing at others' weeping are frequent in Marston's plays.
17   Keith Thomas, "The Place of Laughter in Tudor and Stuart England", *Times Literary Supplement* (January 21, 1977), 77–81; Richard Helgerson, *Forms of Nationhood: The Elizabethan Writing of England* (Chicago: Chicago University Press, 1992), Chapter V, "Staging Exclusion", 195–245, qtn from 226.

still permissible to lose control of your own body, if only for a few moments, as it is taken over by laughing or by weeping.

The second grand narrative is the conception of that body, the early modern body. We are all familiar with the entrenched opposition between "essentialist" interpretations of the body, in which the unchanging basic architecture of the human form over the last 400 years seems to elide the historical distance between then and now, and readings which stress the extent to which "the body" can only be understood in terms of the ideology which produces the categories through which it can be apprehended. The body itself can be seen as textual, as a socially constructed artefact or commodity: "In its own, albeit figurative way ... the newest of England's draperies", in Jean-Christophe Agnew's phrase.[18] But more recent work has sought to shrink the gap between these two intellectual positions, and nowhere more so than in work on early modern theatre as an institution. In particular, some interesting models have been proposed for the ways in which the audience's bodies are part of the meaning of an early modern play. Jeremy Lopez has argued for the importance of the physicality of audience response in this period, drawing attention, for instance, to the pervasive imagery of theatre as food, which implies that it can have a measurable physiological effect on the bodies of its audience. Similarly, in *Drugs and Theater in Early Modern England*, Tanya Pollard traces through pro- and anti-theatrical tracts and through plays themselves an image which figures theatre as a drug, capable of doing good – or harm – to the bodies and minds of its consumers. Again, as Pollard makes clear, the pre-Cartesian world-view of early modern theatre makes for an unclear and non-absolute separation between body and soul, and both Pollard's and Lopez's work dwells on the importance of the physical presence of the audience's bodies in the theatre.[19]

Anthony Dawson, working along related lines, advances an idea of "sacramental participation" to elucidate the relationship between material body and immaterial text in performances of early modern theatre:

The player both puts his body on the line and as it were, retires it – this is demanded by theatrical presentation. He trembles, vibrates with the sheer resonance of the Shakespearean text. The ear vibrates in response. The audience *sounds* the performance ... while audience members are encouraged to construct meaning through the elision of the physical, their bodies are engaged in physical responses: tears, shudders, held breath, laughter.[20]

18 Jean-Christophe Agnew, *Worlds Apart: The Market and Theater in Anglo-American Thought, 1550–1750* (Cambridge: Cambridge University Press, 1986), 85–6.

19 Jeremy Lopez, *Theatrical Convention and Audience Response in Early Modern Drama* (Cambridge: Cambridge University Press, 2003); Tanya Pollard, *Drugs and Theater in Early Modern England* (Cambridge: Cambridge University Press, 2004); Charles Whitney's *Early Responses to Renaissance Drama* (Cambridge: Cambridge University Press, 2006) appeared as this book was going to press. Whitney's account focuses on reaction outside the playhouse: this study, then, is complementary to his, focusing on what happens *inside* the theatre.

20 Anthony Dawson and Paul Yachnin, *The Culture of Playgoing in Shakespeare's England: A Collaborative Debate* (Cambridge: Cambridge University Press, 2001), 21–2; the

In effect, Dawson argues, there is an "incarnational" aspect to the whole idea of theatre which cuts interestingly against the early modern protestant distrust of incarnational ways of thinking in general, and this is one of the factors that make the early modern English playhouse such an interesting place. The bodies of the audience are, in effect, part of the meaning of the play. Dawson's insight fits well with the idea of an acoustic approach – while the imagery of vibrations and sounding-boards in the above quotation is clearly metaphorical, there is also a sense in which it relates back well both to Pollard's and Lopez's stress on the perceived physical effects of early modern theatre, and to Smith's image of the theatre building functioning in a more literal sense as a resonating chamber. As will be seen, imagery of resounding, repeating and reduplicating will echo throughout the early modern texts discussed below. In the early modern theatre, a function akin to that of a sounding-board exists in the relationship between onstage performance of laughter and weeping, and audience response. The projects to recover both the sounds and gestures of stage laughter and weeping, and the sounds and gestures of audience laughter and weeping, reinforce one another.

---

book is a dialogue in which Yachnin offers a competing, more materialist view of the early modern theatre, founded in structures of economic exchange.

Chapter 1

Renaissance constructions of laughter and weeping

In the Introduction to their collection *Reading the Early Modern Passions*, Gail Kern Paster, Katherine Rowe and Mary Floyd-Wilson talk about the difficulties involved in writing a cultural history of emotion, particularly with regard to the early modern period. It is, they write, a mistake to attempt to talk about the passions as if they could be described as coherent entities, or even as coherent states of being: "they comprise, instead, an ecology or a transaction ... [they] transverse the Cartesian division between physiology and psychology."[1] If these dicta apply to a project to discuss early modern passions, then they apply even more strongly to an attempt to write a cultural history of two of the most notable outward manifestations of those shifting and restless ecologies. What follows will move from medical, to religious, to social discourses around laughing and weeping, to build up a sense of the cultural profile of these actions in the period.

Taking cues from pseudo-Aristotelian and pseudo-Hippocratic medical texts, and from rhetorical writings by Cicero and Quintilian, many medical writers of the Renaissance considered the problems of weeping and laughter. While competing accounts differed on points of detail, Quentin Skinner summarises their main points of agreement as follows: "Among the elements common to laughter and weeping, these writers single out the fact that they are peculiar to humankind, that they are largely uncontrollable, and they seem to be almost unnaturally vehement reactions to some inner movement of the soul".[2] Much of the energy, particularly on discussions of laughter, went into attempting to define the nature of the comic stimulus; what it

---

1   Gail Kern Paster, Katherine Rowe and Mary Floyd-Wilson (eds), *Reading the Early Modern Passions: Essays in the Cultural History of Emotion* (Philadelphia: University of Pennsylvania Press, 2004), 18.

2   Quentin Skinner, "Hobbes and the Classical Theory of Laughter", in Tom Sorell and Luc Foisneau (eds), *Leviathan after 350 Years* (Oxford: Clarendon Press, 2004), 139–66, qtn from 143; see also Anne Lake Prescott, "The Ambivalent Heart: Thomas More's Merry Tales", *Criticism*, 45:4 (2003): 417–33; Marjory E. Lange, *Telling Tears in the English Renaissance* (Leiden: Brill, 1996); Keith Thomas, "The Place of Laughter in Tudor and Stuart England", *Times Literary Supplement* (21 January 1977), 77–81; Roberta Mullini (ed.), *Tudor Theatre: For laughs (?)/Pour rire (?): Puzzling Laughter in Plays of the Tudor Age/Rires et problèmes dans le théâtre des Tudor*s (Bern: Peter Lang, 2002); also Manfred Pfister (ed.), *A History of English Laughter: Laughter from "Beowulf" to Beckett and Beyond* (Amsterdam: Rodopi, 2002).

was that made something funny to its recipient. In a sense, the failure even of these contemporary accounts to reach a firm and definitive consensus can be measured against the axioms of Paster, Rowe and Floyd-Wilson, since these accounts tended to look for universal examples of the pathetic or the risible, and sought, in effect, fixity in passions. Learning from their failures, therefore, this account looks to describe not so much the Renaissance pursuit of definitions of the risible and lamentable, nor the psychological mechanisms one might suppose to be invoked by those stimuli, but rather the descriptions of and attitudes to the observable bodily phenomena they caused. Similarly, and for the same reasons, this study stands at something of an angle to the main thrust of most recent writing both on laughter and literature, and on tragic affect and literature. It is not interested in the nature of the comic, or the tragic, or the feelings they produce, so much as in particular and external physical effects.

"Laughter" and "weeping" are both terms which denote syndromes: collections of related physical symptoms with a common cause. A good place to begin is with Renaissance descriptions of those syndromes, using mainly two representative examples of Renaissance medical thought, Timothy Bright's *Treatise on Melancholy*, and, first, the *Traité Du Ris* (1579) of Laurent Joubert (1529–82). Joubert was a Montpellier-based doctor and academic who became personal physician to the King of France.[3] The *Traité Du Ris*, the fullest Renaissance description of the physiological working of laughter, is only one of a number of medical works he published in his lifetime, and is notable for offering an entire theory of laughter, although this theory starts not with the physical reaction itself, but with a discussion of the nature of the ridiculous. For Joubert, laughter is not simply a sign of joy or of sorrow, but arises from a mixture of pleasure and displeasure at this particular kind of stimulus: "Laughter, then, is provoked by deeds or words which have the appearance of ugliness and are not worthy of pity, except perhaps at first blush". In this idea, whose origins are Aristotelian, Joubert is at odds with other theorists who hold that it proceeds solely from joy, and at odds with others who believe that it derives from a form of hatred (a tradition which goes back to Quintilian, and forward to Thomas Hobbes's famous definition of laughter in the later seventeenth century as "a suddaine Glory arising from suddaine Conception of some Eminency in our selves by Comparison with the Infirmityes of others, or with our owne formerly").[4]

Furthermore, following Plato, Joubert believes that "laughter comes from an emotion in the heart and not from the brain"; it is the "laughable matter, carried first to

---

3   Laurent Joubert, *Treatise on Laughter*, trans. Gregory David de Rocher (Alabama: Alabama University Press, 1980), Introduction; I refer to this book throughout what follows as the *Traité*, to avoid confusion with Bright's *Treatise*.

4   Joubert, *Traité*, 62; De Rocher, Introduction, xii, on the Aristotelian origins; Skinner, "Hobbes and the classical theory of laughter", 147, qtn from 155; for instance, Thomas Wright, *The passions of the minde in generall. Corrected, enlarged, and with sundry new discourses augmented* (London: Valentine Simmes, 1604), 61, ascribes laughter purely to joy, adding that "vehement laughter" can be fatal.

the heart through the conduits of the senses", which causes the heart to suffer spasms.[5] Laughter's effects start with these movements (45); these movements are transmitted to the diaphragm (47), thus affecting the lungs and causing heaving of the chest, interrupting the voice, and substituting instead the sound of air being forced out of the lungs. Hence, audible laughter arises straight from the lungs, rather than being produced by the voice or the tongue (50). Then, the effects of this agitation propagate upwards into the head. As a consequence of the need for rapid breathing, the mouth opens, the lips stretch and the chin moves (51); the face wrinkles, especially round the eyes; the eyes themselves sparkle and grow tearful (55–6). The face reddens, coughing may ensue, and one's drink may shoot back down one's nose (58). "The arms, shoulders, thighs, feet and entire body can be moved by dint of laughing" (58), while further effects include an aching stomach, sweating and incontinence. The list of possible symptoms of laughter concludes with loss of consciousness and sudden death (61); laughter, for Joubert, can be a medical emergency.

Joubert's influence can be seen in accounts including *A Treatise of Melancholy* (1586), by Timothy Bright (1549/50–1615), English physician, divine and writer on shorthand as well as on medicine. Bright's book is mainly a medical textbook devoted to the diagnosis and treatment of melancholy, and as such was in turn influential on later texts including Shakespeare's *Hamlet* and Robert Burton's *Anatomy of Melancholy*.[6] While it defers to Joubert on the subject of laughter rather than offering its own description, it does offer a usefully full anatomy of the syndrome of weeping:

> Of all the actions of melancholie, or rather of heauinesse and sadnesse, none is so manifolde and diuerse in partes, as that of weeping. First of all it putteth finger in the eyes, and sheadeth teares; then it baseth the countenance unto the bosome; thirdly it draweth the cheekes with a kinde of convulsion on both sides and turneth the countenance into a resemblance of girninge, and letteth the browes fall vppon the eye liddes; it bleareth the eyes, and maketh the cheekes redde; it causeth the heade to ake, the nose to runne, & mouth to slauer, the lippes to tremble; interrupteth the speeche, and shaketh the whole chest with sighes, and sobbes.[7]

The prime cause of weeping, then, is a humoral imbalance caused by compression in the brain, which leads to the excretion from the brain of a fluid in the form of tears which is also excreted into the nose and mouth to create the runny nose and excessive saliva noted as supplementary symptoms; the excretion of the tears, in turn, alters the

---

5   Joubert, *Traité*, 36; his opinion was not entirely unopposed. For instance, Bulwer, in *Pathomyotamia*, 127–35, notes that most anatomists believe laughter proceeds from the heart, but also marshals others who argue that it starts in the brain and only then proceeds to the heart; he also notes the other widespread opinion of Renaissance doctors, namely that laughter originates in the spleen. See also Joubert, *Traité*, 110–13, and de Rocher's notes *ad loc*.

6   Page Life, "Bright, Timothy (1549/50–1615)", *Oxford DNB*.

7   Timothy Bright, *A treatise of melancholie Containing the causes thereof, & reasons of the strange effects it worketh in our minds and bodies* (London: Thomas Vautrollier, 1586), 135–6.

balance of spirits in the flesh of the face, causing the facial symptoms.[8] As Bright's initial account makes clear, these actions are perceived as happening sequentially ("First ... then ... thirdly"). The expression of the face becomes "a resemblance of girninge" – that is, gurning, or face-pulling. The expelled tears, in turn, have an effect further away still within the body, and are the direct cause of the sobbing: "when matter of grief inforceth teares, the Diaphragme, and the muscles receiue a weakenes, by reason of retraction of spirits, that they are faine for the dilatation of the chest to make mo pulls then one". This produces the respiratory symptoms. Thus, although, as both Bright and Joubert observe, there is in some respects considerable overlap between laughter and weeping in terms of their symptoms, these two accounts ascribe to them quite different fundamental aetiologies; weeping is caused by emotional distress, laughter by a more complex and specific mixture of joy and sorrow. Weeping moves from the brain into the head and downwards, laughter from the heart into the chest and upwards. In weeping, the tears are the first symptom, and audible effects come later: in laughter, the sobbing which makes the audible effects can lead to the tears.[9]

A similar observation of the similarity between tears and laughter is made by John Bulwer more than fifty years later, in a discussion of facial expressions. But again Bulwer differentiates the two, with tears, above all, the distinguishing point:

in the *Face* by Laughter the parts about the *mouth* are more emphatically affected: but in weeping the parts about the *Eye*; which compression expresseth teares, else there is little difference in their lines, as Painters observe, which consequently requires the action of the same Muscles in both.[10]

Joubert, Bright and Bulwer are illustrative examples of a Renaissance orthodoxy which holds that while the symptoms of weeping and laughter are similar, the points of origin are quite distinct.

As direct consequences of humoral imbalance, then, tears and laughter might seem to offer hope of a direct access to the interior experience of the subject. Bright believes that tears cannot be feigned: "tears cannot be counterfetted, because they rise not of any action or facultie voluntary, but natural". And yet, as Bright also notes, there is no easy relation between grief and tears: extreme grief cannot be expressed in tears, which Bright illustrates from the anecdote of King Amasis of Egypt, unable to weep at the death of his son but able to weep at the comparatively minor misfortune of a captured friend.[11] Weeping can also be brought on by joy, as Bright documents,

---

8   Bright, *Treatise*, 147; Lange, *Telling Tears*, 3–19, traces theorists in the 1650s and 1660s advancing an alternative model drawing attention to the importance of glands in the production of tears.

9   Bright, *Treatise*, 157.

10   Bulwer, *Pathomyotamia*, 141.

11   Bright, *Treatise*, 140; for other allusions to the widespread consensus that tears express "only *moderate* grief", see Lange, *Telling Tears*, 39–40.

and he also observes examples of melancholics weeping "without anie outward occasion", so that, even without considering (as he does not) the problem of feigned tears, the question of what weeping *means* is problematic.

Similarly, accounts of laughter are troubled by phenomena such as laughter induced by a chest injury, or what Bright calls "counterfeit and false" laughter caused by

> the midriffe moued disorderly with shaking by anie annoyance; and moueth also the chest, and muscles of the iawes and cheekes by consent of nerues, and so counterfetting a laughinge gesture, wherein the heart taketh no pleasure.[12]

Bright describes the laughter brought on by tickling as of this sort. Here, too, one finds the idea of the sardonic laugh, which is said to take its name from a poisonous herb supposed by Dioscorides to cause its victims to laugh themselves to death.[13] Even grief may cause this inappropriate laughter by making the diaphragm misfire, a phenomenon illustrated by Bright from the story of Hannibal laughing to hear of the distress of Carthage, so that laughter, like weeping, is ultimately ambiguous and mysterious. While in some ways laughter and weeping appear to offer unproblematic, non-linguistic access to subjects' consciousnesses, these accounts are clear that weeping and laughter do not do so reliably, and that they are physiological symptoms, which can have diverse causes. What Marjory E. Lange says about early modern tears is equally true of early modern laughter: both can be "attributes of an abundant variety of mental, physical, and spiritual states".[14]

Both weeping, and laughter, can be dangerous, indeed fatal, in excess. Nonetheless, Bright and Joubert consider moderate weeping and laughter respectively as potentially sanative processes, which work towards restoring humoral balance in the affected body. In this, they are in accordance with the tenor of much Renaissance medical writing. Renaissance medicine's essentially humoral view of both these processes is also pressed into service by both Bright and Joubert to explain "whence it comes that some laugh more often and more suddenly than others", and why some people – healthy adult men, in theory – are less prone to shedding of tears than, for instance, women and children. Joubert alludes to one particularly relevant example of how the same stimulus could cause different effects on two individuals: "Democritus … used to laugh, and Heraclitus to weep, at everything that happened".[15] In a wider Renaissance context, women's supposed propensity to weep is typical of their perceived status as humorally incontinent and therefore inferior "leaky vessels"; and of their habitual failure to live up to neo-Stoic ideals of control over the expression

---

12 Joubert, *Traité*, 79–81; Bright, *Treatise*, 162, 163.
13 Joubert, *Traité*, 88–9; but see *OED*, sardonian *a.*
14 Bright, *Treatise*, 152; Lange, *Telling Tears*, 1.
15 Joubert, *Traité*, 99, 104; Bright, *Treatise*, 144.

of one's emotions.[16] And yet just as laughter and weeping can be healing processes, they can equally well be the symptoms requiring treatment. To take an example from Renaissance drama, the madness of Martha in Richard Brome's comedy *The Antipodes* is expressed "Sometimes in extream weeping, and anon / In vehement laughter", and this is indeed a classic symptom of madness in the period.[17]

Another frequently sounded note in medical and pseudo-medical writing is that laughter and weeping are unique to humans, and therefore, important to what have been called "the borders of the human". In a tradition which goes back to pseudo-Aristotelian texts, the fact that animals neither laugh nor weep is used as evidence of their lack of a human soul, although, as soon as this proposition is made, holes start to appear in it: for instance, Joubert concedes that some animals such as crocodiles are seen to shed tears, but distinguishes this from proper human weeping, proceeding from the brain, and Bulwer concedes that animals show "some signes of exultation and Delight", but denies that these can be considered as laughter.[18] As Gail Kern Paster has demonstrated, attempts by Thomas Wright and others to use humoral theory to rationalise the distinction between humans and animals tend to end up obscuring, rather than clarifying, the difference between them.[19] But in the case of laughter and weeping, Renaissance writers such as Joubert generally believe that these behaviours do distinguish human from animal: "Weeping, then, is peculiar to man, as well as laughter, although there have been people who have never wept, for some have also been found who never laughed ...".[20] In Joubert's formulation, both laughter and weeping are uniquely human and either of them is sufficient, although not necessary, evidence of humanity.

And yet, in wider discourses, laughter and weeping – in that they are involuntary evidence of loss of rational control – are seen as not merely effeminating, but bestialising man. Thomas Wright quoted Plutarch as saying that passions changed men "like *Circes* potions, from men into beastes", while the antitheatrical writer Stephen Gosson, writing specifically about theatre audiences' propensities to

---

16   Gail Kern Paster, "Leaky Vessels: The Incontinent Women of Jacobean City Comedy", *Renaissance Drama*, n.s., 18 (1987): 71–86; Margo Swiss and David A. Kent (eds), *Speaking Grief in English Literary Culture: Shakespeare to Milton* (Pittsburgh: Duquesne University Press, 2003); Jennifer C. Vaught, "Men Who Weep and Wail: Masculinity and Emotion in Sidney's *New Arcadia*", *Literature Compass*, 3 (2005), n.p., online at http://www.Literature-compass.com/viewpoint.asp?section=2&ref=460.

17   Brome, *The Antipodes* (1640), B3v.

18   Erica Fudge, Susan Wiseman and Ruth Gilbert (eds), *At the Borders of the Human: Beasts, Bodies and Natural Philosophy in the Early Modern Period* (London: Palgrave, 2002); Bulwer, *Pathomyotamia*, 105; Joubert, *Traité*, 99; Skinner, "Hobbes and the Classical Theory of Laughter", 139–40.

19   Gail Kern Paster, "Melancholy Cats, Lugged Bears, and Early Modern Cosmology: Reading Shakespeare's Psychological Materialism across the Species Barrier", in Paster, Rowe and Floyd-Wilson, *Reading the Early Modern Passions*, 113–29.

20   Joubert, *Traité*, 99.

laugh and weep, believed that *"Tragedies* and *Commedies* stirre up affections, and affections are naturally planted in that part of the minde that is common to us with brute beastes". For Gosson, an audience's non-verbal responses (most obviously laughter, but potentially weeping as well) turned them into a single, collective, beast, a proverbial "monster of many heads".[21] The quotations below, from, first, Dekker, and then Jonson, illustrate the extent to which dramatists themselves took over this imagery:

> The *Theater* is your Poets Royal Exchange, vpon which, their Muses (y^t are now turned to Merchants) meeting barter away that light commodity of words for a lighter ware then words. *Plaudities* and the *Breath* of the great *Beast*, which (like the threatnings of two Cowards) vanish all into aire.

> What either in the words, or Sense of an Author, or in the language, or Actions of men, is a wry, or depraved, doth strangely stirre meane affections, and provoke for the most part to laughter … jests that are true and natural seldome raise laughter with the Beast, the multitude.[22]

In both of these quotations, from practising professional playwrights, the audience is imagined not as a collection of individuals but as a single *gestalt* organism, a beast. The breath of Dekker's "great *Beast*" is explicitly non-verbal, "a lighter ware then words", although Dekker imagines it as intimately entwined with the words written by the author to be spoken on the stage. The two, in fact, are complimentary and interdependent: "the threatnings of two Cowards", melting away together. As for Jonson's similar imagination of the audience as "the Beast, the multitude", it does not come (as most of the surrounding phrases do) from his summary of the Latin of Daniel Heinsius, but is Jonson's own interpolation. Laughter, or weeping, can thus be read either as guaranteeing the subject's humanity, or as the outward signs of a passion which is having just the opposite effect. Both laughter and weeping are actions which take place on the shifting borders, not merely between soul and body, health and sickness (and in Dekker's formulation, language and non-language), but also between human and animal, individual and crowd.

But despite being, in a medical sense, close siblings, the cultural significances and overtones of laughter and of weeping were also quite different. Theologically, while weeping is in general praiseworthy, implying an appropriate appreciation of the sinful state of the post-lapsarian world, laughter is inappropriately pleasurable and ultimately demonic in origin. William Prynne's distinction between the two applies the lesson specifically to theatres, and even more specifically to audience laughter in theatres, but his terms of reference come from a wider Renaissance culture.

---

21 Wright, *The passions of the minde in generall*, 59; Stephen Gosson, *Playes confuted in fiue actions* (London: Thomas Gosson, [1582]), F1r, D1r.

22 Dekker, *The Guls Horne-Booke* (London: R. S., 1609), 27; Jonson, *Discoveries*, 2642–2646, 2558–2259, cited from H&S; H&S XI.289 reproduces Heinsius' Latin.

His allusion to John 11:35 ("And Jesus wept") is one of the commonest motifs in Renaissance antitheatrical writing:

> Christ *(saith the Scripture)* suffred for us, leaving us an ensample, that wee should follow his steps: *And we follow the steps of our Saviour in Cirques, and in Theaters; as if our Saviour had left us such an example, whom we read to have wept, but that he laughed we never read. And both these for our sakes: because weeping is a pricking of the heart, laughter a corruption of manners.*[23]

Prynne speaks for Puritans in general, and to an extent for religious writers in general, in his dislike and suspicion of laughter. But there are exceptions even to this rule. Christ's failure to laugh could be set against the laughter of God in the Old Testament: "he that sitteth in the heavens shall laugh: the Lord shall have [his enemies] in derision", a passage which lies behind Milton's depiction of a laughing, joking God in *Paradise Lost*.[24] Erasmus' *Praise of Folly*, celebrating Christianity as a form of madness, celebrates also laughter at the joyful absurdity of the mystery of the Incarnation, and this is only part of a much wider tradition of sacred laughter and festivity associated with the medieval and Renaissance church.[25] Indira Ghose, for instance, has read the rise of theatrical laughter, in particular, as a facet of the suppression of popular religious festivity in Tudor England, and, by extension, as a moment in the displacement of the sacred in Western culture.[26]

Similarly, tears enjoyed multiple, competing, cultural significances in early modern England. Imagery of weeping was central, for instance, to the poetic tradition of funeral elegy, and Margo Swiss and David A. Kent, among others, have traced the idea that expression of grief, "grief work", is acknowledged in the period as a healing process.[27] On the other hand, Protestant poetics were suspicious of the whole idea of mourning for the dead, which in Catholic doctrine reflected a concern to help the soul in Purgatory. Reformation Protestants, disbelieving in Purgatory, and not accepting the idea that mourning for the dead had any effect on their fate in the afterlife, had trouble coming to terms with excessive weeping. Weeping for the dead, then, could have Catholic overtones unacceptable to Protestant poetics, and Tobias Döring discusses ways in which the early modern stage displays mourning for the

---

23   William Prynne, *Histrio-mastix, The players scourge, or, actors tragaedie* (London: Michael Sparke, 1633), 526v.

24   John Milton, *Paradise Lost*, ed. Alistair Fowler, 2nd edn (London: Longman, 1998), 2.190–91, 5.735–7 and notes; Suzanne Rupp, "Milton's Laughing God", in Pfister (ed.), *A History of English Laughter*, 47–56.

25   On More, see Prescott, "The Ambivalent Heart"; on Erasmus and "foolosophy", see Jon Haarberg, *Parody and the Praise of Folly* (Oslo: Scandinavian University Press, 1998); cf. also M.A. Screech, *Laughter at the Foot of the Cross* (Harmondsworth: Penguin, 1999).

26   Indira Ghose, "Laughter and Blasphemy in the Shakespearean Theater", *Medieval and Renaissance Drama in England*, 16 (2003): 228–39.

27   See, for instance, Dennis Kay, *Melodious Tears: The English Funeral Elegy from Spenser to Milton* (Oxford: Clarendon Press, 1990); Swiss and Kent (eds), *Speaking Grief*, Introduction, 3.

dead as a coded way of thinking through the theological legacy of the Reformation.[28] Tears could have a valency as objects of erotic and religious veneration in their own right, reflected in the continental Catholic tradition of lachrymatories, so that an excessive interest in tears might even potentially be idolatrous. To that extent, for all that weeping is generally seen as preferable to laughter, it still represents a theologically risky topic.

On the other hand, histories of laughing and weeping must consider not merely medical and religious, but also social history, as Keith Thomas, for instance, has argued in examining the generally disapproving attitudes to public laughter within Renaissance conduct-books, which consider it as an indecorous activity in the same category as spitting or breaking wind:

> Bodily control thus became a symbol of social hierarchy. The new etiquette was meant to distinguish the elite from the vulgar in a way which I think would not have been apparent in the Middle Ages. It stemmed more from a concern with the preservation of social authority than from any deep psychological fear of the body. It was meant to establish that dignified style which contemporaries thought necessary for the maintenance of social respect.[29]

The idea of "folk laughter", an idea perhaps most familiar now from Bakhtinian constructions of carnival, but with, as Bakhtin and his followers have demonstrated, a long pedigree in medieval and Renaissance writing, lies behind this model. Bakhtin describes it as follows: "folk laughter presents an element of victory not only over supernatural awe, over the sacred, over death; it also means the defeat of power, of earthly kings, of the earthly upper classes, of all that oppresses and restricts".[30] Laughter is not merely lower-class, but also potentially socially subversive and capable of causing a world turned upside-down. And yet Bakhtin's model is at odds with the tenor of much of the writing about laughter from within the English Renaissance, which offers a model of laughter as socially corrective and normative.[31] The most famous statement of this point of view in the period is perhaps that of Sir Philip Sidney in the *Defence of Poesy*, who asks rhetorically whether anyone could object to a series of genres including

---

28   Tobias Döring, "*How to do things with tears*: Trauer spielen auf der Shakespeare-Bühne", *Poetica*, 33:3/4 (2001): 355–89.

29   Thomas, "The Place of Laughter in Tudor and Stuart England", 80; Skinner, "Hobbes and the Classical Theory of Laughter", argues that the phenomenon described by Thomas contributes to Hobbes's suspicion of laughter.

30   Mikhail Bakhtin, *Rabelais and His World*, trans. Helene Iswolsky (Bloomington: Indiana University Press, 1984), 92; Ronald Knowles (ed.), *Shakespeare and Carnival: After Bakhtin* (Basingstoke: Palgrave, 2001).

31   On the distinction, see Francois Laroque, "Shakespeare's Festive Comedies", in Richard Dutton and Jean E. Howard (eds), *A Companion to Shakespeare's Works: The Comedies* (Oxford: Blackwell, 2003), 23–46.

the Satiric, who *Omne vafer vitium ridenti tangit amico* [touches every vice in his laughing friend]; who sportingly never leaveth till he make a man laugh at folly, and at length ashamed, to laugh at himself; which he cannot avoid without avoiding the folly; who while *circum praecordia ludit* [he plays around the heart], giveth us to feel how many headaches a passionate life bringeth us to…

Sidney's Latin comes from the poet Persius, writing in turn about the poet Horace.[32] The phrasing is interesting in the context of this discussion because, like Renaissance theory, it places the origin of laughter in the pericardium, rather than the head. Furthermore, whereas Bakhtin celebrates laughter as a force throwing off repression, Sidney believes that laughter is a force for shame and that laughter is, perhaps, ultimately undesirable, since it is a symptom of as well as a warning against a "passionate life". Sidney goes on to describe laughter as a mere "scornful tickling", distinct from delight which is founded on joy. Even so, he argues, it earns its keep in that it makes comic literature into a shaming but morally improving experience. Sidneyan ideas of laughter are developed by Thomas Hobbes, after the end of the period under discussion, into a fully developed theory of laughter as a "sudden glory" over the weakness of another creature, but also make themselves felt in Renaissance drama.[33] For instance, in Jonson's *Cynthia's Revels*, Mercury and Crites propose

to correct,
And punish, with our laughter, this nights sport,
Which our court-*Dors* so heartily intend,
And by that worthy scorne, to make them know
How farre beneath the dignity of man
Their serious, and most practised actions are

And their idea of laughter as a normative, punitive force is aligned with Sidney's assertion that there is a morally corrective aspect to satire and to satirical comedy.[34]

So there is a contradiction at the heart of Renaissance theories of the social value of laughter. It is both normative and subversive; a force which one can use to civilise those at whom it is directed, but at the same time paying the price of becoming uncivilised by doing so. If laughter and weeping are liminal in terms of physiology, and controversial and unfixed in meaning in the terms of religious discourse, then they are equally paradoxical and contradictory considered from the perspective of society.

32 Sir Philip Sidney, *The Defence of Poesy*, in Katherine Duncan-Jones (ed.), *Sir Philip Sidney* (Oxford: Clarendon Press, 1989), 229; *omne vafer vitium ridenti Flaccus amico/ tangit et admissus circum praecordia ludit,/ callidus excusso populum suspendere naso*. Persius, *Satires*, 1.116–18, translated and discussed by Daniel Hooley, "Horace's Rud(e)-imentary Muse: *Sat*. 1.2", *Electronic Antiquity*, 5:2 (October, 1999), at http://scholar.lib.vt.edu/ejournals/ElAnt/V5N2/hooley.html.

33 Sidney, *Defence*, 245; Skinner, "Hobbes and the Classical Theory of Laughter".

34 Jonson, *Cynthia's Revels*, 5.1.17–22.

Figure 1.1 The weeping Heraclitus and the laughing Democritus, from Geoffrey Whitney's *Choice of Emblems* (1586), Emblem 14.

Far from being unhistorical absolutes, they are enmeshed with a whole set of Renaissance debates about the nature of the human animal; the relationship between man and God; and the ways in which society works or should work.

One final pair of emblematic figures, already mentioned in passing in this chapter, encapsulate Renaissance constructions of laughter and weeping – Heraclitus and Democritus, illustrated on the previous page of this book from Geoffrey Whitney's *Choice of Emblems* (1586).[35] Whitney's emblem is one of a number of early modern engravings, paintings and literary accounts juxtaposing Heraclitus, the philosopher who weeps at the follies of the world, and Democritus, the philosopher who laughs at them. Democritus, on the left, makes an expansive hand-gesture; Heraclitus, on the right, has his hands to his face in a version of the gesture later codified by John Bulwer as "finger in the eye". The opposition of Heraclitus and Democritus is a well-established one, going back to Seneca and Juvenal, and a *topos* for discussion in, for instance, Montaigne, who comments tartly that he prefers Democritus,

> not because it is more pleasing to laugh than to weepe; but for it is more disdainefull, and doth more condemne vs than the other. And me thinkes we can never bee sufficiently despised, according to our merite.[36]

Of course, as the above quotation notes, the Renaissance fascination with Heraclitus and Democritus is part of a cultural and philosophical debate which stretches into territory far outside the theatre. Heraclitus and Democritus, therefore, emblematise not merely the medical principle that the same external cause may cause different effects on different individuals, but also an ethical choice about how to relate to society, with Democritus, in particular, becoming a shorthand for a whole mode of satirical discourse, something reflected in Robert Burton's assumption of the mantle of Democritus Junior. But what makes this illustration particularly interesting for the matter at hand is Whitney's accompanying poem. Whereas Whitney's principal source, Alciato, merely comments on the continuing topicality of the two figures, *plus solito*, "now more than usually", Whitney gives the metaphor a specifically theatrical frame of reference by an allusion to the world-as-stage trope:

> The wicked worlde, so false and full of crime,
> Did alwaies moove HERACLITUS to weepe,
> The fadinge joyes, and follies of that time,
> DEMOCRITUS did drive to laughter deepe,
> Thus heynous sinne, and follie did procure
> Theise famous men, suche passions to indure.
> What if they liv'de, and shoulde behoulde this age
> Which overflowes, with swellinge seas of sinne:

---

35 On Whitney, see Andrew King, 'Whitney, Geoffrey (1548?–1600/01)', *Oxford DNB*; John Manning, "Whitney's *Choice of Emblems*: A Reassessment", *Renaissance Studies*, 4 (1990): 155–200.

36 Montaigne, Essay 50, cited from *Essays written in French by Michael Lord of Montaigne*, trans. John Florio (London: Melch. Bradwood, 1613), 3 vols, I.165.

Where fooles, by swarmes, doe presse uppon the stage,
With hellishe Impes, that like have never binne:
I thinke this sighte, shoulde hasten their decaye:
Then helpe us God, and Sathans furie staie.[37]

The "fooles" and "hellishe Impes" that are now to be seen on the stage of life would, Whitney imagines, cause the two philosophers to laugh and weep so hard that it would shorten their lifespans. When Whitney thinks of a place where laughter and tears are to be experienced in all their intensity, he thinks above all of the theatre.

---

[37]   Whitney, *Choice of Emblems*, 14; Alciato, Emblem 152, cited from William Barker *et al.* (eds), *Alciato's Book of Emblems: The Memorial Web Edition in Latin and English*, at http://www.mun.ca/alciato/152.html.

Chapter 2

Laughing on stage

An audience would frequently see and hear laughter represented on the early modern stage. Alan C. Dessen and Leslie Thomson's indispensable *Dictionary of Stage Directions* notes that in their corpus of early modern English drama performed between 1580 and 1642, a corpus containing around 22,000 stage directions, laughter is signalled "roughly forty times, often with no more than the basic term".[1] These explicit stage directions will be discussed below, but first it should be noted that they are outnumbered by a factor of perhaps twenty to one by one implied stage direction, namely the phrase "ha ha ha" and its longer variations.

The first step in investigating this claim is to use the Chadwyck-Healey database *Literature Online* (*LION*) to examine a corpus of English drama performed between 1550 and 1642 which is (approximately) analogous to Dessen and Thomson's, although spanning a larger period of time and containing a slightly different selection of texts.[2] Within this corpus, there occur numerous variants of the family of phrases ranging from "ha ha" to "ha ha ha ha ha ha ha ha ha ha ha". Phrases in this family, it will be argued below, are as a rule grammatically independent interjections; they function as a notation of a non-verbal noise to be made by the actor; and they enable a repertoire of gestures associated with the simulation of laughter.

The most common phrase of the family is "ha ha ha". This chapter begins by examining "ha ha ha" and other such verbal notations of laughter statistically, using *LION*; moves on from there to consider implied stage directions which take other forms; and discusses what can be said about the gestural vocabulary associated with the representation of laughter.

---

1   Alan C. Dessen and Leslie Thomson, *A Dictionary of Stage Directions in English Drama 1580–1642* (Cambridge: Cambridge University Press, 1999), s.v. "laugh". Like Dessen and Thomson, this study starts by treating the early modern stage as a single, almost synchronic cultural phenomenon, in order to gain an overview of what is normal in that set of texts. Only then will it be possible to talk meaningfully about variations through time or in different categories of theatre with regard to the treatment of laughing and weeping.

2   Note that it would not be possible to replicate Dessen and Thomson's results exactly using the *LION* corpus, because of differences in generic criteria, estimated datings, and texts available. This study, therefore, does not attempt to replicate their work, and also allows itself a wider chronological range.

Literal Representations of Laughter

1) Ha ha ha

The "English Drama" collection within the *Literature Online* database contains, at the time of writing, 745 texts which it identifies as first performed between 1550 and 1642, the terminal dates of this study. "Ha ha ha", seemingly the commonest literal representation of laughter in early modern drama, occurs in 255 of the 745 texts, that is to say, in slightly more than a third of the texts in the corpus as a whole.[3] In them, *LION* finds 989 occurrences of the string "ha ha ha". However, it also finds 146 occurrences of the string "ha ha ha ha". Since each "ha ha ha ha" will produce two hits in a search for "ha ha ha", it is necessary to subtract 146 from 989 to produce a count of 843 separate occurrences of "ha ha ha" or of its extended siblings in the collection.[4] Almost all of these 843 phrases, it will be argued below, are instructions to an actor to perform laughter.

To begin with, the context often conveniently removes any doubt that the phrase is indeed representative of laughter. The following three examples show this, although the three different associated formulae also imply subtly differing degrees of agency:

Ha, ha, ha, I laugh at you.

(Daborne, *A Christian Turn'd Turk* [1612], I4r)

Give me leave to laugh: ha, ha, ha

(J.D., *The Knave in Grain* [1640], F4r)

Ha, ha, ha, you make me laugh

(Killigrew, *Thomaso*, in *Comedies and Tragedies* [1664], 364)

On the other hand, almost no examples were noted in which "ha ha ha" is not an instruction to the actor to perform a laugh. *The Spanish Tragedy* furnishes one special case when the unbalanced Hieronimo talks to a Portugese visitor, who assumes he is a madman, and laughs at him. Hieronimo replies, puzzled: "Ha, ha, ha: why ha, ha, ha. Farewell good ha, ha, ha".[5] Indeed, this example gains its force from the fact that it is so unusual, and that the mad Hieronimo is misusing an involuntary sound as if it were a grammatical unit: it is a category mistake of the same sort as Hieronimo's request, in the additions to the play, that the Painter paint a scream.

---

3   As discussed in the headnote to this book, all the figures given here relate to the English Drama collection within the *LION* database as it stood in April 2006. Readers wishing to investigate these figures for themselves should note that, if the same searches are run without limiting *LION* to the English Drama database, the number of hits is spuriously higher, due to (for instance) the inclusion elsewhere in *LION* of extra nineteenth-century texts of Shakespeare.

4   The advantage of this counting is that it works even with longer reduplications: "ha ha ha ha ha ha", for instance, yields four occurrences of "ha ha ha", but three occurrences of "ha ha ha ha", so that it is still represented once in the total of 843.

5   Kyd, *The Spanish Tragedie* (1592), G3v.

In the vast majority of cases, "ha ha ha" is a grammatically independent interjection, an instruction to the actor to laugh.[6] As examples collected in this chapter illustrate, the "ha"s are usually, but not invariably, separated by commas, but given that punctuation in early modern playtexts is usually felt to be compositorial rather than authorial, one should not draw any conclusions from its presence, or absence, in this type of phrase. Conveniently, *LION* searches disregard intervening punctutation, so that a search for "ha ha ha" finds, for instance, "ha, ha, ha" or "ha ha! Ha". As for spelling, uncommon variants of the phrase (which further swell the number of texts involved beyond 255) substitute "a", "ah" or "hah" for the first or subsequent "ha"s, with no obvious shift in meaning, but the sheer frequency of "ha ha ha" makes it the standard verbal form for representing the sound of laughter for both male and female characters in early modern drama.

"Ha ha he" is a string which occurs 156 times across 34 texts, and even though one or two of these occurrences are spurious results, "ha ha he" is still the best-attested alternative to "ha ha ha".[7] For example, the female personification of Vice in Dekker's *Old Fortunatus* bears it written on the insignia she displays:

> *Enter vice with a gilded face ... her garment painted behind with fooles faces & diuels heads: and vnderneath it in the midst this written, Ha, Ha, He.*

The goddess Fortune comments on Vice's appearance, and her power to deceive her victims:

> And if shee once can bring thee to this place,
> Lowd sounds these ha, ha he, sheele laugh apace.[8]

"Ha ha he" has classical warrant, being the way that laughter is recorded in the texts of Terence, and has therefore something of a literary flavour. This can be seen in the fact that the three texts which make heaviest use of "ha ha he" instead of "ha ha ha" – namely, the anonymous comedy *Timon*, Ruggles's comedy *Ignoramus*, and Hausted's tragicomedy *The Rival Friends*, which between them account for 103 of the 156 hits – have provenances from the universities or the Inns of Court. Indeed, while the example from Dekker shows that "ha ha he" is not unknown on the professional stage, it is not the usual notation of laughter in the texts that survive from that stage. When Vice herself laughs in Dekker's play, her laughter is notated not as "ha ha he", as one might expect from her insignia, but in variants of "ha ha ha".

---

6   A second similar example is in Brome, *The New Academy*, 2.2, where Blithe refuses to speak to the buffoon Nehemiah and merely laughs at him repeatedly; finally Nehemiah gives up – "There's ha, ha, ha, ha for you" (Brome, *The New Academy* in *Five New Plays* [1659], 35); songs, such as Pandarus's song discussed in Chapter 8, offer one or two more exceptions.

7   This is from the search "ha ha he" OR "ha ha hee" OR "ha ha hae"; a spurious result might be from a sentence such as, "Ha, ha, he thinks that…".

8   Dekker, *Old Fortunatus* [1600], C3r, H4r; for her own laughter, H3r.

"Ha ha" is also used to denote laughter, a fact which can be illustrated by unambiguous examples listed below. In a handful of cases, "ha ha" clearly does not represent laughter – for instance, when it is part of a speech delivered by a stammerer; or when one of the "ha"s is a speech-prefix. In other cases, it is not clear whether it demonstrates laughter, or some other non-verbal noise. All the same, most occurrences of "ha ha" seem to be associated with laughter. The *Oxford English Dictionary* judges that "ha ha" is "The ordinary representation of laughter" in English, while "ha ha ha" denotes a more sustained laughter, but in this particular subset of texts, at least, "ha ha ha" is a preferred form.[9] *LION* finds 2418 occurrences of the string "ha ha" in the plays, but 989 occurrences of "ha ha ha"; since each of these 989 occurrences gives rise to two of the hits in the search for "ha ha", a calculation shows that there are not more than (2418–1978=) 440 occurrences of "ha ha" when it is not part of "ha ha ha", and of these 155 are accounted for by "ha ha he". At a rough and indicative estimate, then, there are under 300 "free-standing" examples of "ha ha" across the corpus of texts, not all of which denote laughter, compared to the 843 occurrences of "ha ha ha" and its longer siblings.

Metrically, "ha ha" is often, precisely, two syllables long, since it occurs within blank verse. Examples of this include:

Ha, ha: I laugh to see these Kings at jarre

(Anon., *The Tryall of Cheualry* [1605], F2v)

Ha, ha, I smile at my owne foolerie

(Heywood, *2 If you know not me* [1605], H2v)

"Ha ha ha" occurs relatively rarely in verse passages, and when it does, it is often extra-metrical. In some examples where the metre can be pinned down, it, too, often seems to occupy only two syllables of verse time:

Ha, ha, ha, I laugh untill my sides be sore,
For joy that my wives dandiprat is dead

(Heywood, *Love's Maistress* [1636], H2v)

Ha ha ha, I laugh yet, that the Cardinall's vext.

(?Dekker *et al.*, *Lust's Dominion* [1657], C2v)

There are, however, exceptions, which assign to "ha ha ha" a space equivalent to three, or even four, syllables:

Vp? tis a faire preferment, ha ha ha,
There should go showtes to vp-shots; not a breath
Of any mercy, yet? come, since we must...

(Chapman, *Charles Duke of Byron* [1608], R2r)

---

9   *OED*, ha *int.*

Ha, ha, ha, I cannot chuse but laugh,
To see my cosin cosend in this sort.
(Munday and Chettle, The Death of Robert Earl of Huntington [1601], B2r)

While "ha ha", then, appears to indicate a unit of roughly two syllables in length, "ha ha ha" seems to indicate a unit of laughter which is more variable in length even when contained within a verse structure. Twice in Jonson's The Devil is An Ass a ten-syllable line is filled with eight syllables of laughter, and an et cetera sign, the second example being from Act Five:

FITZDOTTEREL: Ha, ha, ha, ha, ha, ha, ha, ha, &c.
SIR PAUL: That is the Diuell speakes, and laughes in him.[10]

"Ha", on its own, is both extremely common (in 552 of the texts, in all), very ambiguous, and, even when it is a literal representation of a noise to be made by the actor, very broad in its range of possible meanings. Occasionally, a single "ha" appears in a context which makes it reasonably clear that it is a representation of a short laugh: thus, the foolish Simplicius in Marston's What You Will laughs, "Ha, ha, ha, God boy good Sinior, what a foole 'tis, ha, ha, what an Asse 'tis, saue you young Gentlemen, is shee comming, will she meete me, shal's incounter ha?" But most occasions on which a single "ha" occurs near the word "laugh" tend to show that the "ha" does not indicate laughter. In Thomas Randolph's Amyntas there occurs the exchange:

MOPSA: Ha ha he!
AMYNTAS: Ha? dost thou laugh old Charon?

Similarly, Fauconbridge in the anonymous Looke About You complains, "Ha laugh they? nay by the rood that is not wel", in a way that seems to indicate emphatically that his single "ha" does not constitute an instruction to laugh.[11] A single "ha", then, usually notates a short non-verbal noise, and that noise sometimes, but by no means often, is a short laugh.

Conversely, longer sequences of "ha"s are certainly possible, denoting, it appears, more sustained laughter. Aside from its appearances in longer sequences, "Ha ha ha ha" occurs 76 times in the corpus; "ha ha ha ha ha" eleven times; and so on for longer strings, including Fulwell's Like Will to Like (1587), C3r, in which the Vice Nichol Newfangle laughs a laugh eight "ha"s long: "Ha ha, ha, ha, ha, ha, ha, ha, / Now three Knaues are gone, and I am left alone". Extended laughter is often, indeed, associated with the Vice, or with madness, or with both, as in Jonson's The Devil is An Ass, when Fitzdotterel feigns demonic possession in the passage already quoted.

---

10   Jonson, The Devil is An Ass, 5.8.27–8.
11   Marston, What You Will (1601), G3v; Randolph, Amyntas (1638), 32; Looke About You (1600), A4r.

One might also note other extended strings including Hausted's *The Rival Friends* (1632), F4r, in which a character laughs: "Ha, ha, ha, he,—O my sides— " (and the dash here does what Jonson's *et cetera* sign does: it marks an aporia in the verbal structure, which may be filled with noise or action). In short, "ha ha ha" is, one might say, a standard-length stage laughter. It is one of a family of instructions to the actor, each of which conveys a different nuance about the duration of laughter required.

2) He he he

"He he he" is a much rarer variant, but when it denotes laughter it seems to have a distinctive flavour. *LION* detects the string in seven texts in the corpus of drama used here, three of which results can be discarded, since in them "he he he" features twice as part of a hunting call, and once as part of a necromantic incantation.[12] Of the four remaining texts, one is *The Rival Friends*, in which it occurs within longer bursts of laughter such as that quoted in the previous paragraph, but the other three texts in which "he he he" occurs use it to represent the laughter of a natural fool: Marston's *Antonio's Revenge*, Middleton and Rowley's *The Changeling*, and Jonson's *Volpone*. Antonio in Marston's *Antonio's Revenge* adopts the disguise of a natural fool, and indeed, seems to suggest that this form of laughter is a marker of that disguise: "I laugh like a good foole at the breath of mine owne lips, he, he, he, he, he." He is marked as laughing again in this manner in the following scene: "I hope sheele liue. If not Antonio's dead, the foole wil follow too, he, he, he".[13] In *The Changeling*, a "genuine" natural fool, also bearing the name Antonio, laughs in this fashion and again, his laughter seems to mark him out:

> LOLLIO: Tonie, Tonie, 'tis enough, and a very good name for a fool, what's your name Tonie?
> ANTONIO: He, he he, well I thank you cousin, he he, he.
> LOLLIO: Good Boy hold up your head: he can laugh, I perceive by that he is no beast.[14]

By "that", of course, Lollio means Antonio's laughing, referring back to Aristotle's statement that animals do not laugh. The third example of "he he he" is from a third play closely related in time to the other two, namely Jonson's *Volpone*. In this play the phrase appears in the song sung by Volpone's retinue at the start of the play, with its punning ending: "Fools they are the only nation ... O who would not be / He he he?", which, as Helen Ostovich notes, puns on the pronoun and on the sound of laughing. Ostovich suggests that these lines are accompanied by pointing at Androgyno, the fool (whose paucity of lines elsewhere in the play suggests that

---

12   The numbers here aggregate the results of searches for the seven possible variant spellings involving substitutions of "hee" for "he".

13   Marston, *Antonio's Revenge* (1602), G3v, H2r.

14   Middleton and Rowley, *The Changeling* (1653), C1v.

he is a natural fool more than a jester).[15] "He he he", then, seems to be a laughter particularly associated with natural fools at this date.

In an interesting symptom of cultural change, this form of laughter, uncommon in pre-Restoration dramatic texts, becomes in Restoration plays a modestly frequent representation of the laughter of normal people. As a rough indication of this, one can take the 469 dramatic texts in the *LION* database with performance dates between 1660 and 1710: "he he he" occurs in 28 of them, usually notating laughter and seemingly without any specific link to natural fools.

Finally, although (for obvious reasons) a moderately common sequence of letters, "He he" and its variants seem rarely, if ever, to denote laughter in early modern dramatic texts. An exception, *The Changeling* (1653), C2r, once again originates from Antonio the natural fool.

3) Ho ho ho

If "He he he" seems to be a form of laugh associated with fools, "Ho ho ho", too, has a particular constituency. The *LION* search produces 46 texts which feature this string or variants of it, although around fifteen of these are fairly clearly examples not of laughter but of hallooing, generally embedded within the calls "so ho ho ho" or "illo ho ho ho".[16] Of the remaining examples of "ho ho ho", a majority are attributed to the Devil himself, or to supernatural creatures such as Robin Goodfellow. For instance, the devil in Thomas Ingelend's morality play *The Disobedient Child* enters to deliver a soliloquy to the audience: "Ho, ho, ho, what a felowe am I? / Geue rowme I saye both more and lesse". Three more times in the ensuing speech, he uses the phrase "ho ho ho" as the start of a new paragraph. An extreme, and thematic, version of this convention used in a Jacobean play is the opening line of Jonson's *The Devil is An Ass*, where Satan laughs, "Hoh, hoh, hoh, hoh, hoh, hoh, hoh, hoh, &c." The persistence of the convention can also be seen, for instance, in J.C.'s *The Two Merry Milke-Maids*, when Landolfe enters, disguised as a spirit, and announces himself as follows: "Ho, ho, ho, Thou foolish Thing without Art …".[17]

Jean-Paul Debax proposes, in a study of interludes, that as a rule of thumb "Ha" or "Ah" is associated with the Vice's laughter, while "Ho" or "Oh" is associated with the Devil's more sinister and more theologically fraught laughter of despair.[18] A fresh look at the *LION* texts suggests that this holds true for the interludes and has interesting

---

15 H&S; Ben Jonson, *Four Comedies*, ed. Helen Ostovich (London: Longman, 1996), commentary *ad loc.*

16 Forty-six texts are found by a search for "ho hoh ho*" OR "hoh hoh ho*" OR "ho ho ho*" OR "hoh ho ho*". The string "ho ho ho" accounts for 41 of these.

17 Thomas Ingelend, *The Disobedient Child* [?1570], F3r; Jonson, *The Devil is An Ass*, 1.1.1; J.C., *The Two Merry Milke-Maids* (1620), B2r.

18 Jean-Paul Debax, "*Oh, oh, oh, Ah, ah, ah*: The Meanings of Laughter in the Interludes", in Roberta Mullini (ed.), *Tudor Theatre: For laughs (?)/Pour rire(?): Puzzling Laughter in Plays of the Tudor Age/Rires et problèmes dans le theatre des Tudors* (Bern: Peter Lang, 2002), 81–93;

implications for some later plays. For instance, in *Antony and Cleopatra*, many critics have noted that Antony's laughter as he tries to cheer up his weeping friends at their last banquet together seems forced: "Ho, ho, ho: / Now the Witch take me, if I meant it thus". In the light of the usual norms around the notation of laughter, his laughter is, almost literally, off-key.[19]

Other examples where "ho ho ho" is clearly mimetic of the sound of humans laughing are rare, although Middleton's *A Mad World, My Masters* provides one when Sir Bountiful laughs in this way at the discomfort of the Constable: "Ho ho ho ho ... Ha, ha ha, by my troth the maddest piece of Iustice gentlemen, that euer was committed." In Beaumont and Fletcher's *The Nice Valour*, Passion and Base sing a song about laughter, in the chorus of which "ho ho ho" is antiphonal to "ha ha ha".[20]

"Ho ho", too, can occasionally denote human laughter, but with a seemingly sardonic or otherwise differentiated tone. Apemantus in *Timon of Athens* laughs like this: "Ho, ho: I laugh to thinke that babe a bastard". So does Caliban, when expressing his regret that he did not succeed in raping Miranda: "Oh ho, oh ho, would't had bene done".[21] If indeed it is the noise of laughter that he makes at this point (and the example is not as conveniently unambiguous as that from Apemantus) then Caliban is laughing in a register with disturbing resonances. "Ho ho ho", and its variants, are a rare but possible way of notating human laughter, although one should be aware of the possibility that they may notate other human noises such as hallooing. And, although this is not an infallible rule, the phrase may carry, potentially, sardonic or even demonic overtones.[22]

4) Hugh and whooh

More exotic forms still are occasionally to be found. In Brome's *The Antipodes*, the amazed and still half-drugged Peregrine utters the phrase "hugh hugh hugh", a phrase which in another context is used by Brome to represent the sound accompanying the

---

a search on *LION* shows no clear examples of a character laughing „oh oh oh", apart from the Devil, of which a good example is Wager, *Inough is as good as a feast* (1570), G1r.

19   F reading of *Antony and Cleopatra*, 4.2.37–8; for an acoustic approach to the play, see Wes Folkerth, *The Sound of Shakespeare* (London: Routledge, 2002), 34–8, 41–3.

20   Middleton, *A Mad World, My Masters* (1608), H3v; Beaumont and Fletcher, *Comedies and Tragedies* (1647), 162.

21   F readings of *Timon of Athens*, 1.2.111; *The Tempest*, 2.1.347. In addition, 30 *LION* texts contain the string "o ho", but none of the examples provides an unambiguous link with laughter of the sort seen in Apemantus's "ho ho".

22   According to an unnamed seventeenth-century source cited in Keith Thomas, "The Place of Laughter in Tudor and Stuart England", *Times Literary Supplement* (21 January 1977), 77, laughter in the forms "hi hi hi", "he he he" and "ho ho ho" is symptomatic of, respectively, melancholic, phlegmatic and sanguine temperaments. However, this does not seem to correspond to the distribution of these phrases on the pre-1642 stage.

stage direction "*cough and spit*". Peregrine's interlocutor seems to interpret it as the sound of laughter:

> PEREGRINE: Hugh, hugh, hugh.
> DOCTOR: What do you laugh?[23]

But the context itself shows that this is untypical, and no other clear parallels to it in drama of the period have been found. And a stage direction in Ruggles's *Ignoramus* appears to use "whooh" as a verbal representation of laughter:

> *They all laugh, whooh, Ha ha he.*[24]

"Whoo", which the *OED* categorises as "an exclamation of surprise, grief, or other emotion", and its variants occur occasionally elsewhere in conjunction with laughter, in texts such as Dekker's *Patient Grisill*, where the clown is dandling a child: "I daunce mine own childe, and I dance mine owne childe, &c: ha ha, whoop olde Master, so ho ho, looke heere, and I dance mine own childe, &c".[25] These uses are, however, infrequent – one might say, unusual forms within the syndrome – and it is clear that this is not a usual way of representing laughter. Reduplicated forms of "ha", "ho" and "he", and variants thereon, are the main verbal representations of laughter in early modern dramatic texts. For all that the pedant in John Marston's *Parasitaster* earns his place on the Ship of Fools for attempting to work out the orthography of laughter, there is such an orthography in early modern drama, and it is an important part of how stage laughter is inflected.

Implicit Stage Directions

In addition to explicit stage directions and to the use of "ha ha ha" and related forms, onstage laughter can also be cued by implicit stage directions. Two examples are given here to illustrate this wider phenomenon. In Beaumont's comedy *The Woman-Hater*, the feisty Oriana is unable to contain her laughter at the eponymous misogynist:

> GONDARINO: Your Ladiships boldnesse in coming, will bee impudence in staying, for you are most vnwelcome.
> ORIANA: Oh my Lord!
> GONDARINO: Doe you laugh, by the hate I beare to you, 'tis true.

A few lines later in the exchange, Oriana does have laughter at Gondarino notated as "Ha, ha, ha". But there is clearly an implied stage direction requiring her to start laughing earlier. Similarly, the Duchess in Chettle's tragedy *Hoffman* reacts to a

---

23 Brome, *The Sparagus Garden* (1640), E1v; Brome, *The Antipodes* (1640), D1r.
24 Ruggles, *Ignoramus* [1662], L4r.
25 *OED*, whoo *int*; cf. *OED*, whoop *int*; Dekker, *Patient Grissill* (1603), G4r.

seduction attempt by the play's villain in terms which are not marked in her lines, but are implicit in Hoffman's response:

> DUCHESS: What my adopted son become my louer?
>   And make a wanton minion of his mother?
>   Now fie vpon you fie y'are too obsceane
>   If like your words, your thoughts appeare vncleane.
> HOFFMAN: By heauen I doe not ieast, goe to, belieue me
>   'Tis well you laugh; smile on, I like this …[26]

Such implied stage directions resist easy quantification, because of their variety of verbal forms, because of the fact that they are frequently combined with other indications such as the phrase "ha ha ha", and because they are not always as completely unequivocal in their implications as the two examples selected above.[27] Although both of the examples listed above could be called second-person implied stage directions, in that a line by an interlocutor makes explicit the fact that the other character is laughing, first-person implied stage directions are also found frequently, such as Dromio's "O Lord, I must laugh" (*The Comedy of Errors*, 3.1.50). Similar formulae used in such first-person implied stage directions include "I laugh at you", and "give me leave to laugh".

From these examples, it follows that there is more to the representation of laughing than merely the notation of the noise. It is to the gestural representation of laughter that this chapter will now turn.

Gesture and Laughter

For detail about gestures associated with emotion, one can consult a source close to the pre-1642 stage, in John Bulwer's *Chirologia* (1644), an "art of manuall rhetoric" which even in its frontispiece acknowledges the interconnectedness of rhetoric and acting. As Andrew Gurr notes, it is not necessary to take *Chirologia* as an indication that all early modern acting was codified and stylised, since the book's taxonomy of gestures is intended explicitly as a set of guidelines rather than a comprehensive practice: nonetheless, it certainly gives some pointers to early modern theatrical custom.[28] At first glance, though, *Chirologia* does not offer any direct clues as to how a speaker might represent gesturally that they are laughing.

---

26 [Beaumont], *The Woman-Hater* (1607), C1v; Chettle, *Hoffman* (1631), L1r–L1v.

27 For example: a search for "do you laugh" OR "dost thou laugh" returns 46 hits from 35 plays, most of them associated with "ha ha ha" or a similar phrase, all of them, seemingly, referring to performed onstage laughter. What is striking about this is how often the phrase draws attention to laughter of other characters which has already been notated.

28 J[ohn] B[ulwer], *Chirologia, or, The naturall language of the hand composed of the speaking motions, and discoursing gestures thereof: whereunto is added Chironomia, or, The art of manuall rhetoricke* (London: Tho. Harper, 1644), 160; see B.L. Joseph, *Elizabethan Acting*,

Clues to facial gestures, though, are to be found in Bulwer's *Pathomyotamia*, a lesser-known sequel to *Chirologia*, dealing with facial expressions. There, Bulwer follows Laurent Joubert in locating the origin of laughter not in the face but in the diaphragm: "the motion of laughter begun within in the middle venter, the terminus ad quem is the extreme part of the Face, where it terminates". Bulwer also offers an interestingly theatrical metaphor for the facial movements:

> In this Dance of the Muscles performed by excessive Laughter upon the Theater of mirth, the Countenance, the Mouth seems to lead the Chorus ... the *Mouth* is more shut than open, that is it is Dehiscent, yet scarce Dehiscent into a Casme, yet the *Lips* are so distended and contracted that they discover the *Teeth*.

Bulwer goes on to give a very detailed description of how almost every muscle in the face is active during laughter: "this Jubilee and vibrations of so many Muscles".[29] If *Chironomia* can be used as a reference point in recovering stage representation of gesture, then *Pathomyotamia* offers a facial equivalent. As will be seen in Chapter 4, the facial expression of the actors is a particularly important element in generating audience laughter: it is interesting, then, that the best description of how to enact laughter on one's own face describes it not as a fixed pose but as a "Dance of the Muscles" led by the mouth. And some evidence that at least one of these facial gestures could be acted on the stage can be gained from Middleton's *Women Beware Women*, where the Ward, fearing his proposed bride Isabella may have rotten teeth, attempts unsuccessfully to make her laugh in the hope of getting to see them.[30]

Stage directions which explicitly mention laughter give a few clues as to what the characteristic gestures accompanying such expressions might be. For instance, two stage directions specify both laughing and pointing, a connection which is also made (as will be seen below) in implicit stage directions:

they point at her, and laugh

(Field, *A Woman is a Weathercock* [1612], H3v)

Enter 3. Lords laughing, and pointing scornfully at Antipater.

(Markham and Sampson, *Herod and Antipater* [1622], K1r)

Bulwer's *Chirologia* does contain a good deal on pointing gestures of the sort implied in the above stage directions, including gestures which suggest scorn, such

---

2nd edn (Oxford: Oxford University Press, 1964), esp. 51, arguing that Bulwer's work is the product of observation; Michael Neill, "'Amphitheatres in the Body': Playing with Hands on the Shakespearean Stage", in *Putting History to the Question: Power, Politics, and Society in English Renaissance Drama* (New York: Columbia University Press, 2000), 167–203.

29 J[ohn] [B]ulwer, *Pathomyotamia, or, A dissection of the significative muscles of the affections of the minde* (London: Humphrey Moseley, 1649), 105–6.

30 Middleton, *Women Beware Women* in *Two New Playes* (London: Humphrey Moseley, 1657), 162.

as "Ironiam infligo … to bend the middle-finger while it stifly resteth upon the thumb, and so in iesting-wise to let it off … a *triviall* expression whereby we with a fillip inflict a *trifling punishment*, or a *scoffe*".[31]

Clapping the hands is mentioned as an actor's gesture accompanying laughter in a stage direction from *Jacob and Esau* (1568), C2r, where, as often, laughing is specified as part of the stage direction for a character's entrance:

> *Mido cometh in clapping his hands, and laughing.*
> MIDO: Ha, ha, ha, ha, ha, ha,
>   Nowe who sawe ere suche an other as Esau?

A second example which corroborates this comes from near the other end of the chronological period under discussion, when an emblematic character named Hilario in the inset masque in William Strode's *The Floating Island* is instructed, in what is in effect a rhymed stage direction, to both clap and laugh: "Hilario clap thy hands and laugh, / Skip, leap, and turn, offer to quaff".[32] Clapping the hands is strictly speaking a sign of joy, rather than part of the symptoms arising from laughter in Joubert's sense: so Bulwer, for example, classifies it in this way. All the same, the two references noted above give us warrant to see it reflected in stage practice associated with laughter, and the representation of clapping and laughing has a particular interest in a theatre in which clapping and laughing are the main ways in which audiences show their approval of a play.

More extreme laughter is often associated with a gesture of holding one's sides, well-attested from implied stage directions in dialogue. In Heywood's *The Silver Age*, a character enters "*extreamly laughing*", according to the stage direction, and the victim at whom she is laughing complains: "What meanes the wretch to hold her sides & laugh,/ And still to point at me?" Another clear example comes from the eponymous Wise-woman in *The Wise Woman of Hogsdon*, who states in soliloquy, "Ha, ha, let me hold my sides, and laugh", and another from Hausted's *The Rival Friends* previously cited: "Ha, ha, ha, he,—O my sides—."[33]

A still more extravagant gesture of helplessness, sometimes outlined in implied stage directions, is to require another character to hold up the laugher. The Vice Sedicyon in Bale's *King Johan* laughs in this fashion as he plots against King John, presumably throwing himself into the arms of the irritated Cardinal:

> SEDITION: Holde me, or els for laughynge I must burste!
> CARDINAL: Holde thy peace, whorson, I wene thu art accurst.[34]

---

31 Bulwer, *Chirologia*, 177, capitalisation silently normalised.
32 Strode, *Floating Island* (1655), D2r.
33 Heywood, *The Silver Age* (1613), F2v–F3r; Heywood, *The Wise Woman of Hogsdon* (1638), D4r.
34 Bale, *King Johan* in *Complete Plays* (1985), 1.73.

In Jonson's *Epicoene*, Dauphine requires similar support while in the grip of a laughter he describes as life-threatening: "Oh, hold me up a little, I shall go away i'the jest else". A third example which demonstrates the spread of this convention both in time and in social register comes from Shirley's *The Ball*, where Lady Lucina laughs at the ridiculousness of her suitors: "Oh *Scutilla*, hold me, I shall fall / In peeces else, ha ha, ha".[35]

Beyond this, it is difficult to generalise about the stage representation of laughter. Sometimes, laughter is acted out as an immobilising, incapacitating force:

> *Trash falls into a laughter*
> (Chamberlain, *The Swaggering Damsell* [1640], H1r)

> *Whilst Trincalo laughes, and fals the staffe, Pandolfo recouers it, and beates him*
> (Tomkis, *Albumazar* [1615], L2r)

However, other stage directions associate it with activity and energy:

> *Divels run laughing over the stage*
> (Kirke, *The Seven Champions of Christendom* [1638], H1r)

> *Enter Bullithrumble, the shepheard running in hast, and laughing to himselfe.*
> (Greene, *Selimus* [1638], H1r)

Similarly, a gestural rhetoric of "pointing scornfully" seems inappropriate for stage directions such as "Shake hands and laugh hartely one at an other" (Preston, *Cambyses* [1570], D4v), where laughter apparently functions to unify, not divide, the characters on stage.

To summarise what can be said: around a third of all English dramatic texts performed in the years 1550–1642 feature the phrase "ha ha ha", almost always functioning as an implied stage direction asking the character to laugh. Laughter is also sometimes notated as "ha ha" and "ha ha he"; in a range of variations on this theme; and, more rarely, in specialised variant forms including "he he he" and "ho ho ho". In addition, onstage laughter is often not merely invited but required in implied stage directions. The representation of laughter is associated with somewhat extreme facial contortions. Stage actions typically associated with laughter's representation include pointing, clapping, holding one's sides, and falling into the arms of another character. The interesting thing about this is that it might make us look afresh at the instruction to the actor, "ha, ha, ha", especially when combined with dashes or the symbol *et cetera*. This is almost a musical notation to the actor: an invitation to improvise, in sounds and gesture, on an established repertoire of effects.

---

35 Shirley's *The Ball* (1639), D2r; Jonson, *Epicoene*, 4.1.20. Richard Dutton glosses the phrase as meaning "die laughing"; Ben Jonson, *Epicene*, ed. Richard Dutton (Manchester: Manchester University Press, 2004), 4.1.20n.

Chapter 3

Weeping on stage

Like laughter, weeping is an action very frequently performed on the early modern stage. Dessen and Thomson's *Dictionary of Stage Directions*, for instance, reports over 100 instances of weeping as an explicit stage direction in English drama from the period 1580–1642. Dessen and Thomson's initial overview runs as follows:

> Over 100 SDs call for a figure to *weep* or presumably to simulate *weeping*, sometimes with happiness, more often in fear, entreaty or sorrow; usually the figure is a woman, and often she, or another calls attention to the *weeping* which the audience is unlikely to see.[1]

The entry raises various problems about the representation of weeping: questions of simulation and reality, questions of interiority and external signification of emotion, and questions of how, in practical dramatic terms, tears are shown. But it is important to note that, as far as instances of weeping are concerned, these hundred or more examples are only the tip of an iceberg, since implied stage directions are by far more common than the explicit ones. For instance, as will be argued in more detail below, variants of the phrase "these … tears", which serves reliably as an implied stage direction, can be found 161 times in the *LION* corpus, so that this one implied stage direction is itself more common than the explicit stage direction.

In order to examine the representation of weeping more closely, it will be helpful to take as a test case Beaumont and Fletcher's tragicomedy *Philaster*, first acted in 1609 or 1610. This play contains no explicit stage directions specifying weeping, but the action of the play encompasses up to eight implied stage directions for weeping, six of which require the representation of weeping for the dialogue of the scene to make sense.[2] In the second act of the play, for instance, Philaster instructs his recently acquired manservant Bellario to take up a new job as servant to Philaster's beloved, Arethusa.

---

1   Alan C. Dessen and Leslie Thomson, *A Dictionary of Stage Directions in English Drama 1580–1642* (Cambridge: Cambridge University Press, 1999), s.v. "weep"; for comparison, the *LION* database used for this study finds 163 stage directions featuring the string "weep*" in plays performed in the period 1580–1642, and 167 for plays performed in the period 1550–1642. In addition, the verb "cry" is occasionally used in its modern sense, as a synonym for "weep". Amid many examples of it being used in its more dominant sense, equivalent to the modern "shout", there are some clear examples where it *does* serve to indicate weeping, including Marston's *Jack Drum's Entertainment*, with the stage direction "*Enter two Pages, the one laughing, the other crying*", discussed in Chapter 1.

2   Beaumont and Fletcher, *Philaster. Or, loue lies a bleeding* (London: Thomas Walkley, 1622); the play is cited from this edition, with cross-references to the line numbering

The young manservant (who is, in fact, a woman in disguise) starts to weep at his parting, as Philaster's speech indicates:

> Thy loue doth plead so prettily to stay,
> That (trust me) I could weepe to part with thee,
> Alas I doe not turn thee off ...
> ... When time is full,
> That thou hast well discharg'd this heauy trust,
> Laid on so weake a one: I will againe
> With ioy receive thee: as I liue, I will;
> Nay, weepe not, gentle boy; Tis more then time
> Thou didst attend the Princesse.

(D1r, 2.1.39–48)

Bellario's weeping is mainly for grief at his parting from Philaster, but he appears to be tipped over into tears by the good news of Philaster's promise to take him back. Bellario's new role is spoiled when enemies of Philaster spread the story that Bellario and Arethusa are having an affair, and in the third act, Bellario weeps again, this time unequivocally for grief, when Philaster threatens to kill him if he ever returns to court; again, this information is conveyed in the dialogue:

> ...through these teares
> Shed at my hopelesse parting, I can see
> A world of Treason practisde vpon you
> And her, and me. Farewell for euermore;
> If you shall heare that sorrow strucke me dead,
> And after finde me loyall; let there be
> A teare shed from you, in my memory.

(F4r–F4v, 3.1.294–300)

In the following scene, another deictic remark draws attention to tears running from the heroine Arethusa's eyes: Arethusa has a soliloquy in which she expresses her distress at being parted from Bellario, and Philaster observes upon his entrance, "He must be more than man, that makes these Christals / Run into riuers", (G1r, 3.2.55). At this point, modern editions, such as Gurr's, have to supply a stage direction to elucidate the speech. In 4.3, when Bellario and Philaster meet again, the dialogue only makes sense if Bellario is weeping, as Philaster warns him:

> Euen so thou wepst, and lookst, and spokst, when first
> I took thee vp; curse on the time. If thy
> Commanding teares can work on any other,
> Vse thy art, I'le not betray it.

(G4v–H1r, 4.3.36–9)

---

of Beaumont and Fletcher, *Philaster or, Love Lies a-Bleeding*, ed. Andrew Gurr (1969; Manchester: Manchester University Press, 2003).

By Act Five, Philaster himself is being comforted by Bellario and Arethusa, and tears of some variety are present:

PHILASTER: Take me in teares betwixt you,
    For my heart will breake with shame and sorrow.
ARETHUSA: Why, 'tis well.
BELLARIO: Lament no more.

(I3v, 5.1.34-7)

But near the end of the play, it is the King's turn to weep, and this time the tears are joyful, or at least in part joyful:

streames of griefe
That I have wrought thee; and as much of ioy
That I repent it, issue from mine eyes;
Let them appease thee.

(K4v, 5.5.12–15)

To these six instances, which require a character to be weeping for the dialogue to make sense, can be added two more which imply that a character is weeping. Another soliloquy by Arethusa on the subject of her miseries is interrupted by the entrance of Bellario, who asks to be pitied: "you that have plenty, / From that flowing store, drop some on drie ground" (H2r–H2v, 4.5.9–10), and while these tears might merely be a figure of speech, the line's implication that Arethusa is shedding tears is certainly in tune with the emotional mood of the scene. A little later, Philaster announces, at the least, an intention to weep when he asks those tending to Bellario (whom he has just wounded):

Would you haue teares shed for you when you dye?
Then lay me gently on his neck, that there
I may weepe flouds, and breath forth my spirit

(I2r, 4.6.120–21)

This last speech also contains a characteristic feature of many implied stage directions indicating weeping, such as 2.1.48 and 3.1.294–300 quoted above, namely that it also alludes to the possibility of others weeping besides the weeper. Later in the same speech Philaster expands on the idea, looking at the wounded Bellario and claiming that the sight of the wounds would induce even queens to weep tears enough to bathe them. It may also be significant that, as will be seen in Chapter 5, two early modern critics praise Bellario, and one in particular the scene of his bleeding, as likely to induce weeping in the audience of the play. Beaumont and Fletcher's *Philaster* is fascinated by weeping to an almost ludicrous extent, and yet it never uses an explicit stage direction to represent the weeping that is so frequent in it.[3]

Philaster is something of an extreme example, but its implied stage directions for weeping are usefully characteristic of their counterparts in early modern drama as a whole. One typical feature is the use of a mixture of first-person and second-person implied stage directions, and elsewhere third-person implied stage directions are also found, of which a good example is *Hamlet*, 2.2.513–14, where the Player's weeping is indicated by third-person remarks by Polonius ("look where he has not turned his colour and has tears in's eyes") and by Hamlet himself. Other typical features exemplified within this sample from *Philaster* include the inventive range of periphrases for the act of weeping, which often mention neither "weeping" nor "tears" directly; the presence of both female, and male, weepers; the presence of tears for sorrow and tears for joy, with the dividing-line between them often far from clear; and the phrasing which implies, not just sobbing, but "Rivers" of running wet tears.

Of the eight implied stage directions collected above, four are first-person and four are second-person. The split is interesting because it speaks to one of the most contested questions of early modern theatre history: whether the prevailing acting style was illusionistic, in the modern sense, with actors remaining in character even when not speaking, or whether it was a very stylised succession of discrete speeches with relatively little interaction.[4] A modern audience would consider a line like, "He must be more than man, that makes these Christals / Run into Rivers", addressed to a character who was not in fact already weeping, to be an absurdity, and the importance of these particular phenomena – their status as, almost, verbal – might lead one to think that they, at least, were enacted, if not enacted naturalistically. Some support for this idea comes from the fragmentary "part" for *Orlando Furioso*, recording the cues and lines of Orlando: during one scene where Orlando orders a clown, first to weep and then to laugh, the clown's weeping is one of very few stage directions relating to other characters to be recorded in Orlando's "part".[5] But there are numerous counterexamples which refer to actors falling out of character when not speaking. Among them, the satirist John Stephens's description of a player is particularly germane here, since it refers to a failure to maintain solemnity: "he hath bin so accustomed to the scorne and laughter of his audience, that hee cannot bee ashamed of himselfe: for hee dares laugh in the middest of a serious conference,

---

3   In addition, offstage weeping is frequently reported in ekphrastic detail, as when Philaster describes Bellario weeping, and Bellario describes Philaster weeping (D4v, 2.3.55–60); indeed, one of Bellario's main responsibilities as a go-between is to weep on Philaster's behalf in front of Arethusa, and on Arethusa's behalf in front of Philaster (F2v, 3.1.184, 3.2.5).

4   See, for instance, B.L. Joseph, *Elizabethan Acting*, 2nd edn (Oxford: Oxford University Press, 1964); Andrew Gurr, *The Shakespearean Stage, 1574–1642*, 3rd edn (Cambridge: Cambridge University Press, 1992).

5   Greene, *Orlando Furioso* (1594), E2r–E3r; W.W. Greg, *Dramatic Documents from the Elizabethan Playhouses*, 2 vols (Oxford: Clarendon Press, 1931).

without blushing".[6] Questions raised here about the degree of stylisation in the representation of weeping are, however, and for obvious reasons, unanswerable from the internal evidence of stage directions alone, whether actual or implied, and it is to other forms of evidence that one must turn to further address this question.

As a transitional step, it is necessary to consider the sound of weeping. Whereas laughter is very often represented by an onomatopoeic instruction to the actor, most commonly by the phrase "ha ha ha", the same is not true, or not so clearly true, of weeping. "Oh", and its variants, seem to cover a broad range of non-verbal noises, including coughing, groaning and (as noted in the previous chapter) laughing. But at least some of the uses of "oh" are specifically coded to represent the noise of sobbing, that secondary consequence (as Bright describes it) of the brain's excretion of tears. Fifty-five occurrences of the phrase "oh oh oh" in drama performed in the period 1550–1642 include, for instance, Wager's *Inough is as Good as a Feast*, in which the Vice Covetise pretends to weep: "Oh Sir, oh good Sir, oh, oh, oh my hart wil breke: / Oh, oh, for sorow God wot I cannot speak".[7] From much later in the period, Magdalen Bumpsey in Brome's comedy *The Damoiselle* provides a conveniently unambiguous example when she gets drunk in a tavern:

> MAGDALEN: O good lack! what will become of us? where are we now, *Jane*?
>   Betray'd! betray'd! Our honours are betray'd. O my poor *Bump.* how will
>   thou take this at my hands, though J carry them never so Courtly?
> DRYGROUNDS: 'Sfoot, she's in her Mawdlin fit: All her wine showres out in teares.
> MAGDALEN: Oh, oh, oh,—
>
>   (Brome, *The Damoiselle* [1653], F4v–F5r)

Of the other 49 examples, it must be said that many if not most, in context, do not refer to the sound of weeping. But in interpreting the ones which are ambiguous, as well as shorter versions of the string such as "oh oh", it is useful to know that "oh oh oh" is sometimes the sound which accompanies weeping. Indeed, a passage from Beaumont and Fletcher's *The Maides Tragedy* conveniently shows not merely that "oh oh" can represent the sound of weeping, but that it can do so in a serious, as well as a comic, context:

> AMINTOR: Forgiue what I ha done;
>   For I am so ore-gon with miseries,
>   Vnheard of, that I lose consideration
>   Of what I ought to do, —oh —oh.
> MELANTIUS: Doe not weep, what ist?[8]

---

6   John Stephens, *Essayes and characters, ironicall, and instructiue* (London: E. Allde, 1615), 299.
7   Wager, *Inough is as Good as a Feast* [1570], D1r.
8   Beaumont and Fletcher, *The Maides Tragedy* (1653), F4v–F5r.

"Ah ah", and its variants, may also denote the sound of weeping. *Cambyses* offers a clear, comic example, although it is complicated by the fact of Ambidexter's knowing insincerity:

> *Enter Ambidexter weping*
> AMBIDEXTER: A, A, A, A, I cannot chuse but weep for the Queene:
>   Nothing but mourning now at the Court there is seen.
>   Oh, oh, my hart, my hart, Oh my bum wil break:
>   Uery greef so torments me that scarce I can speake.
> (Preston, Cambyses [1570], F1v)

Serious examples are less clear-cut, but *Richard III* appears to use a single "ah" as an implied stage direction for an actor to "waile and weepe":

> *Enter the Queene with her haire about her ears, Riuers & Dorset after her.*
> QUEEN: Ah! who shall hinder me to waile and weepe?[9]

As the examples above demonstrate, both "oh", and "ah", and various reduplications of them, can sometimes represent the sound of weeping.[10] Nonetheless, such verbal notation of the sound of weeping is relatively uncommon. *Philaster*, for instance, includes no such verbal indication of noise, and it is also possible to weep in dumb shows. How, then, one might ask, was weeping represented gesturally on the stage? One source of information is provided by the hundred or so stage directions which mention weeping. Some of these offer qualifying descriptions:

> *Ent. ... Eleonora, loose haired, & weeping.*
> (Dick of Devonshire [1955], 30)

> *Chastitie... with her haire disheueled ... wringing her hands, in teares departes*
> (A Warning for Faire Women [1599], E3v)

> *Onælia walking discontentedly weeping to the Crucifix*
> (S.R., The Noble Spanish Souldier [1634], B2r)

> *Enter Violanta at one door, weeping, supported by Cornelia and a Frier*
> (John Fletcher, Four Playes, in Comedies and Tragedies [1647], 35)

> *She weepes, and wrings her hands*
> (John Ford, 'Tis Pitty Shee's a Whore [1633], F3v)

---

9   F reading of *Richard III*, 2.2.34–6.

10   For the sake of completeness, it should be added that this study has found no clear-cut examples of "ha" indicating a noise of woe (although that doesn't confirm that such examples don't exist); and only one clear example of "ho" doing so, as part of the phrase "oh ho", in an example which appears in the very last quotation of this book.

[for joy] *she leanes on him and weepes*

(Thomas Killigrew, *Claracilla* [1641], D5r)

She weeps, and leans upon his breast

(Killigrew, *Thomaso*, in *Comedies and Tragedies* [1664], 368)

Shee rises up weeping, and hanging downe her head

(Suckling, *Aglaura* [1638], 36)

All these more elaborate stage directions, all from "serious" scenes, describe women weeping. Posture (leaning, hanging down of the head) is the most commonly repeated note, also picked up in *The Taming of the Shrew* when the nobleman is giving instructions on how his page-boy should impersonate Sly's wife: "And with declining head into [Sly's] bosom, / Bid him shed tears".[11] Hand-wringing is also required in two of these directions, both times specifically in the context of ideas of guilt. The dishevelled hair of the first two examples (and of the Queen in *Richard III*) is a well-attested stage symbol whose associations with female grief, madness and loss of dignity have been traced more fully by Alan C. Dessen, so that there is a series of overlapping theatrical codes at work in these examples.[12] In a similar vein, representation of the syndrome of weeping is often an element within a larger syndrome of conventional signs indicating love-melancholy, or a similar and related larger syndrome indicating funeral mourning.[13]

In contrast to stage directions from tragic scenes, in which weeping is presented as something of a passive process, the more elaborate stage directions from comic scenes imply a rather different aesthetic of comic weeping:

Let the Vice weep & houle & make great lamentation to the Worldly man.

(Wager, *Inough is as good as a feast* [1570], D1r)

[Rustico] *weepes and howles with hands before his face* ... [Rustico] *hides his face with his hands againe, and so standeth a while sighing and sobbing*

(*Two wise men and all the rest fooles* [1619], 49, 51)

Both of these, as it happens, refer to male characters, but they can be put alongside the excessive weeping and wailing of the distressed Magdalen Bumpsey, and Ambidexter's lines quoted above ("Oh, oh, my hart, my hart, Oh my bum wil break"). All four acts of comic weeping are clearly acoustically excessive, vigorous and amusing, and Rustico's gesture of the hands before the face offers, in overstated parodic form, another interpretation of the gestural rhetoric of weeping.

---

11   Shakespeare, *The Taming of the Shrew,* Induction, 117–8.

12   Alan C. Dessen, *Recovering Shakespeare's Theatrical Vocabulary* (Cambridge: Cambridge University Press, 1995), 43.

13   Dessen and Thomson, *Dictionary of Stage Directions*, s.v. "melancholy", "mourn".

Explicit and implicit references show that a handkerchief is often used as a property to help represent weeping. Three stage directions give explicit information:

> *Antonio and Maria wet their handkerchers with their teares, kisse them, and lay them on the hearse, kneeling*
>
> (Marston, *Antonios Reuenge* [1602], C3r)

> *Hee seems to fall into a passion ... He draws his handkerchiefe (as to wipe his eyes) ... and scatters some small mony*
>
> (J.D., *The Knave in Graine* [1640], M1v)

> *A dull Dutch Lover ... doth often apply his Handkerchiefe to his eyes, as if the griefe of his dispaire did make him weepe*
>
> (Davenant, *The Triumphs of the Prince D'Amour* [1635], 11)

The second and third of these examples seem to feel the need to explain the handkerchief, which could suggest that its appearance as a visual aid is not entirely routine. But a character in Davenant's own *News From Plimouth* sardonically implies it is a *sine qua non* for weeping: "Now can I hardly forbear to cry too, / But that I left my Handkerchief in my / Cabin and want somewhat to dry my Eyes / When they are wet". Lafeu in *All's Well that Ends Well* requires one in what is, in effect, an implied stage direction: "Mine eyes smell Onions, I shall weepe anon: / Good Tom Drumme lend me a handkercher". Other intra-diegetic references to the handkerchief as a natural companion to weeping are frequent, such as that by the word-mistaking Clown in Alexander Brome's *The Cunning Lovers*: "You that lov'd him, out with your eyes, and wipe your handkerchers ... provide for a shower of raine".[14] Unsurprisingly, then, phrases like "dry your eyes" or "dry thine eyes" are frequently used as, in effect, retrospective implied stage directions, and may be taken as in most cases implying the use of a handkerchief or similar property to accompany the weeping.[15]

Considerably later than the period under discussion, and emerging from a very different theatre, is a scene in Sheridan's *The Critic* in which we actually see weeping rehearsed. Tiffany Stern writes that *The Critic* "has nothing to do with rehearsal as practised by Sheridan", since by the time of *The Critic*, rehearsal plays had become a distinct genre in themselves. Thus, the plays cannot be taken as evidence of the practice even of the theatre they purported to represent.[16] This is undoubtedly true. However, Sheridan's scene is worth inclusion here, because it anecdotally illustrates

---

14   Davenant, *News from Plimouth*, in *Works* (1673), 10; Shakespeare, *All's Well that Ends Well*, 5.3.358–9; Alexander Brome, *The Cunning Lovers* (1654), 51.

15   One can use the "FBY" (followed by) search term to construct a search for this: *LION* returns 19 results, for instance, of the search string (dry your FBY.3 eyes) OR (dry thine FBY.3 eyes), almost all of them instructions in the imperative.

16   Tiffany Stern, *Rehearsal from Shakespeare to Sheridan* (Oxford: Clarendon Press, 2000), 241.

a model of how use of a handkerchief *might* work. *The Critic*, of course, dramatises the rehearsal of an amusingly incompetent historical tragedy written by Mr Puff. Its heroine Tilburina, distracted with love, is given a speech which begins with a description of dawn, and moves from there into a description of the beautiful flowers and birds around her ("The lark! / The linnet! chafinch! bullfinch! goldfinch! greenfinch!"). This in turn leads, by a conventional contrast *topos*, to a statement of her own woe which forms the climax of the speech and cues the intervention of her confidante.

> PUFF: Your white handkerchief, madam! —
> TILBURINA: I thought, Sir, I wasn't to use that till, *heart-rending woe.*
> PUFF: O yes madam—at *the finches of the grove*, if you please.
> TILBURINA: Nor lark,
>   Linnet, nor all the finches of the grove! [*Weeps.*]
> PUFF: Vastly well, madam!
> DANGLE: Vastly well, indeed!
> TILBURINA: For, O too sure, heart rending woe is now
>   The lot of wretched Tilburina!
> DANGLE: Oh!—it's too much.
> SNEER: Oh!—it is indeed.
> CONFIDANT: Be comforted sweet lady...[17]

In Sheridan's imagination, at least, a speech that ends with a declaration of the speaker's woe carries an implied cue for weeping at that point, accompanied by a handkerchief. Puff, inappropriately, wants weeping to start earlier during the speech, with bathetic results. Also interesting here is the anecdotal example of theatrical sympathy in partially successful action: Tilburina's "O" is echoed by Dangle and Sneer, her onstage audience, but while Dangle is affected correctly, uttering an "Oh" which is a sigh like hers, Sneer's "Oh" carries quite a different charge. As noted above, *The Critic* cannot really be considered even a witness to the theatrical practice of the 1770s, let alone the theatre of more than a century earlier, but it offers an anecdotal insight into a world in which the handkerchief has a clear symbolic value as a stage property. (That symbolic value, incidentally, means that the handkerchief so essential to the plot of *Othello* must be considered a particularly fraught item not merely in terms, famously, of Desdemona's household linen, but in terms of the norms of stage representation of weeping).

Information on the onstage representation of weeping, from rather closer in time to the Shakespearean stage than Sheridan, can be found in the work of John Bulwer. *Pathomyotamia*, his guide to facial gestures for use in oratory (or acting), remarks that the facial gestures involved in weeping are superficially similar to laughing, resulting in the "whole deformity of the face through grief". *Chirologia*, his guide

---

17 Richard Brinsley Sheridan, *The Critic*, in *Sheridan's Plays*, ed. Lewis Gibbs (1906; London: Dent, 1960), 339.

to hand and arm gestures, offers several designed to represent and to induce sorrow, including a gesture for hand-wringing, another hand gesture, "To beat and knock the hand upon the breast", and a finger gesture, "to put finger in the eye", which is described, and illustrated, as follows:

> To put finger in the eye, is their expression who *crie,* and would by that endeavour of nature *ease themselves* and *give vent to their conceived heavinesse.* The reason of putting finger in the eye in weeping, is, because teares falling from the eye, with their saltnesse procureth a kinde of itching about the carnell of teares, which requireth aid of the *Finger* to be expressed at their first fall: afterward the parts affected with that quality, and one teare drawing on another, such expression is not so necessary.[18]

Incidentally, and I am not aware that this has been noted before, Bulwer's quotation here shows the influence of Timothy Bright's work on the humoral basis of weeping: the whole of the second half of the quotation above is copied *verbatim* from Bright's account of tears in action.[19] "Putting finger in the eye" is, according to Bright, usually an involuntary reflex marking the onset of weeping, but Bulwer argues that a skilful orator (or, by extension, actor) can voluntarily imitate it, and thus communicate the idea of grief. That a form of this gesture was enacted on the early modern stage can be seen, not so much from the stage directions, but from the dialogue: in Thomas Heywood's *The Second Part of King Edward IV*, for instance:

Enter Mistris Shoare weeping, Iockie following.
CATESBY: Why how now mistris Shoare? what, put finger in the eye,
      Nay then I see you haue some cause to crie.[20]

A second particularly clear example indicated by the dialogue, which also confirms the gesture's longevity from at least the 1590s to the 1630s, occurs in Nabbes' *Totenham Court*, where Sam is accusing his sister of being a prostitute: "Heere's halfe a crowne wench; me thinks 'tis a faire rate. Ha! finger in the eye? Keepe thy teares for pennance in *Bride well.* Crye when money's offer'd thee?"[21] Other references to the gesture confirm the extent to which it is part of the stage vocabulary: for instance, Adriana in *The Comedy of Errors* pointedly announces her intention not to "put the finger in the eye and weep, / While man and master laugh my woes to scorn" (2.2.182).

Eye-wiping is also required in Ford's *'Tis Pity Shee's a Whore.* Giovanni walks across the stage while his sister provides a commentary from above:

---

18   Bulwer, *Pathomyotamia*, 141; Bulwer, *Chirologia*, 160, capitalisation silently standardised. Compare Bright's description of the weeping face as having "a resemblance of girninge", quoted in Chapter 1.

19   Timothy Bright, *A treatise of melancholie Containing the causes thereof, & reasons of the strange effects it worketh in our minds and bodies* (London: Thomas Vautrollier, 1586), 153.

20   Heywood, *1 and 2 Edward IV* (1600), I4r.

21   Nabbes, *Totenham Court* (1638), 49.

Sure 'tis not hee, this is some woefull thinge
Wrapt vp in griefe, some shaddow of a man.
Alas hee beats his brest, and wipes his eyes
Drown'd all in teares: me thinkes I heare him sigh.
(Ford, *'Tis Pity Shee's a Whore* [1633], B4r)

Giovanni's combination of actions – eye-wiping, breast-beating and sighing – presents a challenge for a modern actor, since such overdetermined symptoms could well move a modern audience to laughter. But, as has been seen here, the eye-wiping, in particular, is a standard gestural indication of weeping, and one should hesitate to argue that this is a comic moment.

An even fuller catalogue of actions associated with weeping occurs in Marston's *Antonio's Revenge* (1602), C2v, where Pandulpho laughs, rather than weeps, at the discovery of his son dead: an inappropriate laughter-reaction of the sort described by Bright in Chapter 1 of this study. The ensuing exchange, as well as problematising questions of decorum and representation, also gives a catalogue of actorly actions associated with the representation of grief:

ALBERTO : Vncle, this laughter ill becomes your griefe.
PANDULPHO: Would'st haue me cry, run rauing vp & down,
For my sons losse? would'st haue me turn rank mad,
Or wring my face with mimick action;
Stampe, curse, weepe, rage, & then my bosome strike?
Away tis apish action, player-like.[22]

Gestures, then, can describe many aspects of the syndrome of weeping: but that still leaves the problem of the most important element within that syndrome, the tears themselves which early modern physiology believed to be the root cause of all the other elements. On this topic, one of the phrases used in *Philaster* – "these tears" – provides a useful window into representations of weeping, since its deictic quality means that it is unavoidably an indication that tears are expected to be, in some sense, visible in the "here" of the play-world and to the audience. Just as "ha ha ha" serves, reliably, as a first-person implied stage direction for laughing, so, with equal reliability, does "these tears" as an implied stage direction for weeping. One should consider it not merely as a grammatical element within a sentence (although it is that, a respect in which it differs from "ha ha ha"), but also, like "ha ha ha", as a coded instruction to the actor to represent (in some sense) the non-verbal bodily phenomenon of tears.

"These tears"/"These teares" turns out to be a surprisingly common term. Ninety of the 745 plays in the *LION* corpus contain this phrase in one of its two spelling variants, and a slightly more elaborate search – these FBY.3 tears OR these FBY.3 teares – locates all occasions when the word "these" is followed, within three words

---

22 Marston, *Antonio's Revenge* (1602), C2v.

or less, by the word "tears" or "teares". This search finds phrases such as "these blubbring teares", and swells the list to 161 examples from 121 plays.[23] In addition, related terms are also strikingly common, searched for in the same way. "Those ... tears", which often and perhaps usually functions as a second- or third-person implied stage direction, occurs in 78 examples from 66 plays. Phrases such as "my ... tears", "your ... tears" and "thy ... tears" occur hundreds of times across the corpus, not always but sometimes as implied stage directions (as at *Philaster*, 4.3.36–9, quoted earlier in this chapter). Uncountable periphrastic variants of "these ... tears" such as "these waters / That fall like winter storms, from the drown'd eyes" are also very frequent[24] Hence, "these tears" is merely the most distinctive and diagnostically reliable member of a family of phrases which early modern theatre uses to put tears on the stage, and its own 161 appearances are representative of a larger set of related uses. The lines associated with the phrase "these tears" often stress the copiousness and wetness of the tears on display:

Wouldst have me weep?
... when the rage allayes, the rain begins.
These tears are my sweet Rutland's obsequies,
And every drop cries vengeance for his death

(Shakespeare, *3 Henry VI*, 1.4.143–8)

O... that these teares that drissell from mine eyes,
Had power to mollifie his stonie hart

(Marlowe, *Edward II* [1594], E4r)

Still let these knees be wedded to the earth,
Still let these teares run floud-like from mine eies,
Vntill your grace do execute the wretch

(*A knacke to know an honest man* [1596], B1v)

... by these teares,
Which are but springs begetting greater floods,
I doe beseech thee

(Heywood, *The English Traveller* [1633], K2r)

---

23 Consider, though, Wendoll's observation of how Anne is affecting the carters who are taking her away near the end of Heywood's *A woman kilde with kindnesse* (1607), H1r – "she from these rude Carters teares extracts". This example, and perhaps two others out of the 161, are grammatically spurious (although as it happens all of them are in contexts suggesting onstage weeping).

24 Dekker *et al.*, *Lust's Dominion* (1657), G7r–G7v; in addition, as the reader will see by comparing these methods to the examples from *Philaster* with which this chapter started, many implied stage directions indicating weeping would still be undetectable by any automated search along these lines.

Among the examples listed above, the Shakespeare quotation partakes of another characteristic of many of the invocations of "these tears" in early modern drama: characters often read the tears as signs, either of authenticity (characters often swear by their own tears, as Heywood's Wife does in the fourth example above) or of further symbolic meaning, such as when the tears are claimed to be Rutland's obsequies. As Tobias Döring has argued, using the terminology of speech-act theory, tears are often understood almost as a "sincerity condition" within Shakespearean drama – a non-verbal communication more authentic than words. Döring has traced the contemporary debate about whether or not tears could be feigned, arguing that the supposed authenticity of their communication is then fatally compromised both by the general observation that they can be feigned, and by the specific fact of their representation on stage within a fiction.[25] In cases such as the ones discussed above, where the tears are explicitly required to function as an element within the signifying system of the play as a whole, they require some visible corollary in the stage representation, even if only mimed.

This is even more the case since the presence – or absence – of wet tears is sometimes invoked as a distinguishing mark between sincere and insincere weeping. An exchange involving the hypocritical Selina in Lodowick Carlell's *The Passionate Lover, Part II*, is particularly helpful:

SELINA: Your scorn's so just, that I must suffer it:
Seems to weep
CLINDOR: How! Let's see; no moisture! spare, spare your Linen, good *Selina*.
(Carlell, *The Passionate Lovers* [1655], 113)

The reference to linen indicates that Selina's "false" stage weeping uses a handkerchief, just as "genuine" stage weeping does: nonetheless, like other similar stage directions, something about the way the action is performed marks it to the audience as insincere.[26] Within the play, this insincerity is linked to the absence of actual tears. When King Lear asks Cordelia, "Be your tears wet? Yes, faith: I pray weep not", a line which invites stage action drawing attention to the tears, this is another manifestation of the idea that "real" weeping, involving tears, is different from merely sham weeping. R.A. Foakes traces the stage history of performance of this line: "Here Garrick touched her cheek in a moving gesture, and Henry Irving went further, putting his finger to his mouth as if to taste the saltiness of her tears".[27] These production alternatives may be used (with caution) to give a flavour of possible stage practice in Renaissance drama.

25 Tobias Döring, "*How to do things with tears*: Trauer spielen auf der Shakespeare-Bühne", *Poetica*, 33:3/4 (2001): 355–89.

26 For similar stage directions requiring visibly insincere weeping, compare "Hee seems to fall into a passion" (J.D., *The Knave in Graine* [1640], M1v).

27 *King Lear*, 4.7.71, and Foakes's note *ad loc.* in *King Lear*, ed. R.A. Foakes (London: Arden, 1997).

However, not all tears displayed as wet tears are sincere tears. For instance, in Daborne's *A Christian Turn'd Turke*, the duplicitous Voada is attempting to convince the Englishman Ward that her love for him is sincere. Here, the wetness of the tears and their visibility (intra-diegetically at least) are crucial to their supposed meaning:

> VOADA: Do these my teares delight thee then? cruell
>> Hard-hearted man, glut thy relentlesse sight
>> With full-ey'd sorrow.
> WARD: Shee is all amorous, all faire, that she doth loue,
>> Behold those teares whose droppes would pierce the hearts
>> Of Tygers, make them pittifull, They are witnesses she faines not.[28]

Ward's "Behold", in a scene with only himself and Voada on stage, explicitly invites the audience to see the effect that is being described, and to participate, with him, in being deceived about Voada's intentions. This example brings up, more urgently still, the question of how, if at all, tears to accompany the action were produced on the Renaissance stage.

The first and most obvious way to achieve the illusion of tears is for the actor to produce tears themselves from their body. There are several early references which indicate that Renaissance actors, like their classical predecessors and their modern descendants, had the prized ability to cry on demand, an ability mentioned and discussed by Plato, Cicero, Quintilian and Montaigne, among others.[29] The clergyman Thomas Adams, for instance, alludes to this in a sermon about Jesus' weeping: "Let vs not thinke [Jesus] like either of those Mimicks, the Player, or the Hypocrite ... that can command teares in sport." The Bishop of Exeter, Ralph Brownrigg, also alludes to players weeping, in the course of a discussion within a sermon of insincere contrition: "Players on the Stage may howl, and mourn, and wring tears from their eyes, and yet be mad merry fellows among themselves".[30] Such allusions from sermons are corroborated by references within dramatic texts, such as *Hamlet*, which describes an actor shedding "real" tears by a piece of almost method-acting concentration on the story he is telling:

> Is it not monstrous that this player here,
> But in a fiction, in a dream of passion,
> Could force his soul so to his own conceit

---

28   Robert Daborne, *A Christian Turn'd Turke* (1612), E4v.

29   Harold Jenkins (ed.), *Hamlet* (London: Arden, 1996), 481, quoting Montaigne: "Quintilian reporteth to have seen comedians so far engaged in a sorrowful part that they have wept after being come to their lodgings; and of himself, that having undertaken to move a certain passion in another, he had found himself surprised not only with shedding of tears, but with a paleness of countenance and behaviour of a man truly dejected with grief".

30   Thomas Adams, *The deuills banket described in foure sermons* (London: Thomas Snodham, 1614), 230; Ralph Brownrigg, *Twenty five sermons* (London: Thomas Roycroft, 1664), 162. Brownrigg died in 1659, so the theatre he is thinking of is not that of Restoration London.

That from her working all his visage wanned,
Tears in his eyes, distraction in his aspect,
A broken voice, and his whole function suiting
With forms to his conceit?

(Hamlet, 2.2.545–50)

Hamlet's list is almost a checklist of various secondary symptoms of weeping, and implies that all of these were visible (and audible) in the actor. To an extent, the barb here is that most of *Hamlet*'s commentators assume that the tears belong to the actor, and are the consequences of the actor's feelings about the world in which he is immersing himself. In fact, the actor is still playing the part of Aeneas in an (imaginary) play: Aeneas, who retells the story of the fall of Troy, saying of that story that even Ulysses would weep at a retelling of it. The fact that no audience can tell whether the tears and associated symptoms belong to the player or to the character he is personating makes this an especially good example of the description of actorly craft at work.

On the other hand, this is not to deny entirely the validity of the usual interpretation of the passage in terms of an actor personally immersed in an imaginary world. The hypocritical Queen in William Heminges's *The Fatal Contract* describes the same actorly mechanism to induce "real" tears:

QUEEN: tell me *Landrey*, how did I play the mother;
          Did not I seem a *Niobe* in passion,
          A deluge of salt tears?
LANDREY: Most true, you wept.
QUEEN: As a good Actor in a play would do,
          Whose fancy works (as if he waking dreamt)
          Too strongly on the Object that it copes with,
          Shaping realities from mockeries;
          And so the Queen did weep.[31]

The simplest way to achieve what Dessen and Thompson hesitate over – "to *weep* or presumably to simulate *weeping*" – may be indeed for the actor to shed tears. And there would be little point in actors' ability to produce tears on demand, if those tears were not, when produced, visible to the audiences for whom they were produced. As a general proposition, the audience may be "unlikely to see" tears shed directly, but there is certainly the possibility that they might.

While *Hamlet* describes the ability to weep on demand as a mental discipline, a passing remark by the writer Gabriel Harvey appears to suggest that actors used an artificial aid to irritate their eyes and to induce weeping. The context for this is Harvey's *A New Letter of Notable Contents*, a pamphlet mainly given over to personal attacks on Harvey's enemy Thomas Nashe. Harvey is, however, aware that Nashe has

---

31 Heminges, *The Fatal Contract* (1653), D4r.

just published a devotional work, *Christ's Tears Over Jerusalem*, but comments that he is unsure of the sincerity of Nashe's change of heart: "I pray God, the promised Teares of Repentance, proue not the Teares of the Onion vpon the Theater."[32]

Harvey cannot really be called an insider of the professional theatre, nor is his prose entirely clear in its meaning, but his comment requires some consideration, since numerous other sixteenth- and seventeenth-century texts refer to the use of an onion hidden in a handkerchief to help stimulate weeping.[33] Representative examples include Hall's *Virgidemiarum*, where a factor simulates tears for his sick employer, and "Some strong-smeld Onion shall stirre his eyes / Rather then no salt teares shall then arise"; and the comedy *Greene's Tu Quoque* (1615), where we see Bubble's weeping for his dead uncle interrupted when the onions fall out of his handkerchief.[34] And yet both of these examples imagine the onion being used by a "real-life" deceiver rather than a professional actor, and no example yet found offers direct corroboration of Harvey's apparent suggestion that this technique was employed in the theatre. The passage which comes closest to supporting Harvey's allegation is the Induction to *The Taming of The Shrew*, where the Nobleman sets out to trick the drunken Sly into believing that he is himself a rich aristocrat with amnesia and a beautiful wife weeping over him. This passage is particularly interesting since the deception is so clearly metonymic of the theatrical illusion as a whole, and since so many of its details – even down to the page-boy impersonating a woman – reflect the conditions of the theatre which produces not merely the inset play but the events of the Induction as well. The Nobleman wants his page-boy to weep as part of the act:

> And if the boy have not a womans gift
> To rain a shower of commanded tears,
> An onion wil do well for such a shift,
> Which in a napkin being close conveyed
> Shall in despite enforce a watery eye.
>
> (*The Taming of the Shrew*, Induction.123–7)

Elsewhere in Shakespeare, too, onions are associated not just with feigned tears, but with tears as real as any in the fictive world of the play. Enobarbus, for instance, in *Antony and Cleopatra*, comments of an insincere grief, "the tears live in an onion that should water this sorrow". But later, Enobarbus uses the metaphor to describe his own genuine weeping, as Antony's whole retinue are overcome with emotion:

---

32   Gabriel Harvey, *A New Letter of Notable Contents* (London: John Wolfe, 1593), D2r. Of course, Harvey's comment could merely be doubly metaphorical: "his tears are as insincere as the tears of actors, which are themselves as insincere as the tears produced by onions".

33   See Virginia F. Stern, *Gabriel Harvey: His Life, Marginalia and Library* (Oxford: Clarendon Press, 1979) for Harvey's life, and what is known about his links with the theatrical world (such as the fact that he seems to have known Richard Tarlton, and also wrote marginalia about Shakespeare's plays).

34   Joseph Hall, *Virgidemiarum sixe bookes. The three last bookes* (London: Richard Bradocke, 1598), 84.

"Look, they weep; / And I, an ass, am onion-eyed" (1.2.182, 4.2.34–5). Another example is Lafeu's complaint that "my eyes smell onions" (*All's Well*, 5.3.358–9). If Harvey's suggestion that actors used onions to stimulate weeping is correct, then all these passages develop a metadramatic quality.

Furthermore, the idea raised by *The Taming of the Shrew* of an onion conveyed in a handkerchief is not incompatible with the "finger in the eye" gesture described by Bulwer, since the accompanying illustration in *Chirologia* (reproduced in Figure 3.1) shows a man putting a handkerchief to his eye and in the process covering his nose and mouth. Indeed, as has been seen, handkerchiefs are frequently specified as part of stage practice around weeping, so that there is certainly the opportunity to conceal something lachrymatory within it.[35] Nor would application of onion help solely with the tears: it might help generate, for instance, the "broken voice" which Hamlet identifies as another of the symptoms of weeping.

Figure 3.1 "To put finger in the eye", illustrated in John Bulwer's *Chirologia* (1644), 189.

While Harvey and Shakespeare's Nobleman propose onions as a lachrymatory, a different stimulant is proposed by Falstaff, to imitate yet another part of the syndrome of weeping: "Give me a cup of sack to make mine eyes look red, that it may be thought I have wept; for I must speak in passion, and I will do it in King Cambyses' vein". Alluding anachronistically to *Cambyses*, Falstaff links his own performance of a "passion" – and by extension his reddened eyes – to the early modern stage. This same detail is evoked in the "eyes ... red as fire with weeping" which onstage observers note in Antony delivering Caesar's eulogy, and the redness which, in *Measure for Measure*, Lucio sees in Isabella's eyes and interprets as a consequence

---

35   Or, indeed, a small container of a tear-simulating liquid, on the analogies of the concealed glasses of pig's blood used at this period to simulate human blood, and of the modern practice of using glycerine to simulate tears: on the pig's blood, see Andrew Gurr and Mariko Ichikawa, *Staging in Shakespeare's Theatres* (Oxford: Oxford University Press, 2002), 61.

of weeping: "I am pale at mine heart to see thine eyes so red".[36] This symptom, too, could be convincingly produced by onion, if it were produced at all. In the absence of further evidence, though, Harvey's intriguing claim that onions were used on stage must, for the moment, remain not proven.

In some ways, it is fitting that the exact mechanisms for the representation of tears on the Renaissance stage remain mysterious. The frequent references to tears being visible, copious and wet are all always open to being dismissed simply as part of the fiction of the play. Even an allusion to the wetness of tears in a stage direction, such as when, in *Antonio's Revenge*, Antonio and Maria "*wet their handkerchers with their teares*", or when, in Fletcher's *The Night-Walker*, "*The Tears flow from him*", could still be, in the terminology introduced by Richard Hosley, a "fictive" stage direction in which the referent remains only within the fictional world of the play.[37] In *3 Henry VI*, the future Richard III boasts that he can "wet [his] cheeks with artificial tears" (3.2.189), and while this might indeed be a precise metadramatic detail, we, like Richard's victims, have no guarantee that we can understand whether and how they are "real" or illusory either in a psychological or in a dramaturgical sense. To put it another way, Harvey's allegation about the onion is both a claim about theatrical practice and a much wider claim for the insincerity, the displayedness, of all representations of tears in the Renaissance theatre.

What one can say is that weeping is a very common phenomenon on the early modern stage, indicated both in explicit and implied stage directions, and used for both comic and serious effect. The representation of weeping could be achieved partly through non-verbal noises and facial expressions, but more important factors were gesture, properties (notably the handkerchief), and the representation of tears themselves, although it remains unclear to what extent these tears are merely suggested, naturally produced, chemically stimulated, or artificially applied. The next stage of the argument is to move from the stage representation of weeping and of laughter, representation we have seen to be rich and frequent, to consider both those phenomena as they appeared in the audiences who watched the plays where they occurred.

---

36   *1 Henry IV*, 2.4.153–4; *Julius Caesar*, 3.2.95; *Measure for Measure*, 4.3.151–2.

37   Fletcher, *The Night-Walker* [1640], G1v; Linda McJannet, *The Voice of Stage Directions: The Evolution of a Theatrical Code* (Newark: University of Delaware Press, 1999).

Chapter 4

Audiences laughing

This chapter examines early modern accounts of audience laughter, which is by no means the same thing as an examination of "the early modern sense of humour", or of Renaissance comic theory as it is usually understood (that is, in broadly structuralist terms).[1] This chapter does not seek to examine audience laughter as offering any access to the early modern mind; it is instead concerned with documenting that laughter as a phenomenon in itself, using those accounts in which it is described – accounts which are almost always complicated by the fact that they come from "literary" sources, and are without exception complicated by the circumstances of their survival in textual form. Accordingly, this chapter will weigh up what early modern accounts say about questions such as: how important laughter was to the reception of early modern plays; what can be said about what early modern audience laughter sounded like; and in what circumstances early modern audiences laughed.

Some of the most pressing questions raised by such an approach relate to the field of performance criticism. As noted in the Introduction, in recent years, much scholarly work has been done reconstructing the early modern theatre in greater detail than before, but the norms and conventions around audience behaviour are still not yet historicised in detail. And yet, it is particularly important to look for a sense of the history of audience laughter, as, ever since at least the 1970s, scholars have been using evidence from the laughter of modern audiences at modern productions to assess questions of technique, tone and intent in early modern plays. For instance, the director Sam Mendes has said of his 1991 Royal Shakespeare Company production of Jonson's *The Alchemist*:

> When it hit its rhythm ... the timing of the show never changed ... for forty performances it never lost a minute or gained a minute. I've never seen anything like that in the plays I've done. It's always a minute or two either side. It was like clockwork. And they never stopped for laughs. Because actually they grew and grew. So although there was a huge response, they never actually played it. It was just one laugh after another after another. And that's in the writing ... It's a huge, cumulative, farce-like response.

---

1   On this topic, see, for instance, the concise overview of David Galbraith, "Theories of comedy", in Alexander Leggatt (ed.), *The Cambridge Companion to Shakespearean Comedy* (Cambridge: Cambridge University Press, 2002), 3–17; Marvin T. Herrick, *Comic Theory in the Sixteenth Century* (1950; Urbana: University of Illinois Press, 1964); M.J. Sidnell (ed.), *Sources of Dramatic Theory* (Cambridge: Cambridge University Press, 1991).

On the one hand, this is interesting in that Mendes, like his Renaissance precursors, thinks of audience laughter as feeding further audience laughter. But also it is hard not to share Mendes's evident belief that his practice helps illuminate Jonson's intention, and that the details of audience behaviour are, to some extent at least, "in the writing". In a similar vein, the theatre director Peter Barnes writes of Jonson's *Bartholomew Fair* that audience laughter transformed his sense of the apparently minor character Trouble-All, who "zigzags through the fair like a demented ferret ... Each time he was played differently, yet each time he gained the most laughs and was one of the major characters".[2] Experience of how a modern audience reacted is, perhaps inevitably, an interpretative tool for those who are approaching the play with a knowledge of how it has come across in live performance. But, in effect, such analyses tend to treat audience laughter as a transhistorical constant.

A more obviously contentious application of such ideas occurs when looking at early modern tragedies. For instance, Nicholas Brooke's *Horrid Laughter in Jacobean Tragedy* (considered in more detail in Chapter 7) uses audience laughter from modern productions of Jacobean tragedies as part of his evidence for arguing about the plays' intentions to move the audience to laughter. In a similar vein, a chapter in Martin White's seminal book, *Renaissance Drama in Performance*, considers the problem of "Comic (ir)resolutions" in tragedies which appear to provoke incongruous audience laughter, again with reference to modern performance. A notorious example of this effect is *The Changeling*, where twentieth-century productions have tended to play up the comic element. Reviewers praised one 1960s production of the play for its earthiness, producing in its audience "not the expected awe and hush but gales of hearty public school laughter" (and the very fact that the term "public school laughter" sounds so dated is an indication of how quickly the nuances of laughter change). Directorial choices introduced stage business to create *doubles entendres* in lines such as Beatrice-Joanna's "this fellow has undone me endlessly", as the consequence of a "brusque rear-end poke" in simulated onstage sex with De Flores. This led to a critical consensus sarcastically summarised by Roberta Barker and David Nicol: "Although the victim may seem unwilling, in fact it's all a bit of saucy fun: no means yes, and one need not feel pity for a heroine whose corruption is also her awakening to her true nature". Obviously, in the case of *The Changeling*, Barker and Nicol document the extent to which twentieth-century directors have had to twist the text in order to produce this particular effect: but what about the general proposition? Would early modern audiences ever have laughed at tragedies,

---

2   Sam Mendes, interviewed by Brian Woolland, in Richard Cave, Elizabeth Schafer and Brian Woolland (eds), *Ben Jonson and Theatre: Performance, Practice, and Theory* (London: Routledge, 1999), 80; Peter Barnes, "*Bartholomew Fair*: All the Fun of the Fair", in Brian Woolland (ed.), *Jonsonians* (Aldershot: Ashgate, 2003), 43–51, qtn from 44; see also Frances N. Teague (ed.), *Acting Funny: Comic Theory and Practice in Shakespeare's Plays* (Cranbury, NJ: Associated University Presses, 1994) – in the Introduction, Teague notes that five of the essays in her collection use specific modern productions to support arguments about the plays' comic qualities.

for instance, and, while it seems reasonable to suppose that they would have laughed at *The Alchemist*, would they have laughed at the same things in it as a modern audience does? For cases such as these, in addition to accounts of modern performance, it would be helpful to have some historicised sense of the norms around early modern audience laughter, even if that sense is mainly a listing of what we do not know.[3]

This account, then, aims to provide a counterweight to the efforts of reconstructive archaeology undertaken by performance criticism, by simply reviewing some of the available primary evidence about early modern custom and practice. In particular, it aims to illustrate three broad propositions about laughter in early modern theatrical audiences:

- Firstly, by and large, early modern comedy aimed to move laughter, and measured its success by whether or not it had moved laughter. Apparent exceptions to this rule require special discussion, but do not challenge its overall validity.
- Secondly, early modern theatre audiences did laugh, and often with an intensity that observers found potentially alarming both for the loudness of the sound produced, and the bodily harm it seemed capable of inflicting upon the laugher.
- Thirdly, one can be quite precise about the details of what audiences laughed at, at least as far as certain staples of physical comedy: otherwise, accounts of audience laughter tend to be of laughter at the total effect of the production.

Early Modern Comedy Aimed to Move Laughter

Sir Philip Sidney's *Defence of Poesy* is a good place to start, since it is early in the period under discussion, and unequivocal in its implication that most contemporary comedy aimed to move laughter.

> Our comedians think there is no delight without laughter; which is very wrong, for though laughter may come with delight, yet it cometh not of delight, as though delight should be the cause of laughter; but well may one thing breed both together …[4]

Whatever this says about Sidney's poetics, it also constitutes evidence that the theatres of Sidney's day were places where success was measured in terms of audience laughter. There are a group of texts associated with early modern comedy

---

3   Martin White, *Renaissance Drama in Action: An Introduction to Aspects of Theatre Practice and Performance* (London: Routledge, 1998), esp. 186; for a discussion of audience reactions to the play in twentieth-century productions, and this line in particular, see Roberta Barker and David Nicol, "Does Beatrice Joanna Have a Subtext?: *The Changeling* on the London Stage", *Early Modern Literary Studies*, 10:1 (May 2004): 3.1–43, at http://purl.oclc.org/emls/10-1/barknico.htm, qtns from 4, 38.

4   Sidney, *The Defence of Poesy* in Katherine Duncan-Jones (ed.), *Sir Philip Sidney* (Oxford: Clarendon Press, 1989), 245.

which follow Sidney in seeking to downplay the importance of laughter, but before considering them it is worth stressing how out of step such views are with most of the other "statements of intent" from early modern comedy.

Early modern comedy identifies itself, by and large, with the generation of merriment and mirth. While the word "laugh" and its cognates occur frequently in prologues to early modern English drama, the word "mirth" and its cognates occur more often. As its *OED* entry demonstrates, "mirth" covers a range of emotions and affects including pleasure, joy, and even religious bliss, so that the physiological reaction of laughter is only a small subset of what the word can potentially cover.[5] In a sample of 49 prologues from the early modern stage that feature the word "mirth" or its cognates, its meaning is almost invariably positive, although not quite always, as in *Perkin Warbeck*'s solemn rejection of "Vnnecessary mirth", or Habington's protestation that there is no "bawdy mirth" in the tragicomedy *The Queene of Aragon*. By and large, however, "mirth" is seen as a desirable result. Similarly, "sport" is frequently mentioned as a by-product of comedies, usually in a positive sense, although Samuel Daniel, for instance, is eager to assure the queen that the tragicomedy *Hymens Triumph* contains "no wild, no rude, no antique sport, / But tender passions".[6] In a few of these examples, it is explicitly obvious that laughter is central to the construction of mirth and sport, as in the claim in the prologue to Sharpham's *Cupids Whirligig* that the author "onely striues with mirth to please each one, / Since laughter is peculiar vnto man", or the claim of the prologue to Randolph's *Aristippus*: "I come to haue my mirth approu'd, not skill: / Your laughter all I begge".[7] Examples such as these give some warrant to read "mirth" elsewhere almost as a euphemism for "laughter".

An indication of the extent to which laughter is central to comedy in the Renaissance theatre can be seen in the personifications of comedy which are presented there, and this is exemplified by three of the metadramatic scenes in which Comedy is presented in debate with Tragedy. At the start of the anonymous *Mucedorus*, Comedy is unambiguously clear about what she intends her play to do:

Comedie play thy part, and please,
Mak merry them that coms to ioy with thee:
Ioy then good gentilles, I hope to make you laugh.

---

5   *OED*, mirth *n. LION* searches for "laugh*", "mirth*" and "sport*" in the Prologues of drama published in England before 1660 returned, respectively, 42, 49 and 26 entries: these numbers should be taken as indicative, rather than any absolute claim of frequency and relevance.

6   Ford, *Perkin Warbeck* (1634), A4v; Habington, *The Queene of Aragon* (1640), A4v; Daniel, *Hymens Triumph* (1615), A4v.

7   Sharpham, *Cupids whirligig* (1607), A2v; Randolph, *Aristippus* (1630), 3; on the protocols of Prologues in general, see Tiffany Stern, "'A small beer health to his second day': Playwrights, Prologues, and First Performances in the Early Modern Theater", *Studies in Philology*, 101:2 (2004): 172–99.

Laughter is here constructed as the consequence of "joy": this comedy is not Hobbesian. Similarly, the personified Comedy of another late Elizabethan play Induction, *A Warning for Fair Women*, cedes control of the stage to Tragedy with the words: "Tragedie, kil them to day with sorrow, / Wee'l make them laugh with myrthfull ieasts to morrow". Thirty years later, yet a third personification of Comedy, in Thomas Randolph's *The Muses Looking Glasse*, remains equally explicit in her mission statement: "Yes, Laughter is my object: tis a propertie / In man essentiall to his reason."[8]

Numerous early modern comedies assert, in metadramatic moments such as Prologues and choruses, an intention to induce laughter in the audience. One useful example is the Prologue to the anonymous *Wily beguilde*, which specifies laughter so intense as to produce tears in its audience: "Be still a while, and ere we goe, / Weele make your eies with laughter flowe." Other statements of intent from early modern plays claim to move laughter, often distancing themselves in the process from claims of literary merit. The Prologue to Middleton and Dekker's *The Roaring Girl*, for instance, is confident that the play will deliver the intended laughter, and will, indeed, fill the theatrical space with it. However, it uses that laughter as an excuse to limit the promise made to the audience:

> A Roaring Girle (whose notes till now neuer were)
> Shall fill with laughter our vast Theater,
> That's all which I dare promise: Tragick passion,
> And such graue stuffe, is this day out of fashion.[9]

The Prologue to Middleton's *The Widdow* is equally direct in its appeal to an audience sated with entertainments over Christmas:

> to make you merry,
> Is all th'ambition 'thas; and fullest aym
> Bent at your smiles, to win it self a name:
> And if your edge be not quite taken off,
> Wearied with sports, I hope 'twill make you laugh.[10]

A rejection of all genres, including comedy, is to be found in the prologue to Fletcher's *The Captain*:

> This is nor *Comody*, nor *Tragedy*,
> Nor History, nor any thing that may
> (Yet in a weeke) be made a perfect Play:

---

8   *Mucedorus* (1598), A2r; *A Warning for Faire Women* (1599), A3r; Randolph, *The Muses Looking Glasse* in *Poems* (1638), 10. All three of these contests, particularly the first two, see the battle between Comedy and Tragedy in acoustic terms: Comedy's merry music set against the groans and screams that performance of tragedy entails.

9   *Wily beguilde* (1606), A3r; Middleton and Dekker, *The Roaring Girl* (1611), A3r.

10   Middleton, *The Widdow* (1652), K1v.

Yet those that love to laugh, and those that thinke
Twelve-pence goes farther this way then in drinke,
Or Damsels, if they marke the matter through,
May stumble on a foolish toy, or two
Will make 'em shew their teeth.[11]

The showing of teeth, already seen as a symptom of laughter in Bulwer's *Pathomyotamia*, will reappear later in this chapter, cited in other contemporary accounts of audience reaction. And this use of laughter to disclaim all genre, even comedy, is found again in the Prologue to Beaumont and Fletcher's *The Woman Hater*: "I dare not call it Comedy or Tragedy; 'tis perfectly neither: A Play it is, which was meant to make you laugh, how it would please you, is not written in my Part".[12]

Caroline drama provides numerous examples of a stated intention to make the audience laugh. The plays of Richard Brome provide a succession of statements along these lines, often in the context of a refusal to claim literary merit for the work that follows. The Prologue to *The Northern Lass* is typical of several other Brome prologues in its claim that

Though, in the *Muses* Garden [the author] can walke;
And choycest Flowers pluck from euery stalke
To deck the *Stage*; and purposeth, hereafter,
To take your Iudgements: now He implores your laughter.[13]

To this can be added a poem which tends to confirm that Brome's poetics had audible audience laughter at its centre: his elegy for Henry Hastings, printed in 1649, comments that this author is unfit for writing about sadness, since he "never spilt ink, except in Comedie / Which in the packed theatres did appear / All mirth and laughter".[14]

In particular, many Prologues and Epilogues talk about audience laughter as being the audience's contribution to the play. The anonymous play, *The Ghost, or The woman wears the breeches*, requests of its audience:

Sit still, and merrily feed on the Play;
'Tis City-chear, and stead of Wine pray laugh,
And with your money we your healths will quaff.[15]

Similarly, the Epilogue to Thomas Jordan's place-realism comedy *The Walks of Islington* and Hogsdon is clear that the audience's laughter is their contribution to the entertainment:

---

11 Fletcher, *The Captain* in *Comedies and Tragedies* (1647), 73.
12 Beaumont and Fletcher, *The Woman-Hater* (1607), A2r.
13 Richard Brome, *The Northern Lass* (1632), A4v.
14 Richard Brome (ed.), *Lachrymae musarum The tears of the muses: exprest in elegies* (London: Tho. Newcomb, 1649), 74.
15 *The Ghost, or The woman wears the breeches* (1653), A2v.

Well; How is't now? we heard you laugh, but Pray.
Was it at us, the Poet, or the Play?[16]

Jeremy Lopez has documented the importance of audience response in general to the success or failure of early modern plays. In the case of laughter, that audience response is delivered immediately, audibly and publicly. In a play on the paradoxes of laughter similar to that made by Jordan, Alexander Gill celebrates the audible failure of Jonson's *The Magnetic Lady* in 1632. According to Gill, the obvious lack of audience laughter was a fact appreciated by Jonson's enemy Inigo Jones: "Inigo with laughter ther grewe fatte, / That there was nothing worth the laughing att".[17] The negative evidence conveniently puts into relief expectations about the usual behaviour of audiences as active participants in laughing at plays.

The brief sketch given above from Prologues finds no space for the authors who are usually considered as having alternative poetics: the Lylyan poetic of "soft smiling, not loud laughing", or Jonson's dismissal of audience laughter in *Discoveries*. Both of these poetics will be handled separately in a later chapter. The point to note here is that whatever they are, and whatever they mean, they are at odds with the bulk of the evidence from comic prologues, which, when they mention audience laughter, state that they consider it a desirable aim.

Loud Laughing

There is one moment in Renaissance comedy which records the sound of an entire theatrical audience laughing. In Thomas Tomkis's Cambridge University play *Albumazar*, the trickster Ronca is duping the old man Pandolfo with a series of outrageous claims to magic abilities. At one point he furnishes Pandolfo with an "otacousticon" – a supposedly miraculous hearing device in the form of a large pair of asses' ears:

RONCA: ...What heare you?
PANDOLFO: Nothing
RONCA: Set your hands thus
    That the vertex of the Organ may perpendicularly
    Point out our Zenith. What heare you now? ha, ha, ha.
PANDOLFO: A humming noise of laughter.
RONCA: Why that's the Court
    And Vniversitie, that now are merry
    With an old gentleman in a Comaedy. What now?[18]

---

16   Jordan, *The Walks of Islington and Hogsdon* (1657), H4r.

17   Cited from H&S, 11.347, lines 1–8, 17–18; Jeremy Lopez, *Theatrical Convention and Audience Response in Early Modern Drama* (Cambridge: Cambridge University Press, 2003).

18   Tomkis, *Albumazar* (1615), B4v.

The word "humming" can denote sounds of many different volumes at this date, from quiet murmuring to the noise of bells ringing: but its distinguishing feature is that it denotes a sound which one cannot decode into words. Although it is the product of the court and university, the linguistic élite of the country, the laughter is still perceived as noise. A later theatrical anecdote uses a particularly evocative metaphor for this in its account of an accidental double entendre during a (post-Restoration) performance of *Romeo and Juliet*: when the actress accidentally uttered an obscene word, the audience fell "into such a laughter, that London-Bridge at low-water was silence to it".[19]

The loudness and the loss of individuality implied in these accounts of audiences laughing chimes with the antitheatrical writing of the early modern period, in which the evils of laughter form one of the main elements of the attack on the stage as an institution. Rather than listing all of these writings, which tend in any case, as Jonas Barish has noted, to repeat themselves, it will suffice to take as a baseline two of the most influential examples, the antitheatrical tracts of Stephen Gosson and William Prynne. The writings of Gosson in the 1580s, and Prynne in the 1630s, are well separated in time, and valuable possibly as claims about early modern theatrical custom, but certainly as statements of belief about laughter.

"The meaner sorte", warns Gosson in *Plays Confuted*, are

> so easily corrupted, that in the Theaters they generally take vp a wonderfull laughter, and shout altogether with one voyce, when they see some notable cosenedge practised, or some slie conueighance of baudry brought out of Italy. Wherby they showe themselues rather to like it then to rebuke it.[20]

Gosson, then, fears that laughter is an accessory to bawdry, and also, perhaps more surprisingly, that it creates a sort of gestalt in the audience: laughing, they shout "with one voice", as if one organism. Himself a former playwright, Gosson writes with some authority when he describes the effects of theatre, both in terms of audience weeping, and in terms of audience laughter: "Comedies so tickle our senses with a pleasenter vein, that they make us louers of laughter, and pleasure, without any meane, both foes to temperance, what schooling is this?" Expanding on the theme of pleasure, he writes:

> Comedyes make our delight exceede, for at thē many times wee laugh so extreemely, that striuing to bridle our selues, wee cannot; therfore *Plato* affirmeth y^t great laughter breedeth a great change, & ye old prouerbe peraduenture rose of this, much laughter is y^e

---

19   *OED*, hum *v.*; John Downes, *Roscius Anglicanus*, cited in Gāmini Salgādo (ed.), *Eyewitnesses of Shakespeare* (London: Sussex University Press, 1975), 61; at low water, the Thames rushed through the narrow arches of London bridge, creating a loud roaring sound.

20   Stephen Gosson, *Playes confuted in fiue actions* (London: Thomas Gosson, [1582]), C8v–D1r; on Gosson, see Arthur Kinney, *Markets of Bawdry: The Dramatic Criticism of Stephen Gosson* (Salzburg: Universität Salzburg, 1974), Introduction, who situates him as an English humanist, heir to Ascham and Eliot.

cognisance of a foole: where such excesse of laughter bursteth out yᵗ we cannot holde it, there is no temperance, for the time; where no temperance is, ther is no wiseome [sic], nor vse of reason; when we shew our selues voide both of reason, and wisedome, what are we then to be thought but fooles?[21]

Gosson's overwhelming concern is that laughter is irrational, a surrender of the will. His vignette of an audience in which even those who think they know better cannot prevent laughter from bursting out of them imagines theatrical laughter as a visceral, involuntary experience.

One might also look for evidence of theatrical expectations in William Prynne's thousand-page denunciation of stage-plays, *Histrio-mastix*, published in 1633.[22] The tenor of the references in *Histrio-mastix* to laughter – over 150 of them in all – is most economically indicated by its index entry for the topic:

> *Laughter*, prophane, profuse, excessive, censured. p. 290. to 298.123, 403, 404. Christ never laughed. 294.403, 404. this life no time of laughter but of teares. p. 293.294, 404. See Chrysost. Hom. 12. in Collos. 4. an excellent discourse to this purpose: occasioned by Playes. p. 175.290. to 304.403, 404.

It is difficult to take Prynne entirely seriously as a witness to theatrical practice, partly because of his style, well described by Jonas Barish as possessing a "paralyzing repetitiousness from which everything resembling nuance has been excluded".[23] In Prynne's account, for instance, all players, and most audience members, are depraved adulterers. As will be seen later in the chapter, many of his observations are translations (sometimes uncredited ones) from patristic sources rather than the result of direct observation (and as a rule of thumb, Prynne italicises passages which are translated quotations). However, his claims about what it feels like to be in the audience of the early modern theatre remain worthy of attention:

> *Theatricall laughter knowes neither bounds, nor measure; men wholly resigne and let loose the reines of their hearts unto it, glutting, nay tyring their sides and spirits with it: the dissolute profusenesse of it therefore makes it evill ...*

> For what other use doe our most rigid *Play-patrons ascribe to Stage-playes, but to exhilerate the Spectators, by provoking them to laughter.* Or what other pretence have Play-haunters for their resort to Play-houses; (though *many of them ayme at far more sinester respects*) but to passe away the time in mirth? to laugh till their sides doe ake againe, at the Clownes behaviour, or some other merry iests and passages.[24]

---

21 Gosson, *Plays Confuted*, C5r, F5v–F6r.

22 William Prynne, *Histrio-mastix, The Player's Scourge, or actors tragaedie* (London: Michael Sparke, 1633); the quotation that follows is from fol. 6p2r.

23 Jonas Barish, *The Antitheatrical Prejudice* (Berkeley: University of California Press, 1981), 83.

24 Prynne, *Histrio-mastix*, 292–3, 299, marginalia omitted.

Prynne elaborates on Gosson's idea that laughter in a theatre is a surrender of the will, and a triumph of the body. For Prynne, laughter is not merely a failure of the will but an almost addictive high which lets loose the reins of the heart and makes the sides ache. Laughing in a theatre, in Prynne's account, is so intense that it hurts. And once again, Prynne links laughter to lust: "far more sinester respects" is antitheatricalists' code for the association of theatres and brothels.

Something of the antitheatrical fear of laughter's loss of control also inflects Sidney's *Defence of Poesy*, in his account of the distinction between delight and the mere "scornful tickling" of laughter: "in twenty mad antics we laugh without delight". For Sidney, too, laughter can be on the edge of pain, as Sidney imagines circumstances in which (like Gosson in the theatre) "one shall be heartily sorry he cannot choose but laugh, and so is rather pained than delighted with laughter". The metaphor of tickling, used by Sidney and Gosson to indicate a sensation which entails a physical loss of control, occurs too within theatrical writing about the theatrical experience, as in the following Prologue to a tragedy: "No *Comick* Scene shall here salute your eye, / Whose scoffing Vein may tickle, till you lye / Half breathless in your mirth …".[25] According to at least one seventeenth-century writer, it was possible to tickle people to death, an extension of Joubert's idea of death through excessive laughter; Sidney's "scornful tickling", which to us might seem merely to indicate irritation, has potentially darker overtones in this era.[26]

And the idea of the exhausting physical intensity of laughter, particularly the laughter of theatre audiences, can be taken back again to near the start of the period under discussion, and one of the most iconic moments of the early modern stage: the entrance of the clown Richard Tarlton. Tarlton was the most famous clown of his era, both as a solo performer and as an actor who played clown parts within the plays of the Elizabethan stage. Within such performances, one of his most celebrated tricks was to induce audience laughter by making a very protracted first entrance, usually with only his head visible at first, through the curtain at the back of the stage. Early modern writers of all sorts were fascinated by this moment, one which is in many ways liminal: spatially at the edge of the performance area, temporally spanning the moment at which the performance starts, and textually, in that it is an "extra-textual" moment *par excellence* which nonetheless these writers seem determined to record and construct in textual form.[27] Furthermore, because of the very irreproducibility of

---

25 Cosmo Manuche, *The Bastard: A Tragedy* (London: M. M., 1652), A2r; Sidney, *Defence*, 245.

26 Richard Brathwaite, *Ar't asleepe husband? A boulster lecture* (London: R. Bishop, 1640), 273; Joubert, *Traité*, 61; for another anthology of accounts of people dying through excessive laughter, see, for example, Nathaniel Wanley, *The Wonders of the Little World* (London: T. Basset, 1673), 113–14; in a widely publicised case in 1975, a British man died laughing at an episode of the television series *The Goodies*.

27 On Tarlton, see Peter Thomson, "Tarlton, Richard (d. 1588)", *Oxford DNB*; Peter Thomson, "Richard Tarlton and his Legend", in Edward J. Esche (ed.), *Shakespeare and his Contemporaries in Performance* (Aldershot: Ashgate, 2000), 191–210; the useful anthology

the act itself, it provoked detailed descriptions of and imaginations of the audience reaction figured, above all, in terms of loud, sustained laughter.

Thomas Nashe's account of Tarlton in *Pierce Pennilesse* emphasises the duration and uncontrollability of the laughter that Tarlton is supposedly able to induce.

> Amongst other cholericke wise Justices, he was one, that hauing a play presented before him and his Towneship by *Tarlton* and the rest of his fellowes, her Majesties seruants, and they were now entring into their first merriment (as they call it), the people began exceedingly to laugh, when *Tarlton* first peept out his head. Whereat the Justice, not a little moved, and seeing with his beckes and nods hee could not make them cease, he went with his staffe, and beat them round about vnmercifully on the bare pates, in that they, being but Farmers & poore countrey Hyndes, would presume to laugh at the Queenes men, and make no more account of her cloath in his presence.[28]

This anecdote, and those that follow it here, have often been read in terms of what David Mann has called Tarlton's "jiz": the distinctive combination of appearance, sound and actions which gave Tarlton his identity as a performer. Turning the approach on its head, however, one can also read this account for what it says about the behaviour of the audience, imagining them laughing so hard that they become ungovernable.[29] According to another contemporary account, an audience at Worcester "hooted for joy" at Tarlton's performance, while on a third occasion Tarlton's first jest is said to have "brought the whole company into such vehement laughter, that not able again to make them keep silence, for that present time they were fain to break up".[30] Audience laughter, in this last account, is so literally maddening as to overpower the rest of the acoustic environment necessary to make the performance possible.

An elegy on Tarlton by Charles Fitzgeffrey draws attention to the volume of the sound that Tarlton generated:

> Every time Tarlton showed his face in a full theatre, and his witty head, which was not without teeth, the whole heaven echoed with the terrifying laughter (*horrifico ... cachinno*) of the spectators, and the high hall of Jove heard the applause. Even the North and South Poles were stunned and astonished ...[31]

---

of references in Edwin Nungezer, *A Dictionary of Actors and of other persons associated with the public representation of plays in England before 1642* (1929; New York: AMS Press, 1971), 347–65; for more comprehensive accounts of early modern stage clowns, see David Mann, *The Elizabethan Player: Contemporary Stage Representation* (London: Routledge, 1991), and David Wiles, *Shakespeare's Clown: Actor and Text in the Elizabethan Playhouse* (Cambridge: Cambridge University Press, 1987).

    28   Thomas Nashe, *The Works of Thomas Nashe*, ed. Ronald B. McKerrow, rev. F. P. Wilson, 5 vols (Oxford: Clarendon Press, 1958), 1:188.

    29   Mann, *The Elizabethan Player*, 27.

    30   Wiles, *Shakespeare's Clown*, 16, 22.

    31   Charles Fitzgeffrey, *Cenotaphia*, cited from Nungezer, *Dictionary*, 359: *Conspicienda amplo quoties daret ora Theatro / Tarltonus, lepidum non sine dente caput, / Spectantum horrifico*

In a similar vein, Henry Peacham invokes Tarlton as an exemplary generator of extreme, uncontrollable laughter.

> Tarlton when his head was onely seene,
> The Tire-house doore and Tapistrie betweene
> Set all the multitude in such a laughter,
> They could not hold for scarse an houre after...[32]

Neither Fitzgeffrey, born around 1575, nor Peacham, born in 1578, had necessarily seen Tarlton act, but that does not matter for the purposes at hand: these quotations contain within them the unexamined assumption that the theatre is a venue where the laughter is of long duration, and so intense as to be unstoppable, continuing despite the becks and nods of the magistrate, and even the wills of the people involved. Fitzgeffrey describes the sound of the laughter as *"horrifico"* – able to make the hairs stand up on the back of your neck. Bruce Smith has developed two ideas germane to the argument here: firstly, that theatre-going was among the most acoustically intense experiences to be had in early modern England by a population who did not have the constant experience of loud ambient noise which is part of the modern condition, and secondly, Smith argues, the acoustics of the early modern outdoor cylindrical amphitheatre reflected back to audiences the sound of themselves:

> Performers in the reconstructed Globe in London have commented on the way audience response can start in one part of the theater and then spread laterally to the rest. The experience of broad sound comes not only from the actors on stage but from one's fellow auditors.[33]

In the light of this work, one can read Fitzgeffrey's poem as registering astonishment at the sheer decibel level produced by an audience roaring with laughter in a full theatre. According to another contemporary observer, "[Tarlton] was the merriest fellow, and had such jests in store / That, if thou hadst seen him, thou would'st have laughed thy heart sore".[34] Once again, audience laughter could hurt.

Two later accounts of the clown peeping out show that the effect described by Fitzgeffrey and Peacham, and the physical intensity of the experience it was said to generate, by no means died with Tarlton. Simon in Thomas Middleton's *The Mayor of Quinborough* describes his experiences of clowns performing the peeping-out routine:

---

coelum intonat omne cachinno, / Audiit & plausus aula suprema Iovis. Attoniti stupere poli ...

32   Peacham, *Thalia's Banquet*, cited from Nungezer, *Dictionary*, 362–3.

33   Bruce R. Smith, *The Acoustic World of Early Modern England: Attending to the O-factor* (Chicago: University of Chicago Press, 1999), 214.

34   Robert Wilson, *Three Lords and Three Ladies of London*, cited from Nungezer, *Dictionary*, 348.

Oh the Clowns that I have seen in my time!
The very peeping out of one of them would have made
A young heir laugh, though his Father lay a dying;
A man undone in Law the day before (the saddest case that can be)
Might for his 2ᵈ have burst himself with laughing,
And ended all his miseries. Here was a merry world, my Masters![35]

Like many of the other passages collected here, the stress in this account of the peeping-out is on the physical intensity of audience laughing as a bodily experience, as a form of pleasure so delightful that the laugher might actually burst. One final illustration of the intensity with which audience laughter is often described comes from 1638. Two characters are discussing things they enjoy about the theatre, a discussion again focused on the moment of the clown peeping out:

LANDLORD: I 'ave laugh'd
        Untill I cry'd again, to see what Faces
        The Rogue will make: O it does me good…
THRIFT: … I never saw *Rheade* peeping through the Curtain,
        But ravishing joy enter'd into my heart.[36]

This example will be discussed more fully in the next section, for its description of the clown at work, but for the matter at hand what is important is the "ravishing joy" produced by the clown's entrance. Clearly, the characters in this Induction, like Middleton's Simon, are foolish caricatures. Indeed, in Simon's case, he is himself (unknowingly) a clown of the sort whose theatrical performance he praises, so that there is a *mise en abyme* at work. All the same, the idea of audience laughter presented in these accounts is that it could be an experience so intense as to be on the edge of pain, and this opinion of theatrical laughter was one shared by theatre's enemies – Prynne and Gosson – as well as its supporters.

What did Audiences Laugh at?

We have seen that early modern comedies in general sought audience laughter, and seen too that accounts of that laughter often stress its loudness, its intensity, and the loss of self-control it is able to inflict. The question remains, what did early modern audiences laugh at? Again, the approach to this query must keep within the realm of sociological observation, listing and discussing not early modern comic theory in the abstract, but occasions on which an early modern audience is stated to laugh. The chapter has already described one of these occasions – the entry of a clown peeping through a curtain – which was customary in early modern theatre and which is not

---

35 Middleton, *The Mayor of Quinborough* (1661), 63.
36 Goffe, *The careles shepherdess* (1656), 4–5.

customary in modern theatre. What else can be said about the usual and customary occasions for early modern audience laughter?

The best documented cues for audience laughter come from the field of physical comedy, since there are many accounts of such laughter in addition to those already discussed in the previous section with regard to the routine of "peeping out". Four detailed accounts of theatre clowns in action – two Elizabethan, one Jacobean and one Caroline – are presented here, and in two of those cases the play under discussion is extant and identifiable, enabling comparison of the playtext and the account of audience laughter. These accounts form the basis for a provisional taxonomy of what audiences could laugh at in a clown's performance. By extension, this evidence of audiences' laughter patterns also applies to the kinds of physical comedy available to other types of character on the early modern stage.[37]

The clown has a clearly defined role as a laughter-generator in the early modern theatre. But many of his resources, including the entry through the curtain and the jig at the end of the performance, are either not represented at all, or only indirectly sketched out, in the texts of the plays we have in which he features. A useful list of some of these resources is to be found in a passage from Joseph Hall's book of satires *Virgidemiarum*, published in 1597. Again, Hall is fascinated by the auditory texture introduced by the laughter: the contrast between the silent audience of the "frightfull" scenes, and the sheer din of an audience laughing and applauding:

> Now, least such frightfull showes of Fortunes fall,
> And bloudy Tyrants rage, should chance appall
> The dead stroke audience, mids the silent rout
> Comes leaping in a selfe-misformed lout,
> And laughes, and grins, and frames his Mimik face,
> And iustles straight into the Princes place.
> Then doth the *Theatre Eccho* all aloud,
> With gladsome noyse of that applauding croud.
> A goodly *hoch-poch*; when vile *Russettings*,
> Are match't with monarchs, & with mighty kings.
> A goodly grace to sober *Tragick Muse*,
> When each base clown, his clumbsie fist doth bruise,
> And show his teeth in double rotten-row,
> For laughter at his selfe-resembled show.[38]

Even down to the vivid physical detail of the rotten teeth, Hall gives us a warrant to read audible laughter in the comic scenes in Elizabethan tragedy. Hall later imagines

---

37 See also Richard A. Levin, "The Relation of External Evidence to the Allegorical and Thematic Interpretation of Shakespeare", *Shakespeare Studies*, 13 (1980): 1–30, who offers further examples of accounts of audience laughter, and who argues that accounts of affective response from the early modern theatre are often phrased as reactions to characters.

38 Hall, *Virgidemiarum sixe bookes. First three bookes, of tooth-lesse satyrs* (London: Thomas Creede, 1597), 7–8.

the writers sitting watching audience reaction through these scenes, revising the script for future performances accordingly. This is interesting in that it shows the reciprocal, mutually constitutive relationship between audience reaction and playtext – the latter both causes, and changes in response to, the echo of the former – but it also shows that Hall imagines the clown as a scripted element within the drama. Hall's clown brings laughter by non-verbal means: leaping and justling around the stage, grinning and pulling faces, and, indeed, laughing. The same complaint about laughing creating laughter is repeated a few years later in the dialogue of *Hamlet*, when Hamlet warns: "Let not your clowns speak more than is set down for them; for there be of them that will themselves laugh, to set on some quantity of barren spectators to laugh too …". Hamlet goes on to complain about other devices used by clowns, notably "blabbering lips", and repeated catchphrases; but in the light of this book's argument that there is a relationship between onstage laughter and audience laughter, the repetition of Hall's complaint about the effectiveness of onstage laughter as a laughter generator is particularly useful.[39]

Hall's phrase about the clown who "frames his Mimik face" foregrounds face-pulling as a comic technique, and this is interesting, because face-pulling is a comic device which has left textual traces in comedies of the period. For example, in Jonson's *Cynthia's Revels*, performed by the Children of the Revels at Blackfriars in 1600–1601, Amorphus offers a masterclass in pulling faces:

> You shall now, as well be the ocular, as the eare-witnesse, how cleerly I can refell that *paradox*, or rather *pseudodox*, of those, which hold the face to be the index of the mind, which (I assure you) is not so, in any politique creature: for instance. I will now giue you the particular, and distinct face of euery your most noted *species* of persons, as your marchant, your scholer, your souldier, your lawyer, courtier, &c. and each of these so truly, as you would sweare, but that your eye shal see the variation of the lineament, it were my most proper, and genuine aspect.[40]

Amorphus then goes on to pull a series of faces matching the professions he has described. Part of the joke of this scene, then, is that its high linguistic style, typical of the children's companies and of Jonson's writing for them in particular, is applied to a laughter-generating technique which Hall associates dismissively with merely plebeian comedy. Jonson has taken care over the writing-up of this routine, revising the pointing and many minor verbal details from its first appearance in print in quarto in 1601. For instance, in the scene in the quarto which sets this one up, Amorphus can "make the face of any States-men liuing"; in Jonson's revision of the scene for the folio, Amorphus is given a more formal name for this skill which further

39 Shakespeare, *Hamlet*, 3.2.38–40; one Renaissance writer, William Fennor, even complains that ignorant audiences laugh at the sound of themselves laughing: "Let one but ask the reason why they roare / They'll answere, cause the rest did so before", cited in Andrew Gurr, *Playgoing in Shakespeare's London*, 3rd edn (Cambridge: Cambridge University Press, 2004), 275.

40 Jonson, *Cynthia's Revels*, 2.3.11–21.

accentuates the incongruity of its origins in the art of the clown, and he can "tender the face" of any such statesman (1.3.32). Amorphus is not, in other respects, entirely an analogue of Hall's leaping, justling clown: but his name means "shapeless", just as Hall applies the word "misformed" to his clown, and face-pulling is a part of what he does to gain audience laughter.

Face-pulling is again at issue in the second account of laughter to be discussed in detail, from the Cambridge University play *The Pilgrimage to Parnassus*, performed, probably, in 1599. At one point, the manservant Dromo enters, "*drawing a clowne in with a rope*", and explains to the unwilling clown that he must perform:

> DROMO: Clownes haue bene thrust into playes by head & shoulders, euer since Kempe could make a scaruey face, and therfore reason thou shouldst be drawne in with a cart rope.
>
> CLOWN: But what must I doe nowe?
>
> DROMO: Why if thou canst but drawe thy mouth awrye, laye thy legg ouer thy staffe, sawe a peece of cheese asunder with thy dagger, lape vp drinke on the earth, I warrant thee, theile laughe mightilie. Well, Ile turne thee loose to them, ether saie somwhat for they selfe, or hang & be *non plus*.
>
> *Exit.*
>
> CLOWN: This is fine y faith: nowe, when they haue noe bodie to leaue on the stage, the[y] bringe mee vp, & which is worse, tell mee not what I shoulde saye. Gentles, I dare saie youe looke for a fitt of mirthe, Ile therfore present vnto you a proper newe loue letter of mine to the tune of *Put on the smock a mundaye*, which in the heate of my charitie I pende, and thus it begins: O my louely Nigra, pittie the paine of my liuer... [41]

If Hall's account seems to locate the clown, and the laughter he generates, within the drama, this account from *The Pilgrimage to Parnassus* seems to put the clown firmly outside the "they" of the dramatic establishment, and to imagine him as an independent source of laughter which is unscripted ("the[y] ... tell mee not what I shoulde saye"), and entirely an add-on extra to the play. The dialogue says, in particular, that the clown gains laughter through face-pulling, which it describes twice; in the punning phrase "by head & shoulders" it alludes, perhaps to the peeping-out routine; and it states that clowns gain laughter through other sorts of physical routines of an almost silent-comedy style, such as trying to cut a piece of hard cheese. Particularly tantalising is Dromo's description of an audience laughing "mightily" at the clown lapping up drink from the ground, which presupposes a previous set of actions (pouring a drink, spilling a drink) which make this comic moment possible.

---

41   *The Pilgrimage to Parnassus*, cited from J.B. Leishman (ed.), *The Three Parnassus Plays (1598–1601)* (London: Ivor Nicholson & Watson Ltd, 1949), 129–30; the phrase "thrust into playes by head & shoulders" is an admiring quotation of Sidney, *Defence*, 244: "their plays ... thrust in the clown by head and shoulders to play a part in majestical matters".

Of course, this clown isn't a "real" professional theatre clown, in the sense that his part is presumably taken by a university student just like all the other parts. Another marker of the difference is the fact that the comedy routine he then delivers appears to be purely verbal, an intellectual exercise in malapropisms. When, in the third of the *Parnassus Plays*, the character of Will Kemp is introduced, he is firmly associated with the theatrical establishment, and indeed takes part in the audition of the students, so that this scene's depiction of the clown as an entirely separate laughter-generating concern from the rest of the theatrical enterprise is contradicted even within the set of plays from which it comes. All the same, its description of the clown's usual "fit of mirth" is an interesting primary account of what audiences laughed at.

Face-pulling is also complained against once more in the third account to be discussed here, from a pamphlet which falls uneasily between cynical satire and morally improving sermon: *This Worlds Folly*, by I.H., published in 1615. I.H. refers in particular to John Cooke's comedy *Greene's Tu Quoque*, performed by Queen Anne's Men at the Red Bull. For I.H., one of the most upsetting aspects of the theatre is the noisiness of the "oyster-crying audience" of comedies, "oyster-crying" in that oysterwives were proverbial for the loudness of their shouting. But this noisiness in the audience is fed by and is a reflection of the noise of those on stage:

> *Vos Quoque* [*marg.*: *Or, *Tu Quoque*], and you also, who with *Scylla*-barking, *Stentor*-throated bellowings, flashchoaking [*sic*] squibbes of absurd vanities into the nosthrils of your spectators; barbarously diuerting *Nature*, and defacing Gods own image, by metamorphosing humane* shape into bestiall forme. [*marg.*: **Greenes* Baboone.][42]

I.H.'s attack flickers between blaming the clown in the second person singular – "*Tu Quoque … Greenes* Baboone", and blaming "*Vos quoque*" – the work of the whole theatrical troupe around the clown. The laughter that, collectively, they generate is figured as an attack on the respiratory systems of the auditors – fireworks up the nostrils. Cooke's comedy is certainly a play which sets out to generate audience laughter, as is explicit in the final couplet, spoken in the first performances by the clown Thomas Greene in the character of the fool Bubble: "To mirth and laughter henceforth I'le prouoke ye, / If you but please to like of *Greenes Tu quoque*."[43] The performance elements identified by I.H. of loudness and physical grotesquerie survive dimly in Bubble's part as it is recorded in the printed text of the play, within which Bubble is an unexpectedly amiable character, a servant suddenly made rich (as he thinks) whose main function is to be the butt of a series of tricks. Nonetheless, connections can be made between play and attack. For instance, the play requires face-pulling from Bubble, as in the following exchange, in which Staines helps Bubble to prepare to show off his new clothes:

---

42 I.H., *This Worlds Folly Or A warning-peece discharged vpon the wickednesse thereof* (London: William Jaggard, 1615), B2r.

43 Cooke, *Greenes Tu Quoque* (1614), M2r.

BUBBLE: if you will set my face of any fashion, pray'doe it quickly?
STAINES: You carry your face as well as eare an *Italian* in the world, onely inrich it
    with a Smyle, and tis incomparable: and thus much more, at your first apparace,
    you shall perhaps strike your acquaintance into an extasie, or perhaps a laughter: but
    tis ignorance in them, which will soone be ouercome, if you perseuer.

It is not that face-pulling has ceased to be funny, or that comedians have ceased to
make use of it. But it is striking how often face-pulling is mentioned, specifically,
in these accounts of audience reaction to clowns, and how obviously and formally,
sometimes, it is cued in the script. In the example above, indeed, it is not merely
cued, but its potential to cause laughter is alluded to. Bubble's opportunities for
"*Stentor*-throated bellowings" are adumbrated, too, for instance in set-pieces, such
as the scene in which he feigns weeping for his dead relative, a scene which, in
some respects, inherits the tradition of the insincere comic weeping of the Vice
illustrated in the previous chapter. He also has scripted noises, such as when wooing
the unfortunate Joyce: at one point, when he thinks he is making progress, he utters
the lustful interjection "Augh! now shee comes to mee". Also part of Bubble's comic
apparatus, and also unavoidably mentioned by I.H., is his catchphrase, "*Tu quoque*",
equally applicable to all situations, which starts off as a social-climbing affectation
and ends up as a bawdy *double entendre* ("The time is come … [f]or mee to tickle
thy *Tu quoque*").[44]

An odd feature of this attack is that Thomas Greene himself died and was buried
in August 1612.[45] At first glance, I.H.'s information is significantly out of date for
a 1615 publication, and therefore out of touch. Yet it is clear from later revivals
that the play retained its popularity after Greene's death: "*Greenes* Baboone" refers
not (as has been sometimes thought) to a hypothetical lost entertainment in which
Greene performed as a baboon, but to Greene's successor in the clown role, who is,
in the more normal idiom, aping Thomas Greene.[46] And in that case, it again suggests
that the clown's laughter-making techniques, his "squibbes of absurd vanities", are
transferable and to some extent independent of the individual personality.

This is particularly clearly the case with *Greene's Tu Quoque*, since it achieved
a good measure of contemporary fame long after Greene's death, with the printed
edition going through three quartoes; the play itself being revived, and even played
at court in the 1620s; and the performance being remembered by Bubble's adaptation
into one of a series of drolls in Kirkman's *The Wits*, published in 1662. Bubble
appears on the title-page of *The Wits*, in the classic clown pose half through the

---

44   Cooke, *Greenes Tu Quoque*, G2r, D2v–D3r, K2v.
45   Herbert Berry, 'Greene, Thomas (bap. 1573, d. 1612)', *Oxford DNB*; for a sensitive
account of how Bubble's part shares in other stage techniques associated with the Jacobean
clown, such as the onstage claque, see Alexander Leggatt, *Jacobean Public Theatre* (London:
Routledge, 1992), 98–105.
46   See Matthew Steggle, "*Greenes* Baboone: Thomas Greene, baboon impersonator?",
Theatre Notebook, 60 (2006): 72–5.

curtain, and with catchphrase on his lips.[47] The phenomena that drove this success, namely the "mirth and laughter" generated by the opportunities for clowning written into the play, have left their own independent trace in I.H.'s attack.

A fourth description of clowning, and another example which permits comparison between the play in which the clown performed and the description of the clown in action, can be found in the Praeludium to Thomas Goffe's *The Careless Shepherdess*, discussed briefly above for its description of an audience's "ravishing joy". The Praeludium is a short self-contained sketch, probably dating from around 1638, and quite possibly from the pen of Richard Brome, who was at that time the retained dramatist of the Salisbury Court theatre. A dialogue between characters of different social classes on different interpretations of theatrical fashions, it includes two characters, Landlord and Thrift, who represent, respectively, the point of view of the country gentleman and the citizen. It turns out that these two agree on what comic action consists of:

> LANDLORD: Why I would have the Fool in every Act,
> Be't Comedy, or Tragedy, I 'ave laugh'd
> Untill I cry'd again, to see what Faces
> The Rogue will make: O it does me good
> To see him hold out's Chin hang down his hands,
> And twirle his Bawble. There is nere a part
> About him but breaks jests. I heard a fellow
> Once on this Stage cry, *Doodle, Doodle, Dooe*,
> Beyond compare; I'de give the other shilling
> To see him act the Changling once again.
> THRIFT: And so would I, his part has all the wit,
> For none speaks Craps and Quibbles besides him:
> I'd rather see him leap, laugh, or cry,
> Then hear the gravest Speech in all the *Play*.
> I never saw *Rheade* peeping through the Curtain,
> But ravishing joy enter'd into my heart.[48]

In Landlord's imagination, the fool's performance is primarily physical, to the point where "There is nere a part / About him but breaks jests." As a description of physical comedy, this is an admiring counterpart to the hostile checklist of such techniques in William Prynne's *Histrio-mastix*: "*those ridiculous antique, mimicall,*

---

47   John Cooke, *Greene's Tu quoque, or, The cittie gallant*, ed. Alan J. Berman (New York: Garland, 1984), Introduction, xi; Bentley, *JCS*, 1.194; for another allusion to its popularity, see Henry Parrot, *Laquei Ridiculosi* (1613), cited in Nungezer, *Dictionary*, 148.

48   Goffe, *The Careles Shepherdess* (1656), 4–5; Bentley, *JCS*, 4.501–5; G.E. Bentley, "Praeludium for Goffe's *The Careless Shepherdess*", *The Seventeenth Century Stage: A Collection of Critical Essays* (Chicago: Chicago University Press, 1968), 28–41; Matthew Steggle, *Richard Brome: Place and Politics on the Caroline Stage* (Manchester: Manchester University Press, 2004), 120–21.

*foolish gestures, complements, embracements. smiles, nods, motions of the eyes,
head, feete, hands, & whole intire body which Players vse, of purpose to provok
their Spectators to profuse inordinate laughter*".[49] Like many of the other sources
collected here, Landlord heads his list with face-pulling, which he links directly to
audience laughter, but he also imagines physical comedy in posture, in use of the
hands, and in the use of properties (the "Bawble"). Similarly, the comic routine
of peering around the curtain resembles that of Tarlton fifty years earlier. But the
references are less archaic than one might think: the fool here is named as Timothy
Read, who was one of the current actors at Salisbury Court.

Furthermore, the comic routines described, even down to the catchphrase
"*Doodle, Doodle, Dooe*", appear to come from Brome's *The English Moor*,
commissioned for and staged by the Salisbury Court company in 1638.[50] In this play,
the servant and clown-character Buzzard (played by Read) starts off as a servant
of the usurer Quicksands, from whose service he is dismissed when Quicksands
marries a young and beautiful woman. Obsessed with the fear of being cuckolded,
Quicksands also has a guilty secret and a reminder of his own sexual incontinence
in the form of an illegitimate idiot son he keeps isolated in East Anglia. Buzzard
takes on the disguise of the absent son, and bursts into a private entertainment at
Quicksands' house, causing confusion as he "*sings and dances and spins with a
Rock & spindle*".[51] A rock is a three-foot-long staff for use in the spinning of yarn:
it is both a culturally specific property, representing Quicksands' links to the textile
industry of East Anglia, and also a version (according to Landlord) of the traditional
fool's bauble, with obvious potential for lewd horseplay.[52] In addition, there is also
a gestural component to Read's ability to generate laughter, evidenced in Landlord's
description of the changeling's hanging-down hands. This gesture seems to have
been something of a trademark, since it shows up in the illustration of "Changeling"
on the frontispiece of Kirkman's *The Wits*, which appears as Figure 1 in this book.
Face-pulling, posture, gesture and properties combine to create the effect described
in this account of a man who is funny from head to foot.

As for the "craps", presumably scraps of language, and quibbles, the scraps of
language are easy to document, since, both in manuscript and in print versions of the
play, almost all of the changeling's part in this scene consists of the repeated phrases
"hack ye there" and "hey toodle loodle loodle loo" (67).[53] These are Buzzard's
equivalent of Bubble's "*Tu quoque*". And the point about *The English Moor* is that
the changeling's scene of comic mayhem is placed at the heart of the action, important
both thematically (since it emblematises the moral bankruptcy of Quicksands) and also as
a plot device, providing the confusion in which the the usurer is (as he thinks) cuckolded.

---

49   Prynne, *Histrio-mastix*, 877.

50   See Richard Brome, *The English Moore, or, The Mock-Mariage*, ed. Sarah Jayne
Steen (Columbia: University of Missouri Press, 1983), Introduction.

51   Richard Brome, *The English Moor* in *Five New Playes* (1659), 67.

52   *OED*, rock *n*.², bauble *n*.⁴.

53   *OED*, crap *n*.¹ 6, scrap *n*.¹ 2b; Brome, *The English Moor* in *Five New Playes*, 67.

The changeling routines described by Landlord and Thrift are certainly not mere add-ons to the play from which they come. Even though the other characters in the Praeludium to *The Careles Shepherdess* mock Landlord and Thrift for their unrefined tastes, the fact is that the Praeludium comes out of a theatre which very much caters to them, which puts their tastes at the literary heart of the plays it produces, and which measures its success in terms of their laughter.

With consideration of the clown's "craps and quibbles", one starts to move from occasions for laughter derived from physical clowning towards verbal wit. First, though, it is worth summing up what the accounts of audience laughter at physical clowning have suggested. Early modern audiences laughed at clowns for their physical comedy: for their entrances, their movement and their leaping; for their gestures; in particular, for their use of face-pulling, which is specified in all four of these accounts; for the clown's comic weeping, and also (according to Hall and Brome) for the clown's own mannered laughter. Furthermore, opportunities for these routines are encoded within the parts written for clowns in comedies. Cooke's *Greene's Tu Quoque* and Brome's *The English Moor* are merely particularly well-attested examples of this process in action, but the physical repertoire of the clown, and that repertoire's ability to induce audience laughter from particular effects at particular moments, is an implicit part of the assumptions behind any text which includes a clown's part.

While audience laughter in response to non-verbal cues is quite well delineated in accounts such as these, to ask "what sort of verbal effects did audiences laugh at?" is to pose a much harder question. Accounts of audience reaction contain very little which directly links particular sorts of verbal effect to audience laughter, and those accounts which do are almost always dismissive about the value of the effect. By common consent, obscenity was a good way to gain a laugh. For instance, William Cartwright praised Jonson for avoiding obscene verbal effects to obtain cheap audience laughter: in Jonson's comedies, "no rotten talk broakes for a laugh".[54] Puns also delivered audience laughter, according to several sources, including William Davenant in the Prologue to *The Unfortunate Lovers*, a Prologue which also claimed that this was a cheap and low effect, which the following play would eschew. Davenant criticises our "homely ancestors" who *"Laught at a clinch, the shadow of a jest, / And cry a passing good one I protest"*.[55]

In commendatory verses to the 1647 Beaumont and Fletcher folio, William Cartwright wrote of Fletcher:

> When thou wouldst Comick be, each smiling birth
> In that kinde, came into the world all mirth,
> All point, all edge, all sharpnesse; we did sit
> Sometimes five Acts out in pure sprightfull wit,
> Which flowed in such true salt, that we did doubt

---

54   H&S, 11.457.
55   Davenant, *The Unfortunate Lovers* (1643), A3v.

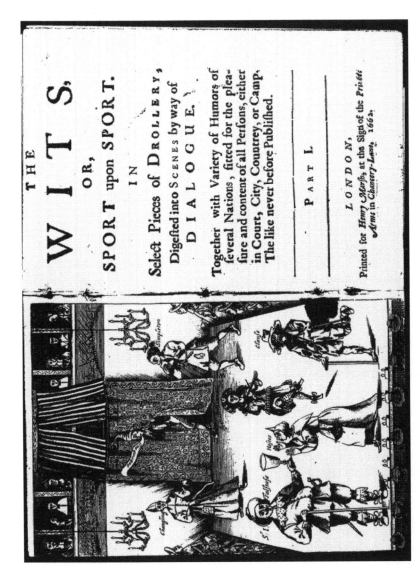

Figure 4.1 Frontispiece of *The Wits* (1662). Note Bubble peeping through the curtain, and "Changeling", with the hanging hands.

In which Scene we laught most two shillings out.
Shakespeare to thee was dull, whose best jest lyes
I'th Ladies questions, and the Fooles replyes;
Old fashion'd wit, which walkt from town to town
In turn'd Hose, which our fathers call'd the Clown;
Whose wit our nice times would obsceanesse call,
And which made Bawdry passe for Comicall.[56]

This is interesting, partly as indirect evidence of what verbal effects in Shakespeare's plays Cartwright regarded as funniest: badinage between lady and clown, such as that found in *Twelfth Night*. Cartwright's dismissal of the clown (and of Shakespeare) is contrasted with celebration of the "pure sprightfull wit" of Fletcher, producing audience laughter spread more evenly across all the scenes. And indeed – and this is a useful transition to the final point concerning audience laughter – often the account of audience laughter is associated not with a particular physical effect, or verbal joke, nor even a particular character, but with the whole experience of the play, to the point where even the audience cannot make up their minds about what they are laughing at. The account of the reception of the antimasque to Beaumont's *Masque of the Inner Temple and Grayes Inne* shares with Cartwright's description the desideratum of a bewildered audience in a state of constant laughter at a spectacle of constant variety:

> the Musicke was extremely well fitted, hauing such a spirit of Countrey iolitie, as can hardly be imagined, but the perpetuall laughter and applause was aboue the Musicke. The dance likewise was of the same strain, and the Dancers, or rather Actors expressed euery one their part so naturally, and aptly, as when a Mans eye was caught with the one, and then past on to the other, hee could not satisfie himselfe which did best.[57]

More dismissive, but in the same spirit, is Nathaniel Tomkyns's eye-witness account of Brome and Heywood's comedy *The Witches of Lancashire*, which he saw at the Globe in the summer of 1634. Tomkyns describes the play as "full of ribaldrie and of things improbable and impossible; yet ... in regard it consisteth from the beginning to the ende of odd passages and fopperies to provoke laughter, and is mixed with diuers songs and dances, it passeth for a merrie and excellent new play".[58] Tomkyns mentions special effects, "odd passages", music and dancing among the pleasures of the play, and describes audience laughter as an important factor in establishing its merriment and excellence. For Tomkyns, as for the majority of those writers

---

56   Beaumont and Fletcher, *Comedies and Tragedies* (1647), d2v.
57   Beaumont, *The masque of the Inner Temple and Grayes Inne* (1613), C3v.
58   Herbert Berry, "The Globe Bewitched and *El Hombre Fiel*", *Medieval and Renaissance Drama in England*, 1 (1984): 211–30, qtn from 212–13; similarly, working from a different set of material, Jeremy Lopez (*in Theatrical Convention and Audience Response in Early Modern Drama*) identifies variety as one of the factors most desired in the Renaissance theatrical experience.

discussed in this chapter, the usual assumption was – for all that Tomkyns seeks to offer a sarcastic critique of that assumption – that the laughter of an audience, preferably loud and sustained, was the badge of success of a comedy.

Chapter 5

Audiences weeping

In the film *Shakespeare in Love* (1998), an early modern audience watches a performance of *Romeo and Juliet*. At the tragic climax of this inset performance, almost all of the spectators – men, women, even the antitheatrical preacher who has been swept into the theatre by mistake – are openly in tears. Just as the previous chapter considered audience laughter, so this chapter poses an apparently narrow and straightforward question: is this scene of *Shakespeare in Love* historically accurate? Is it true that audience members wept in the early modern theatre, and can we say anything about which members did so, to what extent, how often, and under what circumstances?

This topic has been considered before, from various different angles. Andrew Gurr's *Playgoing in Shakespeare's London* provides a collection of over 200 accounts of early modern audiences, a handful of which mention weeping. A second and partially overlapping collection of source material is provided by Richard Levin in a 1980 *Shakespeare Studies* article, material which Levin returns to in his book *Looking for an Argument*.[1] In both pieces, Levin's concern is to demonstrate, by sheer weight of citation of primary sources, that documented early modern audience responses do not support a view of early modern drama as "nonillusionist and hence nonempathetic" (87). The 1980 article directs this evidence against a fashion for allegorical readings of plays, while the book is opposing late-1990s arguments on the nature of early modern subjectivity and selfhood. But in both cases Levin is concerned to demonstrate the affect of early modern drama: the extent to which, surviving evidence suggests, it moved its first consumers. Hence Levin does not need to distinguish between passages describing the experience of consuming early modern drama in the study, or in the theatre, nor between passages which describe drama inducing passions in general, and passages which specifically describe it inducing weeping; all are grist to his mill. Indeed, he ducks altogether the question of whether the passages he collects can be taken as evidence for early modern theatrical custom:

> Of course, the description was a kind of convention (and also an exaggeration – we need not suppose the theaters of that time were actually awash with tears); but the convention itself gives us a significant insight into the "generic expectations" of the contemporary audience.[2]

---

1   Richard Levin, "The Relation of External Evidence to the Allegorical and Thematic Interpretation of Shakespeare", *Shakespeare Studies*, 13 (1980): 1–30; Richard Levin, *Looking for an Argument: Critical Encounters with the New Approaches to the Criticism of Shakespeare and his Contemporaries* (London: Associated University Presses, 2003), 82–94.

2   Levin, "The Relation of External Evidence", 15–16.

For Levin, the quotations he gathers demonstrate that early modern drama in general had affective power upon the minds, which modern criticism has often assumed to be unknowable and unreachable, of its early modern consumers. Other studies which have collected evidence around early modern audience weeping – for instance, the books of Martin White and of Anthony B. Dawson – have used similar sets of quotations to interrogate ideas of affect, performance and subjectivity on the early modern stage.[3] But the interesting thing about the question with which this chapter started, namely whether early modern audiences wept, is that this ought not to be, in the first instance, a matter within the contentious and difficult realm of early modern subjectivity – the grounds of Jonathan Goldberg's attack on Levin's position – so much as a matter of almost sociological observation.[4]

In other words, Levin is interested in accounts of audiences weeping merely as a stepping-stone to the more difficult question of what is going on inside their heads: but what if one shelved (for the moment) any such further step? As has already been argued, even Renaissance accounts of weeping considered it a mysterious and unreliable guide to the state of mind of the weeper. We have accounts suggesting that audience members wept. We need not consider what mental processes this might correspond to, or whether it represents profound emotional perturbation or an easily induced and consensual weeping of the sort represented in a modern idiom by the "three-Kleenex movie". For the moment, it will suffice solely to document references to the phenomenon. As Andrew Gurr comments of audience reaction in general, "Fixing the mental composition of the early playgoers in this period with any precision is not an easy or straightforward task", but "it is certainly possible to identify some of the normative as well as the extreme features of audience behaviour".[5] An examination of norms and extremes around audience weeping should be a useful foundation for anyone looking to think further about the questions for which examples of that weeping might be evidence.

This chapter, therefore, offers a fresh look at the evidence around the weeping of early modern theatrical audiences. For convenience, the evidence is divided into four categories: allusions indicative of general expectations; "eye-witness" accounts, a various and problematic category; references in commendatory poems; and statements of intent from within plays themselves.

---

3   Martin White, *Renaissance Drama in Action: An Introduction to Aspects of Theatre Practice and Performance* (London: Routledge, 1998); Anthony Dawson and Paul Yachnin, *The Culture of Playgoing in Shakespeare's England: A Collaborative Debate* (Cambridge: Cambridge University Press, 2001).

4   Jonathan Goldberg, "Making Sense", in Levin, *Looking for an Argument*, 94–100.

5   Andrew Gurr, *Playgoing in Shakespeare's London*, 3rd edn (Cambridge: Cambridge University Press, 2004), 51–2, 95.

1. General Expectations

It is not controversial to argue that, in early modern discourse in general, tragedy is believed to induce sorrow in those who observe it, and that, as Tanya Hagen has documented, "The language of grief and sorrow establish[es] the emotional atmosphere" of the term *tragedy* in this period.[6] Similarly, among the numerous Renaissance theorists who offered accounts of tragedy's cathartic power, tears were often mentioned as a sign of that effect: according to Lorenzo Valla, the "aim of tragedy is to produce or reproduce tears and lamentations", while Della Casa's *Galateo*, translated into English in 1576, opined that "*these dolefull tales, which wee call* Tragedies, were deuised at first, that when they were plaid in the Theatres (as at that time they were wont) they might draw fourth teares out of their eyes, that had neede to spend them. And so they were by their weeping, healed of their infirmitie".[7]

Two representative examples, standing in for many others, indicate the range and extent of the metaphorical applications of the image of an audience weeping. John Weever's *The Mirror of Martyrs* (1601) and Francis Quarles's *Divine Poems* (1633) both employ imagined audience weeping as a trope. For Weever, the imagined audience are to weep for the martyr Sir John Oldcastle, while for Quarles, they are to weep for the sufferings of Job, but what is interesting here is the way the weeping is constructed in each case:

> Wit, spend thy vigour, Poets, wits quintessence,
> *Hermes* make great the worlds eies with teares;
> *Actors* make sighes a burden for each sentence:
> That he may sob which reades, he swound which heares.
> Mean time, till life in death you doe renew,
> *Wit, Poets, Hermes, Actors*, all adew.[8]

> Wouldst thou behold a Tragick Sceane of sorrow,
> Whose wofull Plot the Author did not borrow
> From sad invention? The sable Stage,
> The lively Actors with their equipage?

---

6   Tanya Hagen, "An English Renaissance Understanding of the Word 'Tragedy'", *Early Modern Literary Studies*, Special Issue 1 (1997): 5.1–30, at http://purl.oclc.org/emls/si-01/si-01hagen.html; for a wider context, see Timothy J. Reiss, "Renaissance Theatre and the Theory of Tragedy", in Glyn P. Norton (ed.), *The Cambridge History of Literary Criticism: The Renaissance* (Cambridge: Cambridge University Press, 1999), 229–47.

7   Valla, cited in Reiss, "Renaissance Theatre and the Theory of Tragedy", 237; Giovanni Della Casa, *Galateo of Maister Iohn Della Casa, Archebishop of Beneuenta*, trans. Robert Petersen (London: Raufe Newbery, 1576), 31.

8   Weever, *The mirror of martyrs, or The life and death of that thrice valiant capitaine, and most godly martyre Sir Iohn Old-castle knight Lord Cobham* ([London]: William Wood, 1601), F3v.

The Musicke made of Sighs, the Songs of Cries,
The sad Spectators with their watry Eyes?
Behold all this, comprized here in one;
Expect the Plaudit, when the Play is done.[9]

Quarles and Weever are particularly good illustrations for our purposes, because both are interested in two aspects of weeping: firstly, weeping as an *auditory* phenomenon, in which the actors' sighs become, in the metaphor used by both poets, a form of music. Both insist, also, on the infectiousness of that weeping, arguing that it will cause the audience to weep, and, by implication, to contribute to the "Musicke made of Sighs". This scenario positions actors as, in effect, agents of transmission between authors (both poems referencing authors as the origin of the plays) and audience, and these initial examples are part of a wide cultural expectation that theatre audiences might, in general, be capable of weeping at a play.

2 First-hand Accounts

There, is, then, an abstract expectation that drama might draw tears in early modern theatres. What one might call "eye-witness" accounts of this effect in action are rather harder to find, and most secondary accounts of audience weeping tend to draw on three or four very well-known primary examples: notably Thomas Nashe's description of audiences weeping at the death of Talbot. This section collects together eleven "eye-witness" accounts in order to put the best-known of them into a better perspective.

One Elizabethan who is known to have wept at a play is the Latin playwright William Gager. Gager was heavily involved in the amateur drama of Christ Church College, Oxford, both as a writer and as an organiser. However, Gager's Oxford University colleague John Rainoldes, a committed antitheatricalist, expressed his displeasure at these plays, and in a letter responding to Rainoldes, Gager denies that the plays are occasions for immoral pleasure in admiring cross-dressing boys. In the process, he makes an admission: "I haue bene often mooved by our playes to laughter, and sometime to teares: but I can not accuse either my selfe, or any other, of any such beastlie thought stirred vp by them."[10] Gager does not weep often, only "sometime". But in a context where he is rejecting charges of effeminacy, it is clear

---

9   Francis Quarles, *Diuine Poems* (London: M.F., 1633), 171. According to the preacher Thomas Playfere in a sermon preached in 1595, "the whole theater of heauen and earth wept" as Jesus suffered, an image he inverts in arguing that "It becommeth vs that are Christians, at the death of Christians rather to reioyce as at a triumph, then to weepe as at a tragedy": Playfere, *The whole sermons of that eloquent diuine, of famous memory; Thomas Playfere* (London: T.S., 1623), 90, 81; his source for the latter quotation is St John Chrysostom.

10   William Gager, quoted in John Rainoldes, *Th'overthrow of stage-playes, by the way of controversie betwixt D. Gager and D. Rainoldes* ([Middleburg]: [Richard Schilders], 1599), 33.

that, for Gager, at least, it was not unreasonable or completely unmanly to weep at the performance of a play.

Another nuanced account of weeping at a dramatic event – although not strictly speaking in a theatre – occurs in a contemporary description of entertainments laid on at Shrewsbury for Philip Sidney's father Sir Henry Sidney in 1581. The account is careful to balance its account of "my Lorde", so that he appears sensitive, yet not too sensitive:

> there weare placid in an Ilett hard by the watersyde ser*ten* apoyntyd scollars of the free scoole beinge aparrelyd all in greene and greene wyllows vppon theire heades mvrningely callinge to hym macking there lamentable orac*i*ons sorrowinge hys departure the *whi*che was doon so pytyfully and of sutche Excellency that truly itt made many bothe in the bardge vppon the water as also people vpon Land to weepe and my Lorde hym selffe to chandge countenance.[11]

However, Gager and Sir Henry Sidney are far from typical playgoers, nor is the theatre described in these two accounts that of the London stage. One gets a little closer to that stage in the case against tragedies made by Stephen Gosson, himself a former writer of plays for the professional theatre: "The beholding of troubles and miserable slaughters that are in Tragedies, drives us to immoderate sorrow, heauines, womanish weeping and mourning, whereby we become louers of dumpes, and lamentation, both enemies to fortitude."[12] Gosson is troubled by the paradox that audiences find the weeping induced by tragedies pleasurable, a paradox encapsulated in his phrase "louers of dumpes". A complaining use of "we" similar to Gosson's occurs in William Cornwallis's essay "Of Discontentments", which alludes to the theatre in the course of its argument that weeping is a sign of the body's inappropriate mastery over the soul:

> alas we are so vsed to this bewayling, as if we haue no cause for what wee feele, we will for what we see, for the losse of money, and things of that kinde: and if these be not readie, we will weepe at a Tale, or at a Puppet play. If the body onely were at this expence, but our soules will accompany them, and bee so foolishly kinde, as to lament for that they neuer knew.[13]

Regardless of whether or not his "we" can be interpreted as possessing the same autobiographical frankness as, for example, Gager's comment, Cornwallis's

---

11   "Dr Taylor's history", quoted in J. Alan B. Somerset, *Records of Early English Drama: Shropshire*, 2 vols (Toronto: Toronto University Press, 1994), 1.228–9, qtn from 229. Taylor also records parts of the boys' songs.

12   Gosson, *Playes confuted*, C5v–C6r.

13   William Cornwallis, *Essayes. By Sr William Corne-Waleys the younger, Knight* (London: Edmund Mattes, 1600–1601), K7r; Cornwallis's phrasing implies a theatre which charges for entrance, and which is usually, but not always, operating. On Cornwallis, essayist and Essex supporter, see Arthur Kincaid, "Cornwallis, Sir William, the younger (c. 1579–1614)", *Oxford DNB*.

allegation would not make sense if early modern playgoers never wept. His formulation, drawing on the early modern idea that the imagination belongs to the body rather than to the soul, reverses the usual modern critical formula whereby bodily reactions (in this case weeping) can be read as symptoms of spiritual passions. In Cornwallis's account, the body weeps in a theatre, and then the soul joins in: tears are not a simple index of affect, but something more complicated and ambiguous.

Audience weeping is alleged both in these last two antitheatrical accounts, and in pro-theatrical discourse, since in *Pierce Pennilesse* Thomas Nashe gives a description of weeping in an Elizabethan professional theatre in the course of an argument for the moral utility of drama. Interestingly, his example is not, strictly speaking, from a tragedy: instead, Nashe describes the audience at a history play, probably Shakespeare's *1 Henry VI*.

> How it would have joy'd brave *Talbot* (the terror of the French) to thinke that after he had lyne two hundred yeare in his Tombe, hee should triumphe againe on the Stage, and have his bones newe embalmed with the teares of ten thousand spectators at least (at severall times) who, in the Tragedian that represents his person, imagine they behold him fresh bleeding.[14]

This is a celebrated quotation, summed up by Andrew Gurr as "the first description of a mass emotion other than laughter in any London playhouse".[15] Nashe's imagery of copious, wet tears recalls that seen in Chapter 3 in onstage descriptions of weeping. For him, the tears act as a chain, making the spectators into a collective: a collective which does not merely include all the audience present at one performance, all of whom are in tears, but all the audience members at a series of performances. Weeping is thus a communal act of remembrance linking the spectators both to the actor and through him to the historical original, Talbot.

Nashe's account excludes any explicit reference to the playwright. But the Prologue of Dekker's *If it be not good, the Diuel is in it* (1612) uses tears as a linking device in a different chain, and a different collectivisation of the audience. Dekker's Prologue is given over to a portrait of contemporary theatre practice, and praises an ideal playwright:

> That Man giue mee; whose Brest fill'd by the *Muses*,
> With Raptures, Into a second, them infuses:
> Can giue an Actor, Sorrow, Rage, Ioy, Passion,
> Whilst hee againe (by selfe-same Agitation)
> Commands the *Hearers*, sometimes drawing out *Teares*,
> Then smiles, and fills them both with *Hopes* & *Feares*.[16]

---

14   Thomas Nashe, *The Works of Thomas Nashe*, ed. Ronald B. McKerrow, rev. F.P. Wilson, 5 vols (Oxford: Clarendon Press, 1958), 1.212.

15   Gurr, *Playgoing*, 165.

16   Dekker, *If it be not good, the Diuel is in it* (1612), A4v. While both the Dekker and May passages occur within playtexts, neither is in a play which sets out to make an audience weep.

For Dekker, the chain runs from inspiration through the writer and on into the actor, who by a process of almost sympathetic resonance induces that same passion in the audience. A passage in Thomas May's comedy *The Heire* (1622) similarly describes a player moving an audience to tears by similar process of reproduction, by feigning grief himself:

> ROSCIO: Has not your Lordship seene
> A player personate *Ieronimo*?
> POLIMETES: By th'masse tis true, I have seen the knave paint griefe
> In such a liuely colour, that for false
> And acted passion he has drawne true teares
> From the spectators eyes, Ladyes in the boxes
> Kept time with sighes, and teares to his sad accents
> As he had truely bin the new man he seem'd.[17]

The play, one may note in passing, is Kyd's *The Spanish Tragedie*, itself very interested in the representation (and the unrepresentability) of weeping. We should not, by now, be surprised to find May describing the representation of weeping as the cause of "true teares" in the audience. Again, the idea that the noise of weeping is almost a musical element within the symphonic theatre comes back, in the idea of ladies who "Kept time" with the grief on stage in their sighs and tears. May's account is also gendered, associating the weeping more particularly with the ladies in the boxes, but leaving open the possibility that "the spectators" more generally shed tears for Hieronimo.

Much later in date, but in a similar vein, is an exchange in George Farquhar's *Love and A Bottle* (1699). The cynical Lyric claims that he enjoys the theatre:

> LYRIC: I laugh to see the Ladies cry. To see so many weep at the Death of the fabulous
> Hero, who would but laugh if the Poet that made 'em were hang'd? On my Conscience,
> these Tragedies make the Ladies vent all their Love and Honour at their Eyes, when
> the same white Hankerchief that blows their Noses, must be a Winding-Sheet to the
> deceased Hero.
> LOVEWELL: Then there's something in the Handkerchief to embalm him, Mr. *Lyrick*,
> Ha, ha, ha.[18]

This is obviously from a different era of theatre, and one in which audiences were perhaps more demonstrative: accounts of audiences weeping in Restoration theatres are relatively easy to find, and are not collected here. The reason for bringing this example in here is partly as a gloss on May's, since it, too, presupposes the women

---

17 Thomas May, *The Heire* (1622), A4r; this is often taken as a description of Burbage, although in fact there is actually nothing distinctive to link it to Burbage rather than to any of the other actors who may have played the lead role in *The Spanish Tragedy*.

18 George Farquhar, *Love and a bottle a comedy* (London: Richard Standfast, 1699), 42; Levin, "The Relation of External Evidence", includes some other Restoration examples.

in the audience to be the most likely to weep, and partly, too, because it shares (in a mocking vein) and illuminates May's sense of the reciprocity of the relationship between stage-fiction and audience. The ladies weep into handkerchiefs (in the manner we see used to represent weeping on the stage), and those handkerchiefs themselves are, in a metaphorical sense, stage properties, serving as a winding-sheet to "embalm" the hero (and Farquhar here falls into the same metaphor as Nashe a century earlier).

While May privileges (and so does Farquhar) the male hero, other descriptions draw attention to the boy-actor playing a woman as a figure particularly likely to induce audience weeping. One example of this is the eye-witness account of a touring performance of *Othello* at Oxford in 1610, written in Latin by the academic Henry Jackson. Normally considered of interest for its description of a boy-actor at work, it also contains within it the unexamined assumption that a performance at a theatre has moved its audience to tears:

> In the last few days the King's Actors have been here. They performed, with the greatest applause, in a full theatre ... they also had tragedies, which they performed with decorum and skill. In them, not just in their speaking, but also in their action, they moved tears [*lachrymas movebant*] ... Desdemona, when dead, was even more moving than when alive, lying on the bed imploring the pity of the spectators even with her expression.[19]

A further account of a boy-actor moving audiences to tears, and another account which, like those of Gager and Cornwallis, uses the first person, is in an anonymous elegy on the actor Walter Clun. The date of Clun's birth is unknown, but according to Wright's *Historia Histrionica* he was an apprentice at the Blackfriars, playing women's parts, late in the pre-Civil-War period.[20] One of these roles is known thanks to a cast-list, rediscovered by David George in 1974, which assigns to him the role of Arethusa in a pre-war production of Beaumont and Fletcher's *Philaster*. He resumed his acting career at the Restoration, playing male roles, and his murder in 1664 prompted an anonymous broadside which recalls his pre-war stage career:

> Thou who in polished words, and Womans dress
> Didst lovers passions to the height express,
> And made us weep, at seeming sorrow swell,
> To hear and see like truth a Fiction fell...[21]

---

19   Gāmini Salgādo (ed.), *Eyewitnesses of Shakespeare* (London: Sussex University Press, 1975), 30. My translation.

20   Edwin Nungezer, *A Dictionary of Actors and of other persons associated with the public representation of plays in England before 1642* (1929; New York: AMS Press, 1971), 94–5; David George, "Early Cast Lists for Two Beaumont and Fletcher Plays", *Theatre Notebook*, 38 (1974): 9–11, estimates it as the mid-1620s; for Clun's career through the Civil War, see Judith Milhous and Robert D. Hume, "New Light on English Acting Companies in 1646, 1648, and 1660", *Review of English Studies*, 42 (1991): 487–509.

21   *An Egley upon the Most Execrable Murther of Mr Clun on of the Comedeans of the Theator Royal* (London: Edward Crouch, 1664).

The essayist Thomas Browne, indeed, sees the sympathy induced by theatre and described in passages such as these as a metaphor for human charity in general, and provides a second example to set alongside William Gager of a named individual who claims personally to have wept in a theatre:

> There is no man that apprehends his owne miseries lesse than my selfe, and no man that so nearely apprehends anothers. I could lose an arme without a teare, and with few groanes, me thinkes, be quartered into pieces; yet can I weep most seriously at a Play, and receive with a true passion, the counterfeit griefs of those knowne and professed impostures. It is not the teares of our own eyes only, but of our friends, also, that do exhaust the current of our sorrowes ... It is an act within the power of charity, to translate a passion out of one brest into another, and to divide a sorrow almost out of it selfe.[22]

The hint of self-mockery in "most seriously" reflects the idea that, for Browne, there is something embarrassing about a man weeping at a play. This is certainly the case in one final account of an audience member weeping, to be found not in the personal meditations of a Thomas Browne, but in the anonymous, schematic world of a Caroline jest-book, *The Book of Bulls* (1636).

> [T]Wo Gentlemen went to see *Pericles* acted, and one of them was moved with the calamities of that Prince that he wept, whereat the other laughed exceedingly. Not long after the same couple went to see the Major of Qinborough, when he who jeered the other at *Pericles* now wept himselfe, to whom the other laughing, sayd, what the Divell should there bee in this merry play to make a man weep. O, replied the other, who can hold from weeping to see a Magistrate so abused?
>
> The jest will take those who have seene these two plaies.[23]

The two plays involved are, of course, Shakespeare and Wilkins's *Pericles* and Middleton's *The Mayor of Quinborough* or *Hengist King of Kent*, Middleton's play having already been cited in this study for its own description of audience laughter at clowning. While *Pericles* is, to modern tastes at least, a problematic play on the cusp between tears and laughter (and Shakespearean tears and laughter will be discussed in Chapter 8), *The Mayor of Quinborough* – at least the part of it related to Simon – is very clearly, to modern and I would argue to early modern sensibilities, a broad comedy about a clown who becomes a magistrate and who is gulled by a group of players. It is ludicrous to weep for the foolish, and very resilient, victim – that's the point of the jest here. And yet in this account of the two plays' stage reception, perhaps, we see what Sidney calls the "sweet violence" of theatre in unusually

---

22 Sir Thomas Browne, *Religio Medici* ([London]: Andrew Crooke, 1642), 127–8.

23 *The Booke of Bulls* (London: Daniel Frere, 1636) F9r–F9v, discussed by Lucy Munro, "A Neglected Allusion to *Pericles* and *Hengist King of Kent* in performance", *Notes and Queries*, 249 (2004): 307–10.

detailed action.[24] There are several interesting details in the account: it is *Pericles* the play which induces weeping, it seems, so that *The Book of Bulls* is among those accounts which credits the play, rather than the actor, with the ability to move tears. Both plays are revivals, and by 1636, open to charges of being old-fashioned, as *Pericles*, perhaps, was from its inception. The tears are embarrassing to the weeper, not entirely routine, and almost against their will ("who can hold from weeping?"). They are also faintly mysterious: the two friends, for all that they go to the theatre together, are differentiated by how they react to what they see, and the first gentleman cannot interpret his friend's reaction to Middleton's comic scenes.

"Eye-witness" is of course a problematic term. All of these accounts are locked into textual conventions of various sorts, even Henry Jackson's personal letter. But the *range* of textual forms involved, from formal poetry to jest-book prose, including accounts which celebrate it, accounts which condemn it, and accounts which merely mention it, does suggest that audience weeping was a centre of interest in the early modern theatre.

3. A Specific Convention

More evidence can be found in a sub-category of accounts excluded so far from the discussion: commendatory verse accompanying play-publication. These are, even more clearly than the accounts collected in the previous section, constrained by generic conventions: conventions that demand they be eulogistic and hyperbolic, and that they praise the author's skill. Nonetheless, and with these *caveats*, they offer some further glimpses of the process of audience weeping.

For instance, Middleton's dedicatory poem to the first edition of Webster's *The Duchess of Malfi* claims that the play provoked tears in the theatre almost against the wills of the spectators: "who e're saw this *Dutchesse* liue, and dye, / That could get off vnder a Bleeding Eye."[25] In a similar vein, a couplet on the title-page of Q3 (1631) of Beaumont and Fletcher's tragicomedy *A King and No King* proclaims: "A Play and no Play, who this book shall read, / Will iudge, and weepe, as if 'twere done indeed."[26] A third useful example from a single-play publication, although it strictly speaking postdates the professional stage, occurs among the commendatory verses to Robert Baron's unacted tragedy *Mirza*, published in 1647. There, one writer expresses an optimistic confidence that, had the play been acted, it would

---

24   Sidney, *The Defence of Poesy*, in Katherine Duncan-Jones (ed.), *Sir Philip Sidney* (Oxford: Clarendon Press, 1989), 230; Sidney is describing Alexander Pheraeus, a cruel tyrant who nonetheless wept at a tragedy.

25   Thomas Middleton, "In the just worth of that well deserver, Mr John Webster, and upon this Master-piece of tragedy", in John Webster, *The tragedy of the Dutchesse of Malfy* (1623), A4r; for more examples, see Levin, "The Relation of External Evidence".

26   Francis Beaumont and John Fletcher, *A King and No King* (London: A.M., 1631), A2r.

have moved the audience "with such a Sympathy / As might extract a deluge from their eyes."[27]

However, the most detailed claims about audience weeping – and claims which bear repeating and re-examining – are to be found in prefatory poems to the 1647 Beaumont and Fletcher folio. There, the playwright Jasper Mayne praises Beaumont and Fletcher's abilities to move tears as an example of their ability to command the audience's sympathies:

> Where e're you listed to be high and grave,
> No Buskin shew'd more solemne, no quill gave
> Such feeling objects to draw teares from eyes,
> Spectators sate part in your Tragedies …

(d1r)

The value, for Mayne, of tears is that they are concrete evidence for the general proposition that the plays were moving. Richard Lovelace, too, praises Fletcher's ability to draw tears.

> Virgins as *Sufferers* have wept to see   [*marg*: Arcas. Bellario.]
> So white a Soule, so red a Crueltie;
> That thou hast griev'd, and with unthought redresse,
> Dri'd their wet eyes who now thy mercy blesse;
> Yet loth to lose thy watry jewell, when
> Ioy wip't it off, Laughter straight sprung't agen.[28]

Lovelace's account alleges audiences could shed tears of joy as well as of sorrow, again the point being that tears from either cause are a "watry jewell" prized by the playwright. It also offers a witty reversal of the usual operation of sympathy: here, while action on stage leads the reaction of the audience, Lovelace imagines that reaction, in turn, influencing by sympathy the mood of the playwright himself. For Lovelace, as for Mayne, spectators are more than observers: their physical reactions, in particular their tears, are part of the theatrical event. Sympathy, again, is central to Thomas Stanley's account of audience weeping at Fletcher's plays:

> He to a Sympathie those souls betrai'd
> Whom Love or Beauty never could perswade;
> And in each mov'd spectatour could beget
> A reall passion by a Counterfeit:

---

27   Robert Baron, *Mirza. A tragedie* (London: Humphrey Moseley, 1647), A5r; see Bentley, *JCS*, 3.10–11, and David Kathman, "Baron, Robert (*bap.* 1630, *d.* 1658)", *Oxford DNB*.

28   Francis Beaumont and John Fletcher, *Comedies and Tragedies* (1647), b2v–b3r; see also a poem influenced by these, *An Elegy on that worthy and famous actor, Mr. Charles Hart* ([London]: Nath. Thompson, 1683), 1, which alleges (Restoration) audiences weeping "A flowing Tide of wo" for the weeping Arbaces and the bleeding Amintor.

When first *Bellario* bled, what Lady there
Did not for every drop let fall a teare?
And when *Aspasia* wept, not any eye
But seem'd to wear the same sad livery;
By him inspir'd the feign'd *Lucina* drew
More streams of melting sorrow then the true ...

(b4v)

And Thomas Palmer goes on to praise the ability of Fletcher's plays to move tears, describing this process as, literally, audience participation in which the audience contributes to the action of the play:

But when thy Tragicke Muse would please to rise
In Majestie, and cal tribute from our Eyes;
Like Scenes, we shifted Passions, and that so,
Who only came to see, turned Actors too.

(f2v)

These four references each describe Fletcher's power to move tears in the audience. For Lovelace, this is a gendered effect: it specifically targets young women. Stanley's account includes an element of gendering, but does not limit the weeping exclusively to women, while Mayne does not at all specify the gender of the spectators who weep, and Palmer's "we" seems certainly to include men.

The weeping is associated with certain characters, and also with certain scenes. A survey of the characters and scenes mentioned reveals a pattern, in that few of the incidents described occur at the end of the play, the place where one might naturally expect audience weeping to break out. Bellario, twice mentioned in the poems above, is wounded in Act Four of *Philaster*, not in Act Five. As discussed in Chapter 3, this scene is accompanied by, probably, onstage weeping, and certainly copious onstage allusion to weeping. Arcas, the eponymous hero of Fletcher's tragicomedy *The Loyal Subject*, does relatively little in Act Five of that play: his bravura moment occurs at the end of Act Four, when he astounds the Duke (and causes him and others to weep onstage) by giving a speech quelling a mutiny even though visibly wounded from the tortures which were being inflicted by the Duke himself when the mutiny broke out. Lucina, in *The Tragedy of Valentinian*, is centre stage for one long, emotional, scene in Act Three of the play, during which she weeps, before leaving the stage to her death. And the weeping of Aspasia in *The Maides Tragedy*, mentioned by Stanley as inducing audiences to weep as well, all occurs in, and is confined to, her set-piece scene which makes up the second half of Act Two of that play. By contrast, when she reappears in Act Five and is killed, she is noticeably cheerful, embracing her death with "a kinde of healthfull ioy".[29] "When Aspasia wept" is a phrase which describes a scene surprisingly early on in *The Maides Tragedy*. On the evidence of

---

29 Beaumont, *The Maides Tragedy* (1619), L3r.

these poems, audience weeping in Beaumont and Fletcher seems to be associated with individual bravura scenes, rather than with (for instance) the fifth-act reunions of the two tragicomedies, or the fifth-act deaths of the two tragedies.

Furthermore, one can take this hypothesis back to the eye-witness accounts collected in Sections 1 and 2 above. In 1 *Henry VI*, the death of Talbot, mentioned by Nashe as inducing audience weeping, is not at the end of the play, but rather at the climax of Act Four. Hieronimo's grieving, which May describes as the cue for audience weeping, takes place substantially in Act Three of that play, more than in the violent catastrophes of the last act. The Duchess of Malfi, famously, dies in Act Four, and not in Act Five, of Webster's play. The death of Desdemona, mentioned by Jackson, is admittedly a last-act event, and the account of *Pericles* is too vague to say whether the "calamities" its spectator wept for were the calamities of Acts One to Four or the recollections of those calamities in Act Five. But, by and large, in the available sample, scenes mentioned as moving tears are not those at the end of the play.

Of course, Levin is clearly right to cast doubt on the reliability of these poems as evidence for pre-1642 theatrical practice. Most of the poems discussed above are written years after the closure of the theatres, in a context where, as Thomas Moisan has discussed with relation to the Beaumont and Fletcher folio, nostalgia and theatricality are both politicised by association with royalism.[30] Like all poems of the genre, these are tied to rules of flattery, and because of their late date they reflect an idealised theatre rather than a current reality. But some at least of what we read may give a picture of early modern audience custom and practice.

4. Statements of Intent

One more class of evidence, used with caution, can help illustrate these ideas: statements of intent within plays themselves. Such statements, of course, are far from unproblematic, and Andrew Gurr warns about the dangers of "the circular argument that finds audience response written into plays, and makes easy assumptions from what it finds there".[31] The following survey bears Gurr's *caveat* in mind, but has, at least, the advantage that what it is seeking are explicit allusions to a visible and audible phenomenon, rather than any indication of mental state.

In contrast to the ubiquitous references linking tragedy and sorrow, and to the numerous references suggesting that early modern audiences might sometimes have wept, remarkably few early modern plays set out an intention to make the audience weep. Many announce in general that the subject is "piteous", "sad" or "a story of ... woe",

30   Thomas Moisan, "'The King's Second Coming': Theater, Politics, and Textualizing the 'Times' in the Dedicatory Poems to the 1647 Folio of Beaumont and Fletcher", in Thomas Moisan and Douglas Bruster (eds), *In the Company of Shakespeare: Essays in English Renaissance Literature in Honour of G. Blakemore Evans* (Madison: Farleigh Dickinson University Press, 2002), 270–91.

31   Gurr, *Playgoing*, 95.

to use three terms from *Romeo and Juliet*, but few specify that they will make the audience shed tears, preferring instead to state far more modest goals of gaining the audience's grace or approval.[32] This section discusses some of the exceptions.

The most notable of these are a group of late-Elizabethan plays which announce an intention to move an audience to tears: *A Larum for London*, *A Warning for Faire Women*, and Yarington's *Two Lamentable Tragedies*. Time in the Prologue to the anonymous *A Larum for London* (performed by the Chamberlain's Men, probably in 1599–1600) warns the audience against laughing at him and promises to "Reforme the mischiefe of degenerate mindes, / And make you weepe in pure relenting kinde."[33] As the phrasing indicates, the weeping is envisaged partly, at least, in terms of penitence and reformation, in a manner which Roslyn Knutson has described as both reaching back towards medieval models of homiletic drama and referring to clear and present political and religious dangers.[34] Whether or not *A Larum for London* made its audiences weep, it certainly announces explicitly an intention to do so.[35]

Another play in this group is the anonymous Elizabethan tragedy *A Warning for Faire Women*, with its Prologue in which a personified Tragedy announces her intentions:

> I must haue passions that must moue the soule,
> Make the heart heauie, and throb within the bosome,
> Extorting teares out of the strictest eyes,
> To racke a thought and straine it to his forme,
> Untill I rap the sences from their course,
> This is my office.

This is an emotional journey which is already cued by the decoration of the theatre, and which even the audience are already priming themselves for: "The stage is hung with blacke: and I perceiue / The Auditors preparde for Tragedie". Tragedy states that the events she will describe are true and recent, and once again emphasises their potential to induce weeping: "many now in this round, / Once to behold me [i.e. these events] in sad teares were drownd".[36]

All three of these plays come from a professional theatre predicated upon entertainment, and are not solely theological tracts, and the inconsistencies this creates can be seen particularly clearly in *A Warning for Faire Women*. This domestic murder play comes to a suitably emotionally intense conclusion, as the play's *femme fatale*

---

32   *Romeo and Juliet*, Prol. 7, 5.3.307, 309.

33   For another, slightly less clear-cut example, see Lodge and Greene, *A looking glasse for London and England* (1594), I4v.

34   Roslyn L. Knutson, "Filling Fare: The Appetite for Current Issues and Traditional Forms in the Repertory of the Chamberlain's Men", *Medieval and Renaissance Drama in England*, 15 (2002): 57–76.

35   Anon., *A Larum for London* (1602), A1v.

36   *A Warning for Faire Women* (1599), A3r, A3v.

Anne Sanders is taken away in tears to her execution. On the one hand, these tears represent her joyful last-minute repentance, since she is now resolved for death. On the other, they have to signify the bitter sorrow of the "warning" promised by the play's title, as she parts from her weeping children ("I am unworthy of the name of Mother").[37] This is a play whose avowed intent to induce pleasurable weeping in an audience seems to take precedence over harnessing that weeping strictly to a single ideological agenda, and also over pinning down what Anne's final tears *mean*. In the same way, the question of what the audience weeping *means* if an audience were to weep at *A Warning for Fair Women* – the question Levin might ask – is secondary, for our purposes here, to the fact that the play states that it sets out to cause that weeping.

Closely akin to *A Warning for Fair Women* is another domestic tragedy dramatising topical events, Robert Yarington's *Two Lamentable Tragedies*. A series of addresses to the audience by Truth through the play insists that they will weep, that they are weeping, and that they have wept. Truth warns at the start that "Our Stage doth wear habilliments of woe", and that the audience will weep: "Gentles, prepare your teare bedecked eyes, / To see two shewes of lamentation."[38] As in Quarles's poem, audience tears are ranked alongside the black hangings of the stage as visual signifiers of a tragic theatre performance. As the domestic tragedy unfolds, and even as Merry, in dumb show, dismembers the body of the neighbour he has murdered, preparatory to hiding the pieces around London, Truth turns to the audience again:

> All you the sad spectators of this Acte,
> Whose harts do taste a feeling pensiuenesse ...
> I see your sorrowes flowe vp to the brim,
> And ouerflowe your cheekes with brinish teares,
> But though this sight bring surfet to the eye,
> Delight your eares with pleasing harmonie,
> That eares may counterchecke your eyes, and say,
> Why shed you teares, this deede is but a playe
>
> (E2v)

The last lines here are interestingly uncomfortable in their problematisation of audience weeping, and the question of whether one can take pleasure in weeping and in what Eiichi Hara has aptly described as a precursor of "splatter movies".[39] Additionally, they seem to identify this scene – the dismemberment scene – as the appropriate moment for audience weeping. A third comment by Truth, at the end, builds on her earlier statements about audience weeping, and implies that the moment for weeping has passed:

37 Ibid, K2v.

38 Robert Yarington, *Two Lamentable Tragedies* (1601), A3r.

39 Eiichi Hara, "The Absurd Vision of Elizabethan Crime Drama: *A Warning for Fair Women, Two Lamentable Tragedies*, and *Arden of Faversham*", *Shiron*, 38 (1999): 1–36, qtn from 17.

See here the end of lucre and desire
Of riches, gotten by vnlawfull meanes,
What monstrous euils this hath brought to passe,
Your scarce drie eyes giue testimoniall

(K2v)

With a neat sleight of hand, Truth appeals to the audience's own participation – their weeping – to guarantee the truthfulness of what they have seen. But Truth's line is also, in effect, a cue to the audience to stop weeping, if they have not done so already; and Yarington's play seems to come from a theatre in which inducing an audience to open lamentation and weeping seems to be very much the object of the exercise.

After this group of three plays, though, plays rarely announce an explicit intention to make the audience weep. Shakespeare and Fletcher's *Henry VIII* offers, guardedly, the possibility that it might:

I come no more to make you laugh. Things now
That bear a weighty and a serious brow,
Sad, high, and working, full of state and woe,
Such noble scenes as draw the eye to flow
We now present. Those that can pity here
May, if they think it well, let fall a tear;
The subject will deserve it …[40]

The Epilogue to Robert Gomersall's *The Tragedie of Lodouick Sforza, Duke of Millan* makes the audacious claim that the play has made its audience weep:

Teares grace a Tragedy, and we are glad
To haue the happy power to make you sad,
Continue it, and our applause is high,
Not from your Hand so much, as from your eye.

And William Lower's tragedy *The Phaenix in her Flames* is similarly confident, claiming in its prologue that it will "make you weepe", and repeating the idea in the Epilogue:

Come, and be welcome still, and let your friends,
Who have not seene as yet our tragicke end,
Come here and weepe with you, untill together,
You make up this a full press'd theater.

---

40   *Henry VIII*, Prologue 1–7; William Shakespeare and John Fletcher, *Henry VIII*, ed. John Margeson (Cambridge: Cambridge University Press, 1990), Introduction; Anton Bosman, "Seeing Tears: Truth and Sense in *All is True*", *Shakespeare Quarterly*, 50 (1999): 459–76, points out the thematic overlap between this Prologue and the pivotal scene in the play of Cranmer's weeping.

Both these last accounts picture audience weeping as part of a dialogue with the stage, and indeed, for Gomersall, weeping is such a definitive intervention by the audience as to constitute a form of applause. With Lower, as with other accounts we have seen, the phrasing makes the weeping into almost a creative act on the part of the audience, in that only by weeping together will they "make up this a full press'd theater". And yet these two plays are exceptions which do reveal more about cultural expectations than theatrical achievement: Gomersall's play is "probably only an academic exercise in dramatization", and "there is no evidence that *The Phoenix in her flames* was ever acted or even considered by the actors".[41] One final reference to audience weeping rounds out the surprisingly small collection by denying any such intention. The Prologue of Richard Brome's bittersweet comedy *A Jovial Crew* is modest in its aims, and hopes that "the dulnesse [of the play] may make no Man sleep, / Nor sadnesse of it any Woman weep."[42] Much recent criticism has noted an almost Chekhovian air of sadness in *A Jovial Crew*, depicting as it does an English countryside under threat. It is, then, striking, and one can now say uncharacteristic for an early modern play, that it should allude, however tentatively, to the possibility of making its audience weep.[43]

5. Provisional Conclusions

The material collected above has been grouped under four headings: general expectations, "first-hand accounts", commendatory verse, and statements of intent from within dramatic works. Summing together all the evidence, some provisional assertions about early modern audience weeping can be made, with a view to testing them against any new evidence that comes to light.

There is a broad cultural expectation that theatre audiences weep at tragedies. More specifically, two accounts in the first-person singular (Gager and Browne), a number of less clear-cut accounts in the first-person plural (Cornwallis, Gosson, Palmer, Clun's anonymous elegist), and a number of third-person accounts (Nashe, Dekker, May, Jackson, *The Book of Bulls*, and the poems from the Beaumont and Fletcher folio), provide descriptions of early modern theatre audience members weeping. The dates of these accounts range from the early 1580s (Gosson) up to accounts written after 1642 purporting to describe the late Caroline theatre (Stanley). In addition, a handful of allusions within plays themselves indicate an expectation that audiences might weep at them.

---

41 Gomersall, *The Tragedie of Lodouick Sforza* (1628), 70; Lower, *The Phoenix in her flames* (1639), A3r, M3r; Bentley, *JCS*, 4.513, 727.

42 Brome, *A Joviall Crew* (1652), A2r.

43 See, especially, David Farley-Hills, *The Comic in Renaissance Comedy* (London: Macmillan, 1981), 147–60; Julie Sanders, "Beggars' Commonwealths and the Pre-Civil War Stage: Suckling's *The Goblins*, Richard Brome's *A Jovial Crew*, and James Shirley's *The Sisters*", *Modern Language Review*, 97 (2002): 1–14.

This evidence associates weeping with a range of settings and venues: amateur university and school drama (Gager and Taylor), professional companies on tour (Jackson), amphitheatre playhouses (Nashe, Dekker, May), and by implication hall playhouses (the favoured settings for the Beaumont and Fletcher plays which form the main subject of Section 3). Three main factors are variously mentioned as making it possible: the subject of the play, the skill of the playwright, and the skill of an individual actor. Weeping is associated with a range of dramatic genres: first of all, tragedies (including *The Spanish Tragedy*, *Othello*, *The Duchess of Malfi*, *The Tragedy of Valentinian*, and *The Maides Tragedy*), but also tragicomedies (*Pericles*, *Philaster*, *The Loyal Subject*) and histories (*1 Henry VI* and *Henry VIII*).

Two subsets of plays stand out clearly. A group of late-Elizabethan plays claim to be setting out to make an audience weep (*A Larum for London*, *A Warning for Fair Women*, *Two Lamentable Tragedies*), in what is, in a sense, an appropriation and aestheticisation of ideas of penitent weeping. In contrast, the plays of Beaumont and Fletcher are frequently linked to audiences weeping for their portrayal of what Clun's elegist calls "lovers' passions".

Across the whole collection of references, a number of scenes are associated with audience weeping. These do not necessarily, or even usually, occur at the end of the play, and generally they feature a character bleeding (Talbot, Bellario), otherwise freshly injured (the raped Lucina, the tortured Arcas), or dying (the Duchess of Malfi and Desdemona). In particular, onstage weeping induces audience weeping, in May's account of Hieronimo, Stanley's account of Aspasia, in the poems of Weever and Quarles. Audience weeping is seen as something which unites the "All you" of an audience into one body, and, indeed, almost as a form of audience participation.

To some extent, audience weeping is gendered and associated with "ladies" and "virgins", and some accounts (the *Henry VIII* Prologue, or *The Book of Bulls*) imagine parts of an audience weeping and parts not, but the frequently desired image is of a theatrical audience all of whom are in tears: Nashe, Middleton, Stanley and Lower state this desideratum particularly clearly, and three of them claim that it has been achieved. For the moment, one can conclude by answering the question which this chapter started: *Shakespeare in Love* has some historical justification for its display of a weeping audience. It is clear that early modern theatregoers sometimes wept, and it is also clear that writers from the Shakespearean period imagined a theatre all in tears as an acme of theatrical achievement.

Chapter 6

Soft smiling?: Lyly and Jonson

The norms established in Chapters 1 to 5 of this book form the basis for discussion, in Chapters 6 to 8, of three more specific topics. The first of these relates to those references, often cited in critical discussions of Renaissance comedy, which explicitly deny that comedy ought to make the audience laugh – references which, as we have seen, seem untypical of the bulk of the material gathered in Chapter 4. In particular, this is a problem relevant to Lyly and Jonson, whose works receive more detailed attention here.

Lyly

Lyly's dictum that "soft smiling, not loud laughing" is the desired audience reaction to comedy can be related to other, earlier, Elizabethan texts, including Sidney's *Defence of Poesy*, whose complaint that "our comedians think there is no delight without laughter" is quoted in Chapter 4. Among other still earlier Elizabethan texts that share this aesthetic, George Gascoigne's comedy *The Glasse of Gouernement*, for instance, warns off mere seekers of entertainment – "[An] Enterlude may make you laugh your fill" – which, incidentally, gives information about the usual expectation of audiences at interludes.[1] Instead, Gascoigne's prologue announces the instructive power of the comedy to follow, although that comedy was probably a closet drama, not intended for performance. Gascoigne's friend George Whetstone's *Promos and Cassandra* (printed 1578) complained in its preface about other comic authors "not waying, so the people laugh, though they laugh them (for their folleys) to scorne: Many tymes (to make mirthe) they make a Clowne companion with a kinge …". As Andrew Gurr points out, this complaint is perhaps tongue-in-cheek, since *Promos and Cassandra* itself makes use of the device of having a clown and a king on stage together.[2] Best-remembered now as a source for *Measure for Measure*, *Promos and Cassandra* was, however, "apparently unperformed" in Whetstone's lifetime.[3] Once again, though it can be taken as evidence for an alternative aesthetic, the preface to *Promos and Cassandra* actually tends to confirm rather than deny the proposition that in practice early modern comic theatre aimed to make its audience laugh.

---

1   Gascoigne, *The glasse of gouernement* [1575], A3v.
2   Whetstone, *Promos and Cassandra* [1578], A2v; Andrew Gurr, *Playgoing in Shakespeare's London*, 3rd edn (Cambridge: Cambridge University Press, 2004), 153.
3   Emma Smith, 'Whetstone, George (*bap.* 1550, *d.* 1587)', *Oxford DNB*.

However, the most important text for the Lylyan aesthetic is the Prologue to *Sapho and Phao*, performed in the early 1580s by a children's company at the Blackfriars. The speaker fears that the audience will be bored by the play, and will

> with open reproach blame our good meaninges: because you cannot reap your wonted mirthes. Our intent was at this time to moue inward delight, not outward lightnesse, and to breede, (if it might bee) soft smiling, not loude laughing: knowing it to the wise to be as great pleasure to heare counsell mixed with witte, as to the foolish to haue sporte mingled with rudenesse. They were banished the Theater at Athens, and from Rome hyssed, that brought parasites on the stage with apish actions, or fooles with vnciuill habites, or Curtisans with immodest words. We haue endeuoured to be as farre from vnseemely speaches, to make your eares glowe, as wee hope you will bee from vnkinde reportes to make our cheekes blush.[4]

"Wonted mirths": again, what this passage really reveals is that laughter is the usual expectation of comedies, even at the Blackfriars. Like Gascoigne, like Whetstone, and indeed like Sidney, Lyly constructs this aesthetic oppositionally, by conscious and mannered contrast against usual practice. Interestingly, though, even this construction of the relation between actors and audience emphasises the physicality: by making their ears glow, actors can affect, even in a small way, their audience's bodies, just as audiences can make the blood rush into actors' cheeks. The bodies of actors and audience are in a physical relationship, even while the actors profess to be attempting to minimise the physical effects, on both sets of bodies, caused by that relationship. Instead, Lyly's concern is with the educative properties of drama, "counsel mixed with wit", in which the *dulce* is the servant of the *utile*. Other Lyly prologues, although less explicit in their denial that they seek laughter, also use the modesty *topos*, hoping for silence, at best, from their hostile and disgruntled audience.[5] If one took these prologues at their word, one would assume Lyly to be a spectacularly unsuccessful playwright. Even so, the Prologue has been taken as evidence that Lyly is seeking an unusual and distinctive relationship with the audience, writing plays which interact differently with audience expectations. David Bevington and G.K. Hunter have described the result, in the case of this play, *Sapho and Phao*, as:

> the very opposite of narrative drama: it is a conversation piece, discursive in form, focusing upon a static concept and all the various possibilities inherent in it. Debate and play of language flourish in such a world of extended stillness.[6]

However, this view of Lyly is open to challenge. For instance, Kate D. Levin reports that Lyly's comedy *Gallathea*, in a college production in New York in 1999, was far more lively than such an analysis of Lyly would suggest, its stichomythia concealing

---

4   Lyly, *Sapho and Phao* (1584), A2r.

5   For instance, the Prologues to *Midas* and *Campaspe*.

6   John Lyly, *Campaspe: Sappho and Phao*, ed. David Bevington and G.K. Hunter (Manchester: Manchester University Press, 1999), Introduction, 189; see 172–5 for a discussion of comedy in the the plays.

unexpected comic rhythms which invited appropriate stage business. For instance, at
one point in that play the nymph Hebe finds herself tied to a tree as a community
sacrifice, expecting to be devoured by a virgin-eating monster. In Levin's production,
Hebe delivered her final farewells to the terrified onlookers, at the end of which, the men
flung themselves to the floor, expecting the terrible death of Hebe. Nothing happened,
and after a long pause the men sat up and Hebe started a second set of farewells, at the
end of which, again, the monster bathetically failed to appear. Levin adds:

> We orchestrated the scene with six such beats. The pauses between each became shorter ...
> and the laughs grew longer each time the men had to fling themselves back down. Finally, the
> Augur sat all the way up and grimly announced the obvious: "The monster is not come".[7]

The production, too, provoked other sorts of audible reaction – "collective sighs of
recognition" from the audience, even groans at the final *coup de théâtre*. As Levin
herself warns, her account is anecdotal, but all the same, it suggests that Lyly's practice
may be less clearly opposed to audience laughter than the Prologue to *Sapho and
Phao* suggests. What is more, that Prologue is not uncompromised by the very play
that succeeds it. While the Prologue eschews apish parasites, the play offers Criticus
and Molus, pages at court, whose obsession with food resembles that of the parasite
in Roman comedy, and whose banter about the relative merits of cheese and fish
could easily be brought to life with the benefit of appropriate action and properties.
Even more strikingly, while the Prologue piously banishes courtesans and immodesty,
the play revolves around the gentlewoman Sapho's unrequited lustful desire for the
supernaturally handsome young ferryman Phao. Sapho falls sick with this desire,
giving rise to a series of potentially very immodest *doubles entendres* (for instance,
when asked where she feels her pain), and culminating in a scene where Phao is
summoned to her bedside, supposedly to give medical advice. Such an episode, and
the extended *doubles entendres* that result, invites comparison to Gosson's description
of an audience's "wonderfull laughter" when they see "a slie conveighance of bawdry"
on the stage at around this date.[8] *Sapho and Phao*, then, does not fulfil the promisese
of the Prologue as regards content, and may not do so as regards audience laughter at
that content. There are problems with taking Lyly's statement at face value: and in this
light, perhaps, the most striking point about Lyly's stated poetic is that it is so at odds
with what Renaissance comedy usually expected.

Lyly's Prologue turns up again, without explanation, in the prefatory material of
Beaumont's *The Knight of the Burning Pestle*.[9] The play was first performed at the
Blackfriars in 1607, and its first quarto was printed in 1611, but the Prologue only

---

7   Kate D. Levin, "Playing with Lyly: Theatrical Criticism and Non-Shakespearean
drama", *Research Opportunities in Renaissance Drama*, 40 (2001): 25–54, qtn from 42.

8   Stephen Gosson, *Plays confuted in fiue actions* (London: Thomas Gosson [1582]),
C8v–D1r.

9   On questions of date and authorship, see the Introduction to Francis Beaumont, *The Knight
of the Burning Pestle*, ed. Sheldon P. Zitner (Manchester: Manchester University Press, 1984).

appears in Q2, printed in 1635, and perhaps associated with a revival which is known to have taken place around that date. Indeed, in Q2 it takes the place of Q1's dedicatory epistle describing the original failure of the play on the stage, "utterly rejected" by the audiences who saw it. The function of the Prologue, here, seems to be to forestall complaints about the play's failure to make people laugh, rather than to advance and practise a new poetic of decorous stillness. To a modern reader, the Prologue seems out of keeping with the broad comic tone of the play as a whole, with its ridiculous metadramatic complications, parodies of bad dramatic speeches, and stage directions such as the wonderfully laconic "*Enter Raph, with a forked arrow through his head*".[10]

And yet caution is required, since such considerations are potentially heretical under the terms of reference of the discussion – since this project is looking to historicise early modern theatre's attitudes to laughter, it should still be reluctant to use the impression that the play makes on a modern sensibility as evidence of an intent to make the audience laugh. However, the title-page of the second quarto (1635) describes the play, unequivocally, as "Full of mirth and delight". One can also observe that Rafe's part contains many opportunities for comic routines of the sort described in Chapter 4 in connection with the fool: his last speech, for instance, is a loquacious account of mortal agony, culminating in "oh, oh, oh, &c.", an invitation to "*Stentor*-throated bellowings" of the sort associated with other Jacobean clowns. And it is also true that *The Knight of the Burning Pestle* celebrates the health-giving qualities of mirth directly in the character of Merrythought, above all, in his songs: "whosoever laughs and sings / Never he his body brings / Into fevers, gouts, or rheums". The last word of the inset play goes to Merrythought, in another song: "Hey ho, 'tis nought but mirth / That keepes the body from the earth".[11] The very fact that the Prologue's poetics of "soft smiling, not loud laughing" is so inappropriate to the mirth, and the celebration of mirth, of *The Knight of the Burning Pestle* is a good indication of the distance between the Lylyan statement of aesthetics and most of the rest of early modern comedy.

Jonson

As for Jonson, we are faced with a paradox about that dramatic author's alleged antitheatricalism, exemplified by Una Ellis-Fermor's description of him as "non-theatrical or not originally theatrical".[12] Jonson's chequered relationship with mere performance is well documented, and a particularly clear example of that might appear to be his attitude to audience laughter, expressed in most detail in a long passage from *Discoveries*, which must be quoted *in extenso* to do justice to the shape of its argument:

---

10   Beaumont, *The Knight of the Burning Pestle* (1613), K3r.

11   *Ibid.*, K3v, E3r–E3v.

12   Cited in Jonas Barish, *The Antitheatrical Prejudice* (Berkeley: University of California Press, 1981), 132.

Nor, is the moving of *laughter* alwaies the end of *Comedy*, that is rather a fowling for the peoples delight, or their fooling. For, as *Aristotle* saies rightly, the moving of laughter is a fault in Comedie, a kind of turpitude, that depraves some part of a mans nature without a disease. As a wry face without paine moves laughter, or a deformed vizard, or a rude Clowne, drest in a Ladies habit, and using her actions, wee dislike, and scorne such representations; which made the ancient Philosophers ever thinke laughter unfitting in a wise man ...

So that, what either in the words, or Sense of an Author, or in the language, or Actions of men, is a wry, or depraved, doth strangely stirre meane affections, and provoke for the most part to laughter. And therfore it was cleare that all insolent, and obscene speaches, jest upon the best men; injuries to particular persons; perverse, and sinister Sayings (and the rather unexpected) in the old Comedy did move laughter; especially, where it did imitate any dishonesty; and scurrility came forth in the place of wit: which who understands the nature and *Genius* of laughter, cannot but perfectly know.

Of which *Aristophanes* affords an ample harvest, having not only outgone *Plautus*, or any other in that kinde; but express'd all the moods, and figures, of what is ridiculous, oddly. In short, as Vinegar is not accounted good, untill the wine be corrupted: so jests that are true and naturall, seldome raise laughter, with the beast, the multitude. They love nothing, that is right, and proper. The farther it runs from reason, or possibility with them, the better it is. What could have made them laugh, like to see *Socrates* presented, that Example of all good life, honesty, and vertue, to have him hoisted up with a Pullie, and there play the Philosopher, in a basquet. Measure, how many foote a Flea could skip *Geometrically*, by a just Scale, and edifie the people from the ingine. This was *Theatricall* wit, right Stage-jesting, and relishing a Play-house, invented for scorne, and laughter; whereas, if it had favour'd of equity, truth, perspicuity, and Candor, to have tasten a wise, or a learned Palate, spit it out presently ... This is truly leaping from the Stage, to the Tumbrell againe, reducing all witt to the Originall Dungcart.[13]

It is not hard to find other disparaging remarks by Jonson about laughter in general (rather than specifically the laughter of dramatic audiences) which appear to back up the extended attack on audience laughter here: for instance, the announcement of *Epigrams* 2.12 that it does not seek the world's "loose laughter, or vaine gaze". Thematically, too, it seems to link to the hostility towards public theatre in general expressed in poems such as the *Ode to Himself*. Furthermore, Jonson's numerous contemporary eulogists were almost unanimous in constructing Jonson as a literary author whose relative lack of success in moving the laughter of "the beast, the multitude" was almost a badge of honour. This is still a view which obtains in much Jonson criticism, in one form or another.

But on the other hand, as many performers of Jonson have reported, in the theatre Jonson's plays seem superbly well engineered to produce waves of audience laughter of the sort apparently despised and rejected in the passage from *Discoveries* and in

---

13   *Discoveries*, 2629–77, marginal notes omitted.

contemporary eulogies on Jonson.[14] For texts by an author who dislikes laughter Jonson's plays seem strikingly successful at inducing laughter, and therein lies the paradox.

One way of making progress towards a more balanced view of Jonson's attitude to laughter would be to downplay the passage from *Discoveries*, for instance by pointing out that it is largely a paraphrase of the Latin of Daniel Heinsius's *Ad Horatii de Plauto & Terentio judicium*, published in 1618, or by drawing attention to Jonson's imitation and praise elsewhere of the Aristophanes that the passage condemns.[15] Another avenue, and the one pursued here, is to collect together the explicit references to audience laughter in Prologues and other forms of explicitly metatheatrical comment within Jonson's dramatic works. Considering these as a group may give a fresh insight into the question of Jonson's relation to audience laughter in particular, especially in relation to the wider picture of audience laughter built up in this study.

1. The Prologue of the F version of *Every Man In His Humour* (originally performed in 1598, and printed in 1616) may well not have been delivered in the theatre, and may well also significantly postdate the play to which it applies: nevertheless, it is a piece which has often been considered, in Robert Miola's phrase, a "poetic manifesto" for Jonson's career, standing at the head of his 1616 *Workes*.[16] In it, the audience are warned that Jonson's play depicts

> Such errors, as you'll all confesse
> By laughing at them, they deserue no lesse;
> Which when you heartily doe, there's hope left, then,
> You, that haue so grac'd monsters, may like men.

(27–30)

One might note the Sidneyan flavour of the word "confesse", activating the idea that laughter is associated with shame, but the really striking word here is "heartily", insisting on the intensity of the laughter that the play will be able

---

14 See above, pp. 57–8. On Jonson's contemporary reception, see H&S, vol. 11; Robert C. Evans, "'This Art Will Live': Social and Literary Responses to Ben Jonson's *The New Inn*", in Claude J. Summers and Ted-Larry Pebworth (eds), *Literary Circles and Cultural Communities in Renaissance England* (Missouri: University of Missouri Press, 2001), 75–91.

15 H&S, 11.289, prints the corresponding passages from Heinsius's Latin; on Jonson and Aristophanes, see Coburn S. Gum, *The Aristophanic Comedies of Ben Jonson* (The Hague: Mouton, 1972), and, better, Helen Ostovich, "Introduction" to Jonson, *Four Comedies*, ed. Ostovich (London: Longman, 1996).

16 Ben Jonson, *Every Man In his Humour*, ed. Robert Miola (Manchester: Manchester University Press, 2000), 244n.; Tiffany Stern, "'A small-beer health to his second day': Playwrights, Prologues, and First Performances in the Early Modern Theater", *Studies in Philology*, 101:2 (2004): 172–99, draws attention to the disposability of Prologues, often apparently written for only a single performance.

to generate – insisting, too, that the presence of that laughter is central to the meaning and purpose of the comedy.

2. In the Induction to *Every Man Out of His Humour* (performed in 1599), another text which is often taken as a foundational statement for Jonson's career, Asper promises the audience not merely to make them laugh, but to make them laugh so hard as to weep: "We hope to make the circles of your eyes / Flow with distilled laughter".[17] Elsewhere in the play another choric figure, Cordatus, defines Comedy as "a thing throughout pleasant, and ridiculous, and accommodated to the correction of manners" – a formulation which, as often in Jonson, uses "ridiculous" in its literal sense of "exciting laughter".[18]

3. The armed Prologue of *Poetaster* (performed in 1601) alludes to laughter in expressing his hope that the play will resist the "coniuring meanes" of "base detractors":

    > 'Gainst these, haue we put on this forc't defence:
    > Whereof the *allegorie* and hid sence
    > Is, that a well erected confidence
    > Can fright their pride, and laugh their folly hence.[19]

This is usually quoted as another statement of Jonson's Olympian pride and solemnity, and yet the moment itself is clearly comic: a small child in a suit of armour, who (according to William Gifford's perceptive imagination of the scene) enters "hastily" to put his foot on an already sinking monster, delivers the sentiment in a quadruple rhyme.[20] The emphasis is more on the "laugh" than the "fright".

4. No-body in the *Althorp Entertainment* (performed in 1603), dressed in a costume of outsize breeches which makes it appear that he literally has no body, expects that the audience will laugh purely at his appearance: "If my outside moue your laughter, / Pray IOVE, my inside be thereafter" (242–3).

5. The *Highgate Entertainment* (performed in 1604) contains a scene set around a "Font of Laughter", guarded by Pan. The font contains a "lusty liquor" which can "force all the myrth of the spleene into the face", and which Pan hands out

---

17 Jonson, *Every Man Out*, Induction, 216–17.
18 Ibid., 3.6.207–9; *OED*, ridiculous *a*. Other examples in Jonson of it in this sense include *The Magnetic Lady*, Third Chorus, 6–8, quoted below, and *Tale of a Tub*, Prol. 4, "our ridiculous play".
19 Jonson, *Poetaster*, Prologue, 11–14.
20 SD of Gifford's edition, quoted from H&S's apparatus: H&S, 4.205.

to the royal audience, inviting them to laugh and delivering a series of risqué comic couplets as he does so.[21]

6. The Prologue to *Volpone* (performed in 1606) builds on the idea of the physiological effects of audience laughter adumbrated in *Every Man Out*:

> The lawes of time, place, persons he obserueth,
> From no needfull rule he swerueth.
> All gall, and coppresse, from his inke, he drayneth,
> Onely, a little salt remayneth;
> Wherewith, he'll rub your cheeks, til (red with laughter)
> They shall looke fresh, a weeke after.[22]

The prologue offers jaunty feminine rhymes; a speech which undercuts itself by stating that there is no gall, and then admitting to a little salt; and a promise to make the audience laugh so hard that their face changes colour for a week.

7. The description of the *Haddington Masque* (performed in 1608) comments on the audience reception of the *Ioci* and *Risus*, twelve boys, "most antickly attyr'd", who (as their names suggest) themselves represent laughter:

> they fell into a subtle capriccious Daunce, to as odde a Musique, each of them bearing two torches, and nodding with their antique faces, with other varietie of ridiculous gesture, which gaue much occasion of mirth, and delight, to the spectators.[23]

This is, in effect, very much the sort of "stage-jesting" condemned in the passage from *Discoveries*.

8. *Bartholomew Fair* (performed in 1614), famously, offers a contract with the audience, a contract into which audience laughter is written without explicit agreement. Anyone seeking to read personal satire in the play, the Book-Holder warns the audience, will themselves become "discovered to the mercy of the *Author*, as a forfeiture to the *Stage*, and your laughter, aforesaid" – a difficult phrase, seemingly implying that people who look for personal satire in the play become fair game for such personal satire.[24] The interesting thing is that this is the

21 Jonson, *Highgate Entertainment*, 193–5.
22 Jonson, *Volpone*, Prologue, 31–6.
23 Jonson, *Haddington Masque*, 158–9, 171–5.
24 Jonson, *Bartholomew Fair*, Induction, 145–8.

first mention of laughter in the contract: audience laughter seems so fundamental to the terms and conditions that it does not even need to be specified.

9. In the masque *Mercury Vindicated* (performed in 1615), 225–9, Nature shows off her twelve sons, and Prometheus comments:

> PROMETHEUS: How many, 'mongst these Ladies here,
> Wish now they such a mother were?
> NATURE: Not one, I feare,
> And read it in their laughters.

As in the *Althorp Entertainment*, this passage clearly expects that the audience *have* laughed. A poetic of "inward delight, not outward lightness" seems incompatible with this emphasis on including the audience in their entertainment through their demonstrative reactions.

10. The Masque in *For the Honour of Wales* (performed in 1618) shares some of the phrasing of *Volpone*, as the Welshmen promise the audience (286–91):

> But what say yow should it shance too,
> that we should leape it in a Dance too,
> And make it yow as great a pleasure,
> if but your eyes be now at leasure;
> As in your eares s' all leave a laughter,
> to last upon yow sixe dayes after?

The Welshmen are interested in the collective *sound* of an audience laughing – they want to generate laughter enough to leave ears ringing with it for six days after. This is explicitly a communally generated, auditory effect.

11. *The Staple of News* (performed in 1625) features an onstage audience of four "gossips", Mirth, Tattle, Censure and Expectation, who compare the play they are watching to their experience of other drama. They twice allude to audience laughter at other plays. Tattle complains that there is no fool in *The Staple of News*:

> I would faine see the *Foole*, gossip, the *Foole* is the finest man i'the company, they say, and has all the wit; Hee is the very *Iustice o'the Peace* o' the Play, and can commit whom hee will, and what hee will, errour, absurdity, as the toy takes him, and no man say, blacke is his eye, but laugh at him.[25]

A little later in the dialogue, the discussion moves on to *The Merry Devil of Edmonton*, and Mirth comments on the fool in that play: "But there was one *Smug*, a Smith, would have made a horse laugh, and broke his halter,

---

25 *The Staple of News*, First Intermean, 23–8.

as they say."[26] In some respects, these references can be linked to many of the other Renaissance references to the laughter-generating power of the fool collected in Chapter 4, and in some respects, too, their interest in the fool and in the animal-like laughter he provokes (since even horses would laugh at him) marks the gossips out as ignorant and unwise. And yet it is hard to be quite so dismissive about the gossips. "They are all fooles", says Expectation of the players, meaning that there is no fool in the play, but suggesting that the fool's functions are distributed among all the characters who do appear (72). Recent readings of the play have suggested that the Gossips are more complex than merely straw women representing points of view inimical to Jonson. Whatever Jonson's views on Mirth, mirth with a small "m" is a quality which Jonson elsewhere prizes and values in the theatre.

12. The Chorus of *The Magnetic Lady* (perf. 1632), like the *Volpone* Prologue, imagines audience laughter as a medicinal effect, in this case a foment or poultice. The Boy reassures Mr Damplay that the audience will laugh: "Give our Springs leave to open a little, by degrees! A Source of ridiculous matter may breake forth anon, that shall steepe their temples, and bathe their braines in laughter, to the fomenting of Stupiditie it selfe, and the awaking any velvet Lethargy in the House." Again, the audience laughter is seen not merely as an effect itself, but as a cause of further effects. It is the laughter of the rest of the audience that will awake any "velvet Lethargy" – that is, as explained by the play's Induction, the mind of any fashionable but dull spectator wearing velvet. In a second allusion to the play's intended effect, a later choric scene comments on Jonson's choice of name for the character of the lawyer: "the ridiculous Mr. *Practise* ... hath rather his name invented for laughter, then any offence, or injury it can stick on the reverend Professors of the Law".[27]

13. Jonson's unfinished Nottinghamshire-set pastoral *The Sad Shepherd* (written around 1636) is explicit in its intention to move laughter, again in the context of a Prologue which is itself aiming to amuse – in this section of the speech, *"the Prologue thinking to end, returnes upon a new purpose, and speakes on"*:

> But here's an Heresie of late let fall;
> That Mirth by no meanes fits a Pastorall;
> Such say so, who can make none, he presumes:
> Else, there's no Scene, more properly assumes
> The Sock. For whence can sport in kind arise,
> But from the Rurall Routs and Families?

---

26   *Ibid.*, First Intermean, 71–2; the expression about the horse is proverbial: *OED*, halter *n.* 1.

27   Second Chorus, 45–8; Third Chorus, 6–8. The play, of course, failed on the stage, and, as noted in Chapter 4, Jonson's enemy Alexander Gill mocked Jonson's failure to attract the hoped-for "Applause and Laughter" (H&S, 11.346–7).

> Safe on this ground then, wee not feare to day,
> To tempt your laughter by our rustick Play.[28]

Even *The Sad Shepherd* expresses an explicit intention to include "mirth" and "sport", and to provoke audience laughter.

Although this list is assembled with a view to making generalisations from it, it is worth pausing a moment to observe how each of these constructions of audience laughter is particularly appropriate to the play from which it comes. To consider three examples from the above list, *Every Man Out*'s Prologue, identifying the most important symptom of audience laughter as tears, is appropriate for a play whose central character Macilente constantly treads a fine line between amusement and disgust:

> Ha, ha, ha? I' not this good? Is't not pleasing this?
> Ha, ha, ha! God pardon me! ha, ha!
> Is't possible that such a spacious villaine
> Should liue, and not be plagu'd?[29]

Volpone's Prologue's description of laughter as medicinal comes back to haunt a play full both of laughter and of misuses of medicines. For Volpone himself, by Act 5, laughter is explicitly paralleled with alcohol, awkwardly poised between medicine and addictive recreational drug:

> … I apprehended, straight, some power had strooke me
> With a dead palsey: well, I must be merry,
> And shake it off. A many of these feares
> Would put me into some villanous disease,
> Should they come thick vpon me: I'le preuent 'hem.
> Giue me a boule of lustie wine, to fright
> This humor from my heart; (hum, hum, hum)
> *He drinkes.*
> 'Tis almost gone, already: I shall conquer.
> Any deuice, now, of rare, ingenious knauery,
> That would possesse me with a violent laughter,
> Would make me vp, againe! So, so, so, so.
> *Drinkes againe.*
> This heate is life; 'tis bloud, by this time: Mosca![30]

---

28 Jonson, *The Sad Shepherd*, Prologue, 31–8.

29 Jonson, *Every Man Out*, 1.3.65–8.

30 *Volpone*, 5.1.6–17; on drugs in *Volpone*, see Tanya Pollard, *Drugs and Theater in Early Modern England* (Cambridge: Cambridge University Press, 2004), 43–54. Elsewhere in the play, Lady Politic also talks about laughter as a health-giving drug.

As for *Bartholomew Fair*, it portrays audience members as potentially the objects of audience laughter: appropriate to a play whose epigraph observes that Democritus, were he alive, would laugh (*rideret*) more at the audience than at the play. As has often been noted, *Bartholomew Fair* problematises the gaze, as observers (from Adam Overdo to Rabbi Busy) constantly turn into participants even by the act of observing.[31] The audience "laughter, aforesaid", which is also unsaid, is particularly appropriate to a play which confounds, one might say, the whole idea of the audience. But to return to using these twelve quotations as the basis for an overall theory of Jonson's attitude to audience laughter, the following observations can be made.

Firstly, Jonson often imagines audience laughter in metaphors of liquid: in terms of something distillable into tears (as seen in the quotation from *Every Man Out*), in terms of washing in a sort of salty ink (as in *Volpone*), and as something that can soak and slosh through the brain (as in *Magnetic Lady*). The drinkable laughter of the *Highgate Entertainment* is merely the most developed version of this image. Elsewhere in Jonson accusations can be "dissolv'd in laughter"; and Volpone suffers from a "fluxe of laughter".[32] Laughter, and particularly audience laughter, for Jonson, is a liquid.

Secondly, as has already been seen in this study, something typical of many early modern accounts of audience laughter is an interest in its sheer noisiness, an interest which occurs here in Jonson's description from *For The Honour of Wales*. Elsewhere in the Jonson canon individual characters' laughter is compared to braying, and to an alarm; Morose, in *Epicoene*, is tortured by laughter as well as by many other noises; and the first line of *The Devil is An Ass* is a long, loud peal of demonic laughter.[33] Jonson, too, is interested in the *noise* of laughter, including audience laughter.

Thirdly, Jonson often imagines audience laughter (perhaps in distinction to individual laughter) as healthy: something that audiences do "heartily", which improves their complexions (with red cheeks), and which applies a stimulating foment to their brains (*EMI, Volpone, Magnetic Lady*). Laughter is associated with pleasure (*Every Man Out*), and with "sport", "delight" and "mirth" (*Sad Shepherd, Haddington Masque, The Staple of News*); indeed, elsewhere in the Jonson canon Laughter is put on stage as one of the handmaidens of Delight (in *The Vision of Delight*).[34] The bodily after-effects of a good laugh can persist for six or seven days (*Volpone, For the Honour of Wales*). Laughter, in these quotations, and as in many other Renaissance representations of laughter, is healthy and pleasurable.

---

31   See especially Peter Happé, "Jonson's On-stage Audiences: *Spectaret populum ludis attentius ipsis*", *Ben Jonson Journal*, 10 (2003): 23–41.

32   *Poetaster*, 3.5, translating Horace; *Volpone*, 1.4.

33   *Epicoene*, 4.1; *Devil is an Ass*, 4.4, 1.1.1.

34   For the sake of completeness, one ought also to mention Gelaia (Laughter), a foolish young nymph who is a peripheral character in *Cynthia's Revels*, and who could be rendered less foolish if she were able to become Aglaia, "kindly conversation ... not without laughter"; *Cynthia's Revels* also contains the lines where Mercury and Crites undertake "to correct, / And punish, with our laughter", quoted in Chapter 1.

In the standard view of Jonson's dramatic theory, that theory is centrally concerned with moral reformation, in which laughter is (as Sidney describes it) an ethical tool to humiliate both the victim of laughter and also the laugher himself.[35] Certainly this was a view taken by several eulogists of Jonson in *Jonsonus Virbius* (1638). According to Jasper Mayne, Jonson's audiences were "laugh'd into *virtue*", while one H. Ramsey, writing in the same collection, figured Jonson's ability to make an audience laugh as a form of personal assault: "His *lines* did relish mirth, but so severe / That as they tickled, they did wound the ear".[36] While some of Jonson's explicit references to audience laughter support this view of laughter as harsh and punitive, most resist reduction into the strict terms of such a theory. The thirteen examples above welcome laughter not just as a judgement against "follies" (*Every Man In* and *Poetaster*), but as a result of a number of other more localised effects which are less easy to subsume under that heading of moral judgement: as a product of dancing (*For the Honour of Wales*, *Haddington Masque*); of costume and stage business (*Poetaster*, *Althorp Entertainment*); and in connection with jokes against stage convention itself – the unexpected twist of a Prologue having second thoughts (*Sad Shepherd*). Laughter can be an end in itself (something shown particularly clearly by the second quotation from *The Magnetic Lady*). As the example from *Mercury Vindicated* shows, audience laughter can even be constructed as part of a dialogue with the fiction, rather than an exclusively one-way reaction. Jonson's practice, and Jonson's theory, is much more inclusive when it comes to audience laughter than the "strict" version of Jonsonian dramatic theory would suggest, and one certainly cannot read Jonson in terms of the poetic advanced (and perhaps not even followed) by Lyly.

In short, the "laughter, aforesaid" of Jonson's audiences is a complicated thing. More than just a means to an end in an edifying literary work, more than a "kind of turpitude" or an unwanted effect of unworthy drama, it is pleasurable and often medicinal; strangely liquid; and potentially ear-ringingly loud.

---

35   This footnote describes just a sample of the work done on Jonsonian ideas of reform through satire: A.L. Dick, *Paideia Through Laughter: Jonson's Aristophanic Appeal to Human Intelligence* (The Hague: Mouton, 1974), offers a rather poor account; Angus Fletcher, "Jonson's Satiric-Comedy and the Unsnarling of the Satyr from the Satirist", *Ben Jonson Journal*, 6 (1999): 247–69, with extensive bibliography; Richard Dutton, "The Lone Wolf: Jonson's Epistle to *Volpone*", in Julie Sanders, Kate Chedgzoy and Susan Wiseman (eds), *Refashioning Ben Jonson* (1999), 114–33, on one of the most influential of Jonson's critical statements (which never mentions audience laughter); Edward Berry, "Laughing at 'Others'", in Alexander Leggatt (ed.), *The Cambridge Companion to Shakespearean Comedy* (2002), 123–38, setting Shakespearean against Jonsonian laughter, and Bakhtinian against Hobbesian; and Murray Roston, "*Volpone*: Comedy or Mordant Satire?", *Ben Jonson Journal*, 10 (2003): 1–22, reading *Volpone* in terms of the *iucunda* and the *idonea*.

36   H&S, 11.453, 472; another contributor, William Habington, figures laughter as a purge administered to the audience.

Chapter 7

Horrid laughter

Chapter 4 of this book looked to establish what can be said, on the basis of early modern accounts of audience laughter, about the norms, conventions and expectations around how, and when, such audiences were expected to laugh. For obvious reasons, most of the accounts of such laughter relate to performances of comedies. This chapter uses that previous one as a springboard to consider the question of audience laughter during tragedies.

As with Chapter 4, the most obvious application of this relates to the field of performance criticism. Nicholas Brooke's influential book *Horrid Laughter in Jacobean Tragedy*, for example, starts by claiming both that audience laughter and weeping are transhistorical constants, and that those phenomena can be linked directly to the emotions felt by those producing them: "Direct human registration of emotion is not, in truth, much wider than that of any other animal: we laugh and we cry. Those two, and those two alone, are universal signs, and universally understood." This observation forms the basis for Brooke's use of his experience of modern performances both to deny comic overtones – "I have never heard of laughter at the end of *King Lear*" – and to justify the detection of those overtones, as in the last act of *The Duchess of Malfi*: "In every performance that I have seen, whether intended or not, there has been laughter before the act is out". This use of observation soon slips over into readings of intentionality: in the performance of *The Duchess of Malfi* at Stratford, Ontario, in 1971, Brooke observes that "the audience laughed in delighted admiration" at the clouds of incense smoke released through the air conditioning system, "which I take to be precisely the right reaction to such a baroque *tour de force*", and he writes of the scene of the skewered heart in *'Tis Pity Shee's A Whore* that it "usually does provoke audience laughter, and the play's intelligence requires that".[1] Brooke's influence, and in particular this idea of authorial intention discernible through modern audience reaction, can be seen in a range of subsequent writings on early modern tragedies, which take for axioms the ideas that those tragedies, or some of them, are intended to make the audience laugh, and that that laughter can be considered a universal sign, "universally understood".[2]

---

1   Nicholas Brooke, *Horrid Laughter in Jacobean Tragedy* (London: Open Books, 1979), qtns from 1, 5, 63, 55, 125.

2   For a survey of and attacks on such readings, see Roberta Barker and David Nicol, "Does Beatrice Joanna Have a Subtext?: *The Changeling* on the London Stage", *Early Modern Literary Studies*, 10:1 (May 2004): 3.1–43, at http://purl.oclc.org/emls/10-1/barknico.htm;

However, this chapter poses the question: is there any evidence from early performance history of tragedies to set against these examples of modern audience behaviour? We have seen that the picture of what audiences can be said to have laughed at in comedies is not quite the same as that obtaining today: is the same true of audience laughter in tragedies, if indeed there was any such laughter? This chapter proposes two basic categories of accounts of audience laughter during tragedies. One relates to the idea of mixed genres, in which a tragic play can include identifiable and generically distinct comic scenes within it, often involving a clown. The second describes audience laughter during scenes which do not have such generic markers. It is this second, more elusive, type of "horrid laughter", dealing with "extreme emotions" whose very intensity means that they "are *liable* to turn over into laughter", that Brooke's book proposes, that must be sought for in early accounts of audience reaction.[3]

Firstly, then, early modern tragedies frequently include scenes of what used to be described as "comic relief". From various contemporary allusions, one can be reasonably certain of what, in any case, is a common-sense assumption, namely that these scenes did indeed move laughter in the theatre. Sir Philip Sidney, for instance, alludes to this: "having indeed no right comedy, in that comical part of our tragedy, we have nothing but scurrility, unworthy of any chaste ears: or some extreme show of doltishness, indeed fit to lift up a loud laughter, and nothing else".[4] The title-page of the tragedy *Cambyses* describes it as "a lamentable tragedy mixed ful of pleasant mirth", and this is reflected in its sharp division between "historical" characters from the Persian royal family, whose troubles are described in relatively realistic style, and a band of allegorical characters led by Ambidexter the jesting Vice.[5] Joseph Hall's description of a 1590s tragedy, quoted at length earlier in Chapter 4, offers a detailed description of a "dead strook audience" revived into acoustic life for the duration of the appearance of a clown. And the admittedly post-Restoration witness Thomas Rymer writes of Fletcher's *The Bloody Brother* that the "serious" scenes of the tragedy are not a great success, but that the "comical part" is:

> We may, I think, conclude the success of this Play due chiefly to the Scenes for laughter, the merry jig under the Gallows, and where the Tragedy tumbles into the Kitchin among the Skoundrels that never saw buskin in their lives before. There the Pantler and Cook give it that relish which renders it one of the most followed entertainments in the Town.[6]

---

for an earlier attack on them, see Richard A. Levin, "The Proof of the Parody", *Essays in Criticism*, 24 (1974): 312–16.

3   Brooke, *Horrid Laughter*, 3.

4   Sidney, *The Defence of Poesy*, in Katherine Duncan-Jones (ed.), *Sir Philip Sidney* (Oxford: Clarendon Press, 1989), 245.

5   Later Renaissance observers, of course, found *Cambyses* funny not so much for the scenes with Ambidexter as for the overblown fustian of the "tragic" elements, "King Cambyses' vein", parodied by Falstaff in *1 Henry IV*.

6   Thomas Rymer, *The tragedies of the last age consider'd and examin'd by the practice of the ancients and by the common sense of all ages* (London: Richard Tonson,

But all of these accounts suggest a conscious mixing of elements: Sidney's account of doltishness, Hall's account of the "lout" sharing a stage with princes, and Rymer's mention of the kitchen, imply a class difference between a tragic plot which conventionally, in the Aristotelian formula, involves high-status characters, and a comic plot which does not.

On the other hand, the sort of laughter Brooke argues for, truly "horrid laughter" which can be shown to propagate to a theatre audience, is much harder to document. When characters in plays talk about the possibility of laughing at tragedies, it generally implies a failure of tragedy: thus Chapman's foolish Monsieur D'Olive, invited to see the dead Countess lying in state, frets that "I should laugh and spoyle the Tragedie". And Domitian in Massinger's *Roman Actor* states explicitly that he will not weep for the death of Paris:

> I shall looke on your Tragedie vnmou'd,
> Peraduenture laugh at it, for it will proue
> A Comedie to me. [7]

However, these are only metaphorical uses. What one would prefer are "eye-witness" accounts of tragedies moving laughter, but one of the few accounts which does approach this area suggests that such laughter is distinctly unacceptable. In *The Guls Horne-booke*, Dekker satirically advises anyone looking to make a name for themselves in London:

> It shall crowne you with rich commendation to laugh alowd in the middest of the most serious and saddest scene of the terriblest Tragedy: and to let that clapper (your tongue) be tost so high that all the house may ring of it: your Lords vse it; your Knights are Apes to the Lords, and do so too. [8]

Of course, there is no easy relationship between this satirical advice and observed truth (a more recent comparison, perhaps, being Gerard Hoffnung's mock advice to tourists, "have you tried the famous echo in the Reading Room of the British Museum?"). As satire, it cannot be taken as straightforwardly true. The point about the passage is that Dekker considers such behaviour anti-social, a disruption of the communally generated acoustic ambience which is essential to the enjoyment of a tragedy.

There are also several stories of audiences laughing during tragedies as a result of unexpected performance mishaps. These often concern university tragedies, such as this jest-book anecdote:

> [A] Master of Art in one of the Vniuersities, hauing acted in a Tragedy, and his body lying seeming dead on the Stage, for the time, was not yet come that hee should be taken

---

1678), 55; similarly, speakers in John Dryden, *Of dramatick poesie, an essay* (London: Henry Herringman, 1668), 31, regard scenes of comic relief in English tragedies as indecorous.

7   Chapman, *Monsieur D'Olive* (1606), E2r; Massinger, *The Roman Actor* (1629), G1v.

8   Thomas Dekker, *The guls horne-booke* (London: R.S., 1609), 30.

away, a passion took him that he was forced to cough so loud that it was perceived by the generall auditory, at which many of them falling into a laughter, hee rising vp excused it thus: you may see Gentlemen what it is to drinke in ones porridge, for they shall cough in their graue.[9]

The point about this laughter, though, is that it destroys the dramatic illusion entirely, and stops the tragedy in its tracks. The same is true of the anecdote told by Edward Gayton, in which two university scholars, suffering extreme stage fright while playing ghosts in a "Spanish tragedy ... of Petrus Crudelis", held up the performance for half an hour and "put the Auditory into such a shaking with laughing, that they had almost died with the excessive motions of the Diaphragme".[10] Two anecdotes in a Restoration play attributed to John Tatham, *Knavery in all Trades*, are also relevant, because while they allege similar effects in two plays on the pre-war professional stage, they present the actors as retaining some control over proceedings:

> FIFTH CUSTOMER: *Fowler* you know was appointed for the Conquering parts, and it being given out he was to play the Part of a great Captain and mighty Warriour, drew much Company; the Play began, and ended with his Valour; but at the end of the Fourth Act he laid so heavily about him, that some Mutes who stood for Souldiers, fell down as they were dead e're he had toucht their trembling Targets; so he brandisht his Sword & made his *Exit;* ne're minding to bring off his dead men; which they perceiving, crauld into the Tyreing house, at which, *Fowler* grew angry, and told 'em, Dogs you should have laine there till you had been fetcht off; and so they crauld out again, which gave the People such an occasion of Laughter, they cry'd that again that again, that again.

> FOURTH CUSTOMER: I but what d'ye call him was the man; he plaid the devil in Doctor *Faustus,* and a fellow in the Gallery throwing a Tobacco-Pipe at him; I hope to see thee (quoth He) e're long as bad as I am, what's that quoth the fellow? the Son of a Whore quoth He.

> OMNES: Ha, ha, ha.[11]

The context of these anecdotes in a Restoration comedy, and the onstage laughter that they are wrapped in, does not invite complete confidence in their veracity, or in the picture they appear to present of the pre-Restoration playhouse as a venue within which audience laughter occurred during "serious" plays, and within which suspension of the dramatic illusion during a play was a regular occurrence. But other Restoration anecdotes point in the same general direction as regards audience laughter at tragedies. When, in the performance of Tate's *King Lear*, the actress

9   Archie Armstrong, attr., *A Baquet of Jeasts. Or Change of Cheare. Being a Collection of Moderne Jests. Witty Jeeres. Pleasant Taunts. Merry Tales* (London: Richard Royston, 1630), 103.

10   Edmund Gayton, *Pleasant Notes Upon Don Quixote* (London: William Hunt, 1654), 95.

11   John Tatham, *Knavery in all trades, or, The coffee-house a comedy* (London: J.B., 1664), D4v–E1r.

Elizabeth Barry, playing Cordelia, referred to her "virgin innocence", the audience is said to have responded with "a horse-laugh".[12] And this is John Dryden's observation of Restoration practice:

> I have observ'd that in all our Tragedies, the Audience cannot forbear laughing when the Actors are to die; 'tis the most Comick part of the whole Play. All *passions* may be lively represented on the Stage, if to the well-writing of them the Actor supplies a good commanded voice, and limbs that move easily, and without stifness; but there are many *actions* which can never be imitated to a just height: dying especially is a thing which none but a Roman Gladiator could naturally perform upon the Stage when he did not imitate or represent, but naturally do it; and therefore it is better to omit the representation of it.[13]

The main thrust of Dryden's speaker in this passage is the discussion of the desirability of neo-classical decorum, but what is most striking is the casualness with which he states that in "*all* our Tragedies" – not just some performances, but as a matter of course – "the Audience cannot forbear laughing". "Forbear" is a telling choice of words in that it implies an audience who are trying to participate, rather then merely laughing destructively in the manner of most of the audiences so far listed. Of all the passages discussed in this section, it is Dryden's which would give most help and succour to readings of tragedies which posit that they generate the sort of horrid laughter proposed by Brooke and subsequent writers, and yet it comes from the Restoration theatre, not the theatre of the years before 1642. For whatever reason – rhetorical inconvenience, perhaps – accounts of audience reaction in the early modern stage hardly ever talk about laughter at a tragedy except as marking the failure of that tragedy. And yet many of the tragedies of the early modern period appear to modern sensibilities to be very funny.

One approach which might be of use in making further progress into this apparent impasse is the idea, mooted in the earlier chapters of this study, that stage laughter generally anticipates and shapes audience laughter. One can develop this idea by means of a close analysis of one representative tragedy: the anonymous *Lust's Dominion*.

Lust's Dominion, or the Lascivious Queen was first printed in 1657, ascribed on its title-page to Christopher Marlowe. That title most likely dates from the 1650s (although it will be retained throughout the following discussion), and the Marlowe attribution has always seemed improbable and is made particularly unlikely in the light of the play's long-recognised indebtedness to a pamphlet first published in 1599.[14] Most scholars have concurred with J.P. Collier's suggestion that the

---

12   Paula R. Backscheider, "Barry, Elizabeth (1656x8–1713)", *Oxford DNB*; see also the anecdote recorded in Chapter 2 above, in which a Restoration audience roars with laughter at an unintentional obscenity in *Romeo and Juliet*.

13   Dryden, *Of dramatick poesie*, 32–3.

14   See, in particular, two articles by Charles Cathcart: "'You Will Crown Him King That Slew Your King': *Lust's Dominion* and Oliver Cromwell", *Medieval and Renaissance Drama in England*, 11 (1999): 264–74, and "*Lust's Dominion: or, the Lascivious Queen*: Authorship,

play can be identified as the otherwise lost *Spanish Moor's Tragedy*, a payment in connection with which is recorded in Henslowe's *Diary* for February 1600. However, uncertainty remains about other possible authors involved in the play, the date of its original composition, and the date of possible revisions to it. Discussion of it here implicitly accepts the recent arguments of Charles Cathcart, who argues that Henslowe's payment is indeed associated with the origin of the play (rather than a revision of an existing piece dating from the early 1590s); that the play is of multiple authorship, involving Dekker, Day, Haughton and John Marston; and that it was probably revised around 1606, perhaps reflecting a revival on the stage at that date. For the matter at hand, the most important of the points at issue is merely a broad indication of the date, placing this as a late-Elizabethan tragedy. *Lust's Dominion* charts the rise and fall of Eleazer the Moor, an exuberant Machiavellian villain who is likely to remind modern readers of Shakespeare's Richard III or the Barabas of Marlowe's *The Jew of Malta*, and this somewhat generic quality is useful, because it means that conclusions drawn from this play are potentially applicable to those others which make use of similar characters.

The play is alluded to in Dekker's *Satiro-mastix*, in which "Horace" (Dekker's satirical version of Jonson's Horace from *Poetaster*, and therefore, in some senses, a caricature of Jonson), complains about it. Recent commentators, including Charles Cathcart, agree that the "Innocent Moore" is a reference to *Lust's Dominion* under its title *The Spanish Moor's Tragedy*:

> Crispinus, that Crispin-asse and Fannius his Play-dresser ... cut an Innocent Moore i'th middle, to serue him in twice; & when he had done, made Poules-worke of it, as for these Twynnes these *Poet-apes*:
> Their Mimicke trickes shall serue
> With mirth to feast our Muse, whilst their owne starue.[15]

Given the layers of irony at work here in Dekker's fictional creation attacking a play apparently co-authored by Dekker, and the uncertainties about what process of revision is being described in the play being cut "i'th middle", one should hesitate to extrapolate very much from this piece of theatrical shop talk. But in making the tragedy a subject of fun, and in juxtaposing, even in an ironic way, *Lust's Dominion* with "mimick trickes" and "mirth", Dekker accommodates a view of *Lust's Dominion* which is different from the classical seriousness one might more usually associate with tragedy – certainly different from the po-faced seriousness of Horace/Jonson's theory as presented in *Satiromastix*.

Date, and Revision", *Review of English Studies*, 52 (2001): 360–75; the play is cited from the first edition, but see also the text in Thomas Dekker, *The Dramatic Works of Thomas Dekker*, ed. Fredson Bowers, 4 vols (Cambridge: Cambridge University Press, 1953–61), and the commentary in Cyrus Hoy, *Introductions, Notes and Commentaries to Texts in 'The Dramatic Works of Thomas Dekker'*, 4 vols (Cambridge: Cambridge University Press, 1980).

15   Dekker, *Satiro-mastix* (1602), E3r.

Lust's Dominion contains a number of scenes which fit the template of a generically distinct comic strand as outlined in the first section above. Of these, the most obvious relate to Friar Crab and Friar Cole, two corrupt and foolish Friars who appear as a pair, and who finish each other's sentences in an evidently comic patter. They are "scoundrels", as Rymer would call them, and of a lower social class than, for instance, the Cardinal, whose minions they are. Their final scene, in which they are assassinated by the equally comic double-act of Eleazer's henchmen, Zarack and Balthazar, is a good example of what we would recognise as comic style, with a running series of jokes about the guns – "is thy cock ready" – intercutting with the banter (D10v). But *Lust's Dominion* also seems explicitly to invite audience laughter in its main plot, and that is what makes it interesting to this study.

A programmatic example of this is the opening scene of the play. From as early as the opening stage-direction, Eleazer is set up as a figure who does things that make Elizabethan audiences laugh.

> *Enter Zaracke, Baltazar, two Moors taking tobacco: musick sounding within: enter Queen Mother of Spain with two Pages, Eleazar sitting on a chair suddenly draws the curtain.*

Eleazer's sudden entrance achieves surprise, and also links him to the tradition of the clown's manipulations of the curtain on a first entrance, discussed in Chapter 4 above as a cue for audience laughter. Eleazer then argues with his lover the Queen Mother of Spain, expressing rage at her lascivious attentions:

> ELEAZER: Nay prithee good Queen leave me,
>   I am now sick, heavie, and dull as lead.
> QUEEN: I'le make thee lighter by taking something from thee.
> ELEAZER: Do: take from mee this Ague and these fits that hanging on me
>   Shake me in pieces, and set all my blood
>   A boiling with the fire of rage: away, away
>   Thou believ'st I jest: and laugh'st, to see my wrath wear antick shapes:
>   Be gone, be gone.

The Queen's lewd *double entendre* is another well-marked invitation to audience laughter – rotten talk broking for a laugh, as William Cartwright describes such moments. But then Eleazer's speech functions as a form of retrospective implied stage direction, both for the Queen Mother and for himself. In order for his last speech to be credible, the Queen must be laughing on stage; and he must have performed physical actions – the "antick shapes" he mentions – which are obviously the cause of that laughter, and which the audience can apprehend are actions one might laugh at. By implication, the audience can be expected to have found these antics funny, and perhaps to have laughed. And if that audience *does* laugh, making their own acoustic contribution to the play so far, then Eleazer's angry reaction to the Queen's laughter is also a reaction to their laughter, setting up in this opening moment an antagonistic and yet complicit relationship with them. As in the exchange from

Jonson's *Mercury Vindicated*, quoted in Chapter 6, audience laughter is a mechanism whereby the audience are incorporated into the action. In this case, one can use the onstage laughter as a guide to the anticipated audience laughter.

It should also be noted – although these details are, of course, less compelling than direct onstage references to laughter – that as *Lust's Dominion* unfolds it would make a modern audience laugh in several places. These moments come in various forms. For instance, at one point Eleazer and the Queen Mother are plotting the murder of her husband the King, in order to make their love affair easier. The Queen Mother reminds Eleazer that he too is married, to Maria, and raises the possibility that Maria, too, might be "cut off". Eleazer replies: "Stay, stay, cut off; let's think upon't, my wife? / Humh! Kill her too!" (C7v). It is the bathos, and in particular the inbuilt pause before the bathos, which makes this line a gift to an actor looking to move laughter, and a potential liability to one who is not. Of course, as Richard Levin warns us *a propos* of the works of Marston, such effects might simply be the result of bad writing rather than of an intention to raise hilarity.[16] But one is on slightly safer ground in considering the rivalry between Eleazer and the Cardinal, which is expressed in tart asides – "Cardinal, I'll shorten thee by the head for this" (B11r) – and a handshake marking their supposed rapprochement which we know to be comically insincere. The fat, lustful and Catholic Cardinal is clearly a figure that the audience might be expected to despise, and Eleazer is more than happy to laugh at him when he bests him:

> CARDINAL: Curses shal fal like lightnings on your heads:
>   Bell, book and candle, holy water, praiers,
>   Shal all chim vengeance to the of Court Spain [*sic*]
>   Till they have power to conjure down that feind;
>   That damned *Moor*, that Devil, that Lucifer,
>   That dares aspire the staffe, the Card'nall swaid.
> ELEAZER: Ha ha ha, I laugh yet, that the Cardinall's vext.
> PHILIP: Laughts thou base slave, the wrinckles of that scorn
>   Thine own heart blood shall fill.

> (C2r–C2v)

Eleazer's laughter possibly indicates that the Cardinal's fuming rage, expressed in terms stereotypical of those used in anti-Catholic mockery, is calculated, not merely to please the audience's anti-Catholic prejudices, but also to make them laugh: it certainly demonstrates that onstage laughter is one way in which *Lust's Dominion* manipulates the sympathies of its audience, aligning them here with Eleazer against the prelate and the royal family of Spain.

Indeed, Eleazer comes to laugh more and more as the play goes on. He laughs at his own cleverness; laughs at the carnage on the battlefield; and, in Act Five, becomes more explicit about the relationship in his mind between tragedy and laughter.

---

16   Levin, "The Proof of the Parody".

Congratulating himself on his "jocund spleen", he comments: "Murder be proud, and Tragedy laugh on, / I'le seek a stage for thee to jett upon" (F12v). Eleazer's idea of tragedy is not, then, incompatible with laughter. Again, as he gathers his victims for a final mass execution, he reflects on the genre of tragedy:

> The Scene wants Actors, I'le fetch more, and cloth it
> In rich Cothurnall pompe. A Tragedy
> Ought to be grave, graves this shall beautifie.[17]

The bad pun on "grave" indicates Eleazer's lack of sympathy with conventional ideas of gravity in tragedy. A third, and even more extended metathcatrical allusion by Eleazer imagines Tragedy in terms of "Crimson jollitie", and is topped and tailed with jokes and with the Moor's own laughter.

> ELEAZER: Farewell my Lords, meet there so ha, ha, ha. [*Draws his Rapier*]
> Now Tragedy thou Minion of the night,
> Rhamnusias pew-fellow; to thee I'le sing
> Upon an harp made of dead Spanish bones,
> The proudest instrument the world affords;
> When thou in Crimson jollitie shalt Bath,
> Thy limbs as black as mine, in springs of blood… Ha, ha, ha.
> PHILIP: Damnation tickles him, he laughs again, *Philip* must stand there and bleed to death: Well villain I onely laugh to see, that we shal live to out-laugh him and thee.[18]

Eleazer sees laughter as part of tragedy, and Philip sees the final act of the play in terms of a laughter competition. Indeed, Eleazer's over-reaching is brought about by an excessive sense of humour, when he makes the mistake of having himself and his supporters make mocking impersonations of those chained up: "Oh! fit, fit, fit, stay a rare jest, rare jest. *Zarack*, suppose thou art *Hortenzo* now? I pray thee stand in passion of a pang, to see by thee how quaintly he would hang". From there, it is a small step to Eleazer letting himself be chained up, for a joke, and finding that his Moorish henchmen are really merely his enemies wearing black make-up. One may imagine Eleazer's opportunities for face-pulling when he discovers the deception. The disguised Spaniards then set free the others – "we have not laughs enough" – who regard Eleazer with "mirth". Even when chained and defeated, Eleazer still has lines which can only be described as jokes – the Queen Mother announces that she will torture him by denouncing him, and Eleazer quips that "I know thee then: / All womens tongues are tortures unto men". Indeed, even when stabbed, Eleazer

---

17   *Lust's Dominion*, G5r; Cathcart, "*Lust's Dominion*", 362, argues that "cothurnal" is a word specifically associated with Marston.
18   *Lust's Dominion*, G10r–G10v; "jolly" is of course a loaded and multivalent word in Renaissance literature, with its *locus classicus* being Spenser, *Faerie Queene*, 1.1.1.8.

does not abandon ideas of entertainment: he dies announcing his intention to "out-act" all the devils of Hell in his continuing villainy.[19]

Interestingly, the motif of a deceiver tricked into letting himself be tied up is itself a recognisable convention – a recognisable cause of laughter – in Renaissance drama. An originary example is Pedringano in *The Spanish Tragedy*, who consents to mount the scaffold for his execution, falsely believing that his associates will halt his execution at the last minute. The scene is set by a Boy, who explains to the audience in soliloquy that he knows Pedringano is deceived, and who also makes it plain that *he* expects the next scene to be an occasion for laughter: "I cannot choose but smile ... Wilt not be an odd iest ... Alas poore *Pedringano*, I am in a sorte sorie for thee, but if I should be hanged with thee, I cannot weep" (F2r). The influence of Kyd's scene in particular can also be seen in Daborne's *A Christian Turn'd Turk*, where the Jew and Rabshake the Turk murder three people, laughing and jesting as they do so, in a scene whose uneasy genre is summed up by an exchange between the two of them which is comparable to Eleazer's musings on the nature of tragedy quoted above:

> JEW: ... How lik'st this Tragedy, *Rabshake*?
> RABSHAKE: Rarely, if it do not proue a Tragedy to vs sir, its but a Comedy hitherto: the setting off is all.
>
> (I1r)

The Jew, still laughing, then tells Rabshake that they must find a convincing cover story to enable the two of them to escape justice and "laugh at the silly world". It must appear, argues the Jew, that someone has tried to kill the two of them as well: Rabshake must wound the Jew lightly with a knife (which he does), and Rabshake must put his head in a noose, as if someone has tried to hang him. Rabshake is unhappy with this plan, as he suspects a trap: "I haue seene the play of *Pedringano* sir, of *Pedringano* sir". The Jew eventually persuades him to put his head into the noose all the same, and once he is in the noose, hangs him:

> I could euen cracke my sides with laughter. This will affoord me mirth vnto my dying day. The play of *Pedringano*? How the weesell hangs! Ha, ha, ha. Theeues, theeues: Murder, murder. I shall betray my selfe with laughter. Were you caught *Rynard*? Are you in the noose?
>
> (I2r)

Daborne's staging of this scene appeals for precedent not just to *The Spanish Tragedy*, but also to the fable of Reynard the fox. In *Lust's Dominion*, then, the equivalent scene can be viewed not just as an event on its own, but as a specimen of a recognisable trope, a trope which in the case of both the *Spanish Tragedy* and *A Christian Turn'd Turk* is associated with the laughter of observers. In *Lust's Dominion*, the trapping of Eleazer is regarded as an occasion for laughter by its perpetrators, similarly, and

---

19   *Lust's Dominion*, G10v, G11r, G12r.

by all the other laughers on stage. None of this is as good as a report of audience reaction, but together the three examples suggest that this type of scene (of which *Lust's Dominion* offers one example) is one which might be expected to be a cue for laughter in a theatrical audience.

In marked contrast to these scenes, the subplot in *Lust's Dominion* concerning the death of the relatively sympathetic Maria is conducted in a scene with no onstage laughter, and, rather, copious onstage weeping, described by the King as "these waters / That fall like winter storms, from the drown'd eyes" (G7r–G7v). This corresponds well with what one might call a common-sense assumption that the scene is sadder and more sentimental than the frenetic carnage of most of the rest of the play. Using stage laughter and weeping as signposts to audience laughter and weeping produces, in the case of this play, what would appear to be a fairly reasonable reconstruction of the tone of each scene. No very detailed accounts of audience reaction survive from the early modern stage for any play, and indeed very little is known of any form of performance history for this particular play. Nonetheless, *Lust's Dominion* does have a poetic in which tragedy can coexist with laughter, and it does use onstage laughter as a way of showing shifts in the balance of power among the characters. If we are to recover the profile of the original audience laughter in this play, the best pattern we have is that of onstage laughter and weeping.

Thus, for Brooke's "horrid laughter", a phenomenon which is almost invisible both in Renaissance literary theory and in eye-witness accounts of the Renaissance stage in action, *Lust's Dominion* is an unusually helpful test case. Eleazer's comments about the "Crimson jollitie" of a laughing Tragedy offer, in a sense, the germ of a contemporary literary theory describing such a form, and while there are no eye-witness accounts of an audience laughing at this play, allusions to onstage laughter – particularly the opening exchange, which sets up a situation in which Eleazer can react against audible laughter from the spectators – suggest that this is a tragedy to which audience laughter is important, not just in a subplot of comic relief but in the main plot too. In developing such readings of other Renaissance tragedies besides this one, one might pay attention not just to metadramatic statements such as Eleazer's discussions of tragedy, and not just to the implicit cues for audience laughter, but to the representation on stage of weeping and of laughter.

Chapter 8

Shakespeare's theatre of sympathy

The study so far has argued that early modern drama in general is fascinated by laughter and weeping, very frequently displaying both actions, and associating them with a rich theatrical vocabulary, involving associated phrases of dialogue, gestures, and even properties such as the handkerchief. Also, contemporary accounts of and allusions to early modern theatre are fascinated by audience laughing and weeping, which is considered an important element within the performance occasion; by the volume and intensity of audience laughter; and by the mysterious nature of audience weeping. As a general principle, by and large, audience laughter is cued by stage laughter, and audience weeping is cued by stage weeping. This eighth and final chapter asks: what are the implications of these ideas for study of Shakespeare?

Examination of a concordance quickly demonstrates that both weeping and laughter are represented or referred to hundreds of times in the works of Shakespeare, and a full taxonomy of those references would be a book-length study in its own right. A sampling of examples might include Jacques, weeping at the weeping deer and laughing at the fool; Talbot, laughing as he turns the tables on the treacherous Countess of Auvergne; and the weeping male heroes – Pericles, Lear, Othello and Coriolanus, for example – all weep.[1] Some of the laughing and weeping is intimately domestic, such as Rosalind's threat to Orlando that "I will weep for nothing, like Diana in the fountain, and I will do that when you are disposed to be merry; I will laugh like a hyena, and that when thou art inclined to sleep". Elsewhere, the frame of reference is more abstract and symbolic, as in Henry V's reaction to the tennis-balls sent by the Dauphin: "His jest will savour but of shallow wit / When thousands weep more than did laugh at it".[2] This chapter aims to survey Shakespearean weeping and laughter, and it will do so by focusing on examples of Shakespeare's interest in the mechanisms that cause laughter and weeping, with particular reference to onstage audiences. *Hamlet* and *A Midsummer Night's Dream* both feature allusions to onstage audiences being made to laugh, while *Julius Caesar*, *Titus Andronicus* and *The Winter's Tale* all explore the causation of and representation of weeping, although – as will be seen in several of these plays – a characteristic of Shakespeare is to confound tears and laughter.[3]

---

1   *As You Like It,* 2.1.65, 2.7.30; *1 Henry VI*, 2.3.43.
2   *As You Like It*, 4.1.145–8; *Henry V*, 1.2.295–6.
3   Previous work on tears and laughter on stage in Shakespeare includes essays in Roberta Mullini (ed.), *Tudor Theatre: For laughs (?)/Pour rire (?): Puzzling Laughter in Plays of the Tudor Age/Rires et problèmes dans le théâtre des Tudors* (Bern: Peter Lang, 2002);

Hamlet, for example, although it seems to have more to do with weeping than with laughter, starts, figuratively at least, with an uneasy combination of the two simultaneously: with "mirth in funeral and dole in marriage" (1.2.12). As discussed in Chapter 3, the Player in *Hamlet* narrates and performs a scene of tears so effectively as to induce weeping, perhaps in some of his audience, but certainly in himself – or, at least, he gives the impression that the weeping belongs to himself rather than to his character. But *Hamlet*'s interest in the theatricality of laughing and weeping does not stop there, since, in a sense, the Player's counterpart within *Hamlet* is another professional entertainer whose outward displays of the signs of these syndromes are linked to his ability to induce them in others: Yorick the jester. Thus, in Act Five, Hamlet addresses Yorick's skull:

> Where be your gibes now? your gambols? your songs? your flashes of merriment,
> that were wont to set the table on a roar? Not one now, to mock your own grinning? quite
> chopfallen? Now get you to my lady's chamber and tell her, paint an inch thick, to this
> favor she must come. Make her laugh at that.[4]

There are certainly some points of intersection between the language used here by Hamlet and the language we have already seen used elsewhere in Renaissance theatrical writing to describe the activities of clowns. In particular, Hamlet anticipates the image of a firework used by "I.H." to accuse the clown Bubble of "flash[ing] choking squibbes of absurd vanities" in the nostrils of his spectators. The response that Yorick has obtained from those flashes is instant, auditory and roaringly loud, for all that it is imagined as taking place in the context of an informal entertainment rather than a theatre. Hamlet imagines even Yorick's skull as still performing, pulling faces which might be merely grotesquely exaggerated ("chopfallen"), but which also reference the tradition that fools create laughter by showing the signs of merriment themselves, like Joseph Hall's fool who "laughes, and grins, and shows his Mimik face", or like the theatrical clowns referred to earlier in *Hamlet* itself who "shall make those laugh whose lungs are tickle o'th sear … will laugh themselves, to set on some

---

Indira Ghose, "Licence to Laugh: Festive laughter in *Twelfth Night*", in Manfred Pfister (ed.), *A History of English Laughter: Laughter from "Beowulf" to Beckett and Beyond* (Amsterdam: Rodopi, 2002), 35–46, relating laughter to ideas of folk festivity; Tobias Döring, "*How to do things with tears*: Trauer spielen auf der Shakespeare-Bühne", *Poetica*, 33:3/4 (2001): 355–89, which discusses several Shakespeare plays; Anton Bosman, "Seeing Tears: Truth and Sense in *All is True*", *Shakespeare Quarterly*, 50 (1999): 459–76, on weeping in *Henry VIII*. For accounts of Shakespeare relative to audience reaction, see, for example, David Richman, *Laughter, Pain, and Wonder: Shakespeare's Comedies and the Audience in the Theatre* (Newark: University of Delaware Press, 1990), although this tends to treat audience reaction as transhistorical; and several essays in Frances Teague (ed.), *Acting Funny: Comic Theory and Practice in Shakespeare's Plays* (Cranbury, NJ: Associated University Presses, 1994).

4   *Hamlet*, 5.1.188–92.

quantity of barren spectators to laugh too".[5] Yorick, then, is a counterpart of the weeping player of Act Two: and the two figures, one grinning (and clearly that grin is no longer "sincere" laughter), one weeping (and weeping tears whose sincerity is problematic), are emblematic of *Hamlet*'s much broader interest in the slipperiness of performances of emotion in general, and, indeed, in the theatricality of the world.[6]

Another play famous for its play-within-a-play, and also interested in what causes audience laughter, is *A Midsummer Night's Dream*. As has often been noted, *A Midsummer Night's Dream* as a whole is very interested in processes of sympathetic influence, as, for instance, in the connections between the welfare of the fairy world and the welfare of the human world. Indeed, when the play-within-a-play is first discussed, Bottom's immediate assumption is that it will work according to a principle of sympathy, so that tears on stage will provoke tears in the audience. Hence his reaction to the part of Pyramus: "That will ask some tears in the true performing of it. If I do it, let the audience look to their eyes. I will move storms; I will condole in some measure." And the part of Pyramus does indeed "ask some tears in the true performing of it", for at the climax of *Pyramus and Thisbe* Pyramus is given an implied stage-direction requiring him to weep:

> O wherefore, Nature, didst thou lions frame?
> Since lion vile hath here deflower'd my dear,
> Which is—no, no—which was the fairest dame
> That lived, that loved, that liked, that looked with cheer.
> Come, tears, confound,
> Out, sword, and wound
> The pap of Pyramus...[7]

For all that its effect is comic, Pyramus' speech is a clear first-person implied stage-direction requiring weeping, of the sort seen in Chapter 3 to be typical of early modern drama. We may imagine Bottom acting it out using any or all of the resources to represent weeping described in that chapter. Furthermore, Bottom says that the audience must look to their own eyes, which, as well as being a neat piece of sensory confusion which anticipates his later speech about Bottom's Dream, is also orthodox Renaissance dramatic theory: the display of weeping will produce, or ought to produce, weeping in others, by the process of sympathy which Bottom describes using the word "condole". Thus far, Bottom's ideas are perfectly in accordance with the advice offered by Horace in the *Ars poetica*. But although he does move tears from Philostrate in rehearsal, it is for the wrong reasons, since Philostrate says of the play:

---

5   *Hamlet*, 2.2.324–5; 3.2.40–41; *OED*, grin *v.*[2], on the two competing significations of "grin" at this date.

6   On this topic, see the still-classic study of Jackson I. Cope, *The Theater and the Dream: From Metaphor to Form in Renaissance Drama* (Baltimore: Johns Hopkins University Press, 1973).

7   *A Midsummer Night's Dream*, 1.2.21–3; 287–93.

Which when I saw rehears'd, I must confess,
Made mine eyes water; but more merry tears
The passion of loud laughter never shed.

(5.1.68–70)

The "tragical mirth" of *Pyramus and Thisbe* moves laughter in spite of displaying the opposite on stage. In this sense, Act Five of *A Midsummer Night's Dream* depicts a breakdown of the usual process of sympathy underlying dramatic representation – a breakdown thematically related to the earlier problems of the lovers, where Lysander's onstage weeping ("Look... I weep") is misinterpreted by Helena as displaying a form of "derision" (3.2.123–4). Such a breakdown is, of course, partially recuperated by Theseus' awareness of the wider social functions of the performance of *Pyramus and Thisbe*, and by Puck's framing epilogue. All the same, *A Midsummer Night's Dream* is certainly interested in exploring unusual cases of the causation and reception of weeping and laughter: and it depicts a world in which the two states are strangely close together.

A Midsummer Night's Dream presents what ought to be a sad stimulus, which causes an onstage audience to laugh, and the same, in a sense, is true of *Titus Andronicus*, which examines these processes in greater and more destructive detail. Act Three, Scene One of *Titus Andronicus*, in particular, rings a series of virtuoso changes on the idea of what weeping and laughter mean, and how they might be caused, propagated, represented and understood, in a play whose own relationship in performance with audience laughter has been famously difficult.[8]

In Act Three, Scene One of the play, Titus is weeping in front of the judges, in the hope that they will spare his sons' lives. His weeping is conveyed in another classic example of a first-person implied stage direction: "For these bitter tears, which now you see / Filling the agèd wrinkles in my cheeks ..." (3.1.6–7). These tears are perceived as tokens, indeed as a form of writing, and, as with the examples collected in Chapter 3, the emphasis is very much on the visibility and the wetness of what Titus sheds from his body.

For these, tribunes, in the dust I write
My heart's deep languor and my soul's sad tears.
Let my tears stanch the earth's dry appetite;
My sons' sweet blood will make it shame and blush.

(3.1.12–15)

---

8   For an argument that the play *is* designed to make audiences laugh, see Carol Chillington Rutter, "Looking like a Child – or – *Titus*: The Comedy", *Shakespeare Survey*, 56 (2003): 1–27; see also Natália Pikli, "The Crossing Point of Tears and Laughter, A Tragic Farce: Shakespeare's *Titus Andronicus*", *AnaChronist* (2000): 51–69, cited from the Thomson Gale database *The Shakespeare Collection*, at http://shakespeare.galegroup.com. Pikli argues that the play's interrelation of the "universal signs" of tears and laughter is related to an aesthetic of the grotesque; see also Richard J. Brucher, "'Tragedy, Laugh On': Comic Violence in *Titus Andronicus*", *Renaissance Drama*, 10 (1979): 71–91; Brucher's title quotation comes from *Lust's Dominion*, and he sees Shakespeare's play, too, as likely to provoke "bitter laughter" in its audience.

Even their warmth is mentioned in subsequent lines. In spite of appearing to be the unmediated effusion of his soul ("my soul's sad tears"), this weeping fails to move the sympathy of those to whom they are directed, to the extent that even the stones seem more sympathetic, for they at least "humbly at my feet / Receive my tears and seem to weep with me" (3.1.20, 41–2).

Into this episode, without a break, Marcus then enters, announcing an event which invites further weeping: "Titus, prepare thy agèd eyes to weep". He introduces the mutilated Lavinia, herself in tears, and unable to perform that weeping in the way in which it would be conventionally represented on stage, as Titus' speech tellingly indicates: "Thou hast no hands, to wipe away thy tears" (3.1.59, 106). In the world of *Titus Andronicus*, weeping and laughter appear to offer hope of a non-verbal, non-linguistic form of signification, but Marcus and Titus soon find that they cannot understand even the weeping of Lavinia:

> TITUS: When I did name her brothers, then fresh tears
>   Stood on her cheeks...
> MARCUS: Perchance she weeps because they kill'd her husband;
>   Perchance because she knows them innocent.
>
> (3.1.111–15)

The interpretation of those tears is impossible for the characters, but that does not alter their intra-diegetic reality, or the requirement to represent them.

Titus imagines the surviving Andronici weeping together around a fountain, their cheeks "stained, as meadows, yet not dry, / With miry slime left" (3.1.125–6), their tears resembling and indeed polluting the flow of the fountain. The weeping goes on:

> LUCIUS: Sweet father, cease your tears; for, at your grief,
>   See how my wretched sister sobs and weeps.
> MARCUS: Patience, dear niece. Good Titus, dry thine eyes.
> TITUS: Ah, Marcus, Marcus! Brother, well I wot
>   Thy napkin cannot drink a tear of mine,
>   For thou, poor man, hast drown'd it with thine own.
>
> (3.1.136–41)

Here we have infectious weeping, with Lavinia's weeping, allegedly, caused by the weeping of Titus which it helped to engender. A handkerchief appears, used as a stage property, and interesting too is the retrospective implied stage direction of Titus' speech: the actor playing Marcus has not had any direct instructions to use a handkerchief himself (particularly not if we restrict ourselves to a reconstruction of his "part"), and yet the scene falls apart at this point if he has not so far been doing so. Lucius' handkerchief is so wet that it will not serve when he serves to dry Lavinia's cheeks with it, evidence that Lucius too has already been weeping: as Marcus comments, "O, what a sympathy of woe is this" (3.1.148). There may well be a comic element in this scene – Natália Pikli observes that this moment might move laughter, since "Marcus's sympathy is comically impotent, and its latent ridiculousness is enhanced by the repetition of the gesture" – and yet, in assessing this possibility, it should be borne in mind that the gestural vocabulary of the handkerchief is an entirely accepted stage convention of the early modern theatre.[9]

Titus, at least, believes that there is a direct connection between his inner self and the outward appearance of that self, something exemplified by his weeping: "I am the sea. Hark, how her sighs do blow ... my bowels cannot hide her woes, / But like a drunkard must I vomit them" (3.1.225, 230–31). But within a few lines this connection appears to have snapped, at the arrival of the severed heads of his sons.

> MARCUS: Now is a time to storm; why art thou still?
> TITUS: Ha, ha, ha!
> MARCUS: Why dost thou laugh? it fits not with this hour.
> TITUS: Why, I have not another tear to shed:
>   Besides, this sorrow is an enemy,
>   And would usurp upon my watery eyes
>   And make them blind with tributary tears.
>   Then which way shall I find Revenge's cave?[10]
>
> (3.1.263–70)

In a few lines, Titus' relationship to his sorrows, to how he possesses them, has changed completely. The outward sign of laughter caused by excessive grief is, as noted in Chapter 1, something that fascinates theorists such as Timothy Bright. More disconcerting than that is the change from a world-view in which outward weeping passively registers distress, to one in which weeping is limited both by physiological factors ("I have not another tear to shed") and by tactical considerations of how to gain revenge.

In succeeding scenes, Shakespeare continues to play with the gestural vocabulary of weeping – the gesture of breast-beating, mentioned by Bulwer as one available to orators to indicate grief, and a range of non-verbal noises, as well as the tears. Back at the Andronicus family home, Titus addresses his daughter in a speech which cues, not merely her actions, but his own:

> When thy poor heart beats with outrageous beating,
> Thou canst not strike it thus to make it still.
> Wound it with sighing, girl, kill it with groans
>
> (3.2.13–15)

Titus here causes young Lucius to weep in sympathy, not at the original stimulus, but at the sight of others weeping. This detail, a textbook example of the effect described by Marmontel, is introduced in a third-person stage-direction: "Alas, the tender boy, in passion moved, / Doth weep to see his grandsire's heaviness" (3.2.48–9).

---

9   Pikli, "The Crossing Point of Tears and Laughter", n.p.

10   *Titus Andronicus*, 3.1.263–70: the F reading of Titus' laugh is "Ha, ha, ha,". It is generally agreed that punctuation is compositorial in these texts, but all the same it is striking that the speech ends not with a full stop but a comma.

These displays of sympathy are counterpointed by Aaron's speech in Act Five, which draws attention to the physiological similarities between laughter and weeping discussed in Chapter 1, and to the difficulties of interpretation when seeing a character apparently weeping.

I ... drew my selfe apart,
And almost broke my heart with extreame laughter.
I pried me through the crevice of a wall
When for his hand, he had his two sons' heads,
Beheld his tears, and laughed so heartily
That both mine eyes were rainy like to his;
And when I told the Empress of this sport,
She swoonèd almost at my pleasing tale,
And for my tidings gave me twenty kisses.

(5.1.111–20)

Aaron's imagination moves smoothly from weeping, to laughter, to the erotic swooning and kissing of the Empress. Like Philostrate, Aaron's pleasure depends on antipathy, not sympathy – the signs of emotion which Philostrate observes in the context of a simulation and Aaron observes for real. The situation is further complicated by the fact that Titus was not even weeping at this moment – we have seen Titus, not weeping, but laughing at the moment of receiving the heads. So profound is Aaron's displacement, that he cannot even read the signs which he hopes to react against, and when he tries to share his laughter with the Empress her reaction in turn takes the form of almost swooning – a state more usually associated with extreme grief than extreme joy. "Horrid laughter" may be hard to find documented in accounts of audience reaction, as detailed in Chapter 7, but one can certainly see it represented on the stage at moments such as this. This scene confounds the audience's usual expectations about the registration of joy and grief.

Titus Andronicus closes with a scene which aims to bring closure by asserting the proper action of sympathy in a ritual form, the weeping of the three surviving Andronici over the body of Titus. Lucius weeps first, shedding "These sorrowful drops upon [the] blood-stain'd face" of the dead Titus; then Marcus follows, "tear for tear" (5.3.134; 136). Lucius insists to his son young Lucius that weeping is contagious, and that weeping is sincere: "Come hither, boy. Come, come, and learn of us / To melt in showers. Thy grandsire loved thee well..." (5.3.160–61). Young Lucius' weeping is seen as finishing the process of mourning – "have done with woes". But the preceding play has complicated this view of weeping as in any sense a straightforward activity: it is, as Lucius' speech suggests, something learned, and associated with particular codes such as the handkerchief, rather than in any sense natural.

By the political implications of the public mourning displayed for "friends" as a prelude to resuming government, the last scene of *Titus Andronicus* also speaks to the idea raised by Paster, Rowe and Floyd-Wilson of "emotional expression as either a generic marker of social status or the sentient matter of communal bonds".[11] And if such displays are public, and communal, then they are also political currency. This is a topic to which Shakespeare returns in another Roman play, *Julius Caesar*. The clearest example of this effect in the play is of course Mark Antony's oration, a masterclass in moving tears. But this scene does not stand alone in *Julius Caesar*: rather, it sits in a matrix of scenes in which the operations of sympathy are explored, this time for audiences seen in specifically political terms.

Julius Caesar sets up a world in which, as Lloyd Davis notes, the reading of external signs of emotion in the body is an important, and somewhat mysterious, part of the political process.[12] Brutus points out to Cassius signs to be read on the faces of the other characters on stage:

> BRUTUS: But look you, Cassius,
>   The angry spot doth glow on Caesar's brow,
>   And all the rest look like a chidden train.
>   Calpurnia's cheek is pale, and Cicero
>   Looks with such ferret and such fiery eyes…
> CASSIUS: Casca will tell us what the matter is.

These signs are made particularly difficult to read by the fact that they are hard for the actors directly to represent. (The actor playing Caesar can simulate anger, but he will be doing well to make a visible spot glow on his brow, the thing that Brutus claims he can see.) Caesar, for his part, is suspicious of Cassius, because he cannot read Cassius' body language, in particular his body language as regards laughter: "Seldom he smiles, and smiles in such a sort / As if he mocked himself, and scorned his spirit / That could be moved to smile at anything". And when Casca arrives, supposedly to explain to Brutus and Cassius what has happened at the meeting from which they have all come, the story itself consists of a series of failures to understand the non-verbal reactions of others. Casca cannot understand and does not share the hooting and the "stinking breath" of the crowd's reaction to Caesar, nor the smiling of those who understood Cicero's oration.[13] This is truly a world in which external signs cannot easily be equated with an internal self, and Brutus, of course, falls into a theatrical metaphor when explaining this to his co-conspirators as they set out: "Let not our looks betray our purposes, / But bear it as our Roman actors do". Moments before his death, Caesar cannot read the smile of Popilius Mena.[14]

---

11   Gail Kern Paster, Katherine Rowe and Mary Floyd-Wilson, "Introduction", in (eds), *Reading the Early Modern Passions: Essays in the Cultural History of Emotion* (Philadelphia: University of Pennsylvania Press, 2004), 13.

12   Lloyd Davis, "Embodied Masculinity in Shakespeare's *Julius Caesar*", *EnterText*, 3:1 (2003): 161–82, online at http://people.brunel.ac.uk/~acsrrrm/entertext/3_1_pdfs/davis.pdf.

13   *Julius Caesar*, 1.2.205–7, 243–4, 279.

14   *Julius Caesar*, 2.1.226–7; 3.1.24.

Antony, whom Trebonius has wrongly predicted will "laugh at this hereafter" (that is, the murder, 2.1.193) – a guess which, as well as being wrong, naively collapses the difference between outward expression and inward feeling – enters to meet the conspirators after the murder. He seems himself surprised at the fact that he is not weeping, particularly since he is presented with what we know from Chapter 5 to be a cue for that weeping in the form of freshly bleeding wounds:

> Had I as many eyes as thou hast wounds,
> Weeping as fast as they stream forth thy blood,
> It would become me better than to close
> In terms of friendship with thine enemies.
> Pardon me, Julius!

(3.1.201–6)

Antony stands over Caesar's body, prophesying a civil war in which the normal significations of laughing and weeping will break down: "Mothers shall but smile when they behold / Their infants quartered with the hands of war, / All pity choked with custom …" (3.1.269–71). And when he finally does start to weep, it is weeping at the sight of his servant weeping, rather than at the original grief.

> Thy heart is big. Get thee apart and weep.
> Passion, I see, is catching, for mine eyes,
> Seeing those beads of sorrow stand in thine,
> Began to water.

(3.1.284–7)

This last line is a crux, with many editors reading "begin" rather than F "began". In either case, the point is that Antony seemingly cannot weep at the primary cause of grief, but only through sympathy of others' weeping: once again, Marmontel's image of the "five hundred mirrors sending to one another the light that they reflect".

Examined from this perspective, Antony's oration can be seen as a masterclass in moving weeping. Whereas Brutus claimed that he wept for Caesar, Antony instead does weep for Caesar, or at least displays symptoms from the syndrome of weeping – a quiet voice, eyes which an observer says are "red as fire with weeping", and an inability to speak which he ascribes to being overwrought ("Bear with me: / My heart is in the coffin there with Caesar, / And I must pause till it come back to me").[15] Once he has started to move the crowd, he moves on to showing them Caesar's blood-stained mantle, in a way which reflects the particular association between blood and audience tears documented in the descriptions of Nashe and others recorded in Chapter 5. Indeed, just as Yarington's play *Two Lamentable Tragedies*, also discussed in Chapter 5, cues audience weeping in explicit instructions to start to weep, and in instructions that the audience are weeping, so Antony cues and directs

15   *Julius Caesar*, 3.2.24, 26, 65, 115, 104–6.

audience weeping in two instructions. The first is for weeping in the imminent future – "If you have tears, prepare to shed them now" (3.1.166) – and the second requires weeping in the present:

> Oh, now you weep, and I perceive you feel
> The dint of pity. These are gracious drops.
> Kind souls, what weep you when you but behold
> Our Caesar's vesture wounded? Look you here!
> *He lifts Caesar's mantle*

Of course, the tears that Mark Antony induces are harnessed to a particular, and violent, political agenda: a "flood of mutiny".[16] They cannot be said to be the result of a long-standing internal grief, since Antony is able to create them, and they do not mean what the crowd think they mean. Furthermore, Antony is able to manipulate them precisely because there is some artifice in his use of them: his own private assessment of the scene, that "Fortune is merry" (3.2.267), dramatically deflates his previous display of grief. It is generally accepted that *Julius Caesar* explores the theatricality of politics: one might also add that a central element of this is the display, the reading, the moving of, and the ability to appear to be responding to, signs of external emotion in others, and prominent among these signs are the highly ambiguous and highly theatrical syndromes of laughter and weeping.

To set alongside the other plays, a final example of Shakespeare's interest in the operations of sympathy in inducing weeping, which also speaks to the condition of the theatre itself, can be taken from *The Winter's Tale*, itself a play founded on the (mis)interpretation of external signs of emotional affect. Leontes foolishly believes he can use signs of laughter and weeping as an infallible guide to internal psychological reality. Among the catalogue of reasons for his belief that Hermione is unfaithful, he asks whether anyone could doubt that she has been "stopping the career of laughter with a sigh? – A note infallible / Of breaking honesty".[17] Hermione, for her part, says that she is constitutionally unapt for weeping, even though she knows that if she did so it might move sympathy in her accusers; even though her ladies weep as she is committed to prison; and even though we are told that a devil would have wept, would have "shed water out of fire", at what Leontes had done.[18] In a sense, the play is founded on a misfiring of the normal operations of signs of joy and sorrow, and the numerous other references in the play to laughing and weeping contribute to this overall sense that Leontes' damaged kingdom is a place where the normal operations of sympathy have failed, in contrast to the pastoral Bohemia.

16   *Julius Caesar*, 3.2.194–8; F reading "O now you weepe"; 3.2.212.
17   *The Winter's Tale*, 1.2.285–7; cf. also 1.2.115–17.
18   Ibid., 2.1.105–14, 119; 3.2.193; with Hermione's declaration, cf. Timothy Bright, *A treatise of melancholie Containing the causes thereof, & reasons of the strange effects it worketh in our minds and bodies* (London: Thomas Vautrollier, 1586), 144.

Of course, the play brings redemption to Sicily, and does so partly in an extended offstage scene narrated in ekphrastic terms and describing, rather than showing, the weeping, first of Leontes and Polixenes, then of the Shepherd (described as a conduit of others' rains), then of Paulina, then of Perdita, and finally of everyone else present including the narrator. We learn of the reunion of Leontes with his daughter only in this report from a Gentleman, who observes that he was in the "audience" to see this scene "acted":

> There might you have beheld one joy crown another, so and in such manner that it seemed Sorrow wept to take leave of them, for their joy waded in tears. There was casting up of eyes, holding up of hands, with countenances of such distraction that they were to be known by garment, not by favor ... One of the prettiest touches of all and that which angled for mine eyes – caught the water though not the fish – was when, at the relation of the queen's death, with the manner how she came to't bravely confessed and lamented by the king, how attentiveness wounded his daughter; till, from one sign of dolour to another, she did, with an "Alas!" I would fain say, bleed tears, for I am sure my heart wept blood. Who was most marble there changed color; some swooned, all sorrowed. If all the world could have seen't, the woe had been universal.[19]

This moment has been frequently discussed in terms of Shakespeare's dramatic artistry and baroque technique, and one might additionally note that the tears in question are delicately poised between joy and sorrow, to the point where even the participants cannot tell what has caused them. Shakespeare's list of gestural and facial representations of weeping – held-up hands, unrecognisably distorted faces – might be considered a late entrant to the gestural catalogue of weeping outlined in Chapter 3 of this book. But the second part of the described scene is also, in effect, a particularly extreme implementation of Horace's maxim. Hermione's death, the tragic event, is seen, as it were, through a whole series of mirrors: what we see is a narrator telling a story about a scene of weeping, an "act" which he has seen "acted". Even this reported "act" is only a relation at second hand of the originary cause of sorrow. The number of people weeping increases from two (Leontes and Polixenes) to three and then four (with the additions of the shepherd and Paulina), and five with the narrator, whose initial weeping is described as a rather superficial surrender to the "prettiest touches" of the scene as he watches Perdita listen. At the sight of Perdita herself starting to weep, the narrator's weeping intensifies too with a much more visceral self-description – "I am sure my heart wept blood" – and the number of people affected suddenly expands beyond those personally involved to include the whole court and then, potentially, the whole world ("if all the world could have seen't" – and the "it" is the weeping, rather than the original sad event – "the woe had been universal"). Marmontel's metaphor of amplification is particularly apt for this process, especially since, by implication, the whole effect is being transmitted to

---

19   *The Winter's Tale*, 5.2.44–7, 82–92.

the theatre audience. Or, as Horace's maxim puts it, "If thou wouldst have me weep, bee thou first dround / Thy selfe in teares".

But *The Winter's Tale* explores not merely the mechanisms which propagate weeping, but also the mysterious interconnectedness of weeping and laughter. Writing about *Cymbeline*, Roger Warren very aptly quotes Underdowne's translation of Heliodorus' *Aethopica*, as giving a clue to the tone of the end of that play. It would also make an apt description of the treatment of laughter and weeping in Shakespeare's other late tragicomedies, as, one might say, concrete onstage (and in-audience) analogues of the incomprehensibility of providence. The Gods, according to Heliodorus, "made very contrary things agree, and joined sorrow and mirth, tears and laughter, together, and turned fearful and terrible things into a joyful banquet in the end: many that wept began to laugh, and such as were sorrowful began to rejoice." C.A. Patrides, working from a different perspective, notes the frequency of combined onstage weeping and laughter in Shakespeare's plays, and suggests that "action that terminates in tears or laughter or – given the nature of the human condition – tears and laughter inseparable". Yeats, according to Patrides, is close to the mark when he describes even Lear, in a sense, as "gay".[20] I would make the point here that this approach to the philosophically ineffable is rooted in players, and audience, enacting in their bodies syndromes of laughter and of weeping.

This study started by quoting, and attacking, Elizabeth Barrett Browning's description of Shakespeare's "brow sublime / With tears and laughter for all time." And yet in some respects, Barrett Browning's formulation hits the nail on the head precisely. Not merely are Shakespeare's plays frequently among those said to move laughter, and tears, in early audiences (as documented in Chapters 4 and 5), but they are also consistently interested, as this chapter has endeavoured to show, in representing both weeping and laughter in descriptions and in action. Shakespeare's plays use the full range of techniques available in early modern theatre to explore the processes by which laughing and weeping work on stage and in the audience.

If it is possible to talk about a distinctively Shakespearean aspect to those plays' treatment of weeping and laughter, then one note which is frequently sounded, and which provides an appropriate note on which to end this study, is that Shakespeare, of all early modern playwrights, does seem (as Patrides suggests) particularly interested in the similarity between the physiological states of tears and laughter, and the ease with which one may be interchanged for the other. Many examples of this have already been given in this chapter (Philostrate, Aaron and Rosalind, for instance), but two final examples sum up the range of these plays' interests in these two states and in what they mean.

---

20   William Shakespeare, *Cymbeline*, ed. Roger Warren (Oxford: Clarendon Press, 1998), Introduction, 61; C.A. Patrides, "Shakespeare: The Comedy Beyond Comedy", in Claude J. Summers and Ted-Larry Pebworth (eds), *Figures in a Renaissance Context* (Ann Arbor: University of Michigan Press, 1989), 47–73, qtn from 63.

Isabella in *Measure for Measure* does not know whether to laugh or weep at human activity as a whole, stuck, like the whole universe to which she belongs, between Democritus and Heraclitus:

> … man, proud man,
> Drest in a little brief authority,
> Most ignorant of what he's most assured,
> His glassy essence, like an angry ape,
> Plays such fantastic tricks before high heaven
> As make the angels weep; who, with our spleens,
> Would all themselves laugh mortal.[21]

The motif that man as a whole "Plays… before" an audience who could laugh, or weep, at one and the same performance takes us back to Geoffrey Whitney's emblem of Heraclitus and Democritus suffering bodily harm while watching "the stage" of life. But Isabella goes further in stressing the physicality and embodiedness of audience reaction, even in this extended metaphor. Whitney imagined an audience whose physical reactions were so intense that they might shorten their lifespan; Isabella entertains the idea that angels might lose their immortality, laughing and weeping like a theatre audience.

Pandarus in *Troilus and Cressida*, light years away from Isabella in social circumstances and moral outlook, does, however, share Isabella's sense that weeping and laughter are fundamentally interchangeable in a universe poised between those two actions. The song he sings in Act Three of *Troilus and Cressida* constructs laughing and weeping in corporeal terms, celebrating them both as the stuff of life. Weeping and laughter are both related, by Pandarus, to the noise of lovemaking, and are both so similar to each other that it is hard to discern whether a lover is laughing or weeping. In a small textual detail symptomatic both of this confusion, and of Shakespeare's wider attention to laughing and weeping, the last two words quoted below are a textual crux. They have been recognised as part of the song, but they have also been considered as a notation of a noise to be made by Pandarus at the end of the song indicating how that song has affected him – and if so, is that a noise indicating a sigh, or a laugh?[22] While characteristically Shakespearean, this song could also serve as an emblem of all Renaissance drama's wide and deep interest in weeping and laughter: in how those actions are caused, in how they can be represented, in how they can be transmitted, and in the many problems of interpretation that they create.

---

21 *Measure for Measure*, 5.2.121–8.
22 *Troilus and Cressida*, 3.1.114–26, quoted below as it appears in Q, with terminal comma changed to full stop. Bevington considers the "hey ho" an interjection rather than part of the song, as does Kenneth Muir in William Shakespeare, *Troilus and Cressida*, ed. Kenneth Muir (1982; Oxford: Oxford University Press, 1994).

Loue, loue, nothing but loue, still loue still more
For o loues bow. Shoots Bucke and Doe.
The shafts confound not that it wounds
But ticles still the sore:
These louers cry, oh ho they dye,
Yet that which seemes the wound to kill,
Doth turne oh ho, to ha ha he,
So dying loue liues still,
O ho a while, but ha ha ha,
O ho grones out for ha ha ha—hey ho.

Bibliography

Adams, Thomas. *The deuills banket described in foure sermons* (London: Thomas Snodham, 1614).

Agnew, Jean-Christophe. *Worlds Apart: The Market and Theater in Anglo-American thought, 1550–1750* (Cambridge: Cambridge University Press, 1986).

Alciato, Andrea. *Alciato's Book of Emblems: The Memorial Web Edition in Latin and English*, ed. William Barker *et al.*, at http://www.mun.ca/alciato/

Anon. *A Larum for London, or the siedge of Antwerpe* (London: William Ferbrand, 1602).

_____ *A most pleasant comedie of Mucedorus the kings sonne of Valentia and Amadine the Kings daughter of Arragon with the merie conceites of Mouse* (London: William Iones, 1598).

_____ *A newe mery and wittie comedie or enterlude, newely imprinted, treating vpon the historie of Iacob and Esau* (London: Henrie Bynneman, 1568).

_____ *A pleasant comedie, called Wily beguilde* (London: Clement Knight, 1606).

_____ *A pleasant commodie, called Looke about you* (London: William Ferbrand, 1600).

_____ *A pleasant conceited comedie, called, A knacke to know an honest man* (London: Cuthbert Burby, 1596).

_____ *A Warning for Faire Women* (London: Valentine Sims, 1599).

_____ *An Egley upon the Most Execrable Murther of Mr Clun on of the Comedeans of the Theator Royal* (London: Edward Crouch, 1664).

_____ *An Elegy on that worthy and famous actor, Mr. Charles Hart* ([London]: Nath. Thompson, 1683).

_____ *Lusts dominion, or, The lascivious queen a tragedie* (London: F.K., 1657).

_____ *The Booke of Bulls* (London: Daniel Frere, 1636).

_____ *The Ghost or The woman wears the breeches. A comedy written in the year MDCXL* (London: William Bentley, 1653).

_____ *The history of the tryall of cheualry with the life and death of Caualiero Dicke Bowyer* (London: Simon Stafford, 1605).

_____ *The Play of Dicke of Devonshire* (Oxford: Malone Society, 1955).

_____ *Two wise men and all the rest fooles: or A comicall morall* (London: n.p., 1619).

Armstrong, Archie (attr.). *A Banquet of Ieasts. Or Change of Cheare. Being a Collection of Moderne Jests. Witty Jeeres. Pleasant Taunts. Merry Tales* (London: Richard Royston, 1630).

B[ulwer], J[ohn]. *Pathomyotamia, or, A dissection of the significative muscles of the affections of the minde* (London: Humphrey Moseley, 1649).

_____ *Chirologia, or, The naturall language of the hand composed of the speaking motions, and discoursing gestures thereof: whereunto is added Chironomia, or, The art of manuall rhetoricke* (London: Thomas Harper, 1644).

Bacon, Sir Francis. *Opera* (London: John Havilland, 1623).

Bakhtin, Mikhail. *Rabelais and His World*, trans. Helene Iswolsky (Bloomington: Indiana University Press, 1984).

Bale, John. *The Complete Plays of John Bale*, ed. Peter Happé (Bury St Edmunds: St Edmundsbury Press, 1985).

Barish, Jonas. *The Antitheatrical Prejudice* (Berkeley: University of California Press, 1981).

Barker, Roberta, and David Nicol. "Does Beatrice Joanna Have a Subtext?: *The Changeling* on the London Stage", *Early Modern Literary Studies*, 10:1 (May, 2004): 3.1–43, at http://purl.oclc.org/emls/10-1/barknico.htm

Barnes, Peter. "*Bartholomew Fair*: All the Fun of the Fair", in Brian Woolland (ed.), *Jonsonians* (Aldershot: Ashgate, 2003), 43–51.

Baron, Robert. *Mirza. A tragedie* (London: Humphrey Moseley, 1647).

Beaumont, Francis. *The knight of the burning pestle* (London: Walter Burre, 1613).

_____ *The Knight of the Burning Pestle*, ed. Sheldon P. Zitner (Manchester: Manchester University Press, 1984).

_____ *The Maides Tragedy* (London: Richard Higgenbotham, 1619).

_____ *The masque of the Inner Temple and Grayes Inne* (London: F. K., 1613).

_____, and John Fletcher. *A King and No King* (London: A.M., 1631).

_____, and John Fletcher. *Comedies and tragedies written by Francis Beaumont and Iohn Fletcher* (London: Humphrey Robinson, 1647).

_____, and John Fletcher. *Philaster or, Love Lies a-Bleeding*, ed. Andrew Gurr (1969; Manchester: Manchester University Press, 2003).

_____, and John Fletcher. *The maides tragedy* (London: Richard Higgenbotham, 1619).

_____, and John Fletcher. *The woman hater As it hath beene lately acted by the Children of Paules* (London: John Hodgets, 1607).

Bentley, G.E. "Praeludium for Goffe's *The Careless Shepherdess*", in *The Seventeenth Century Stage: A Collection of Critical Essays* (Chicago: Chicago University Press, 1968), 28–41.

_____ *The Jacobean and Caroline Stage*, 7 vols (Oxford: Clarendon Press, 1942–68).

Berry, Edward. "Laughing at 'Others'", in Alexander Leggatt (ed.), *The Cambridge Companion to Shakespearean Comedy* (2002), 123–38.

Berry, Herbert. "The Globe Bewitched and *El Hombre Fiel*", *Medieval and Renaissance Drama in England*, 1 (1984): 211–30.

Bertrand, Dominique. "Contagious Laughter and the Burlesque: From the Literal to the Metaphorical", in Claire L. Carlin (ed.), *Imaging Contagion in Early Modern Europe* (London: Palgrave, 2005), 177–94.

Bosman, Anton. "Seeing Tears: Truth and Sense in *All is True*", *Shakespeare Quarterly*, 50 (1999): 459–76.

Brathwaite, Richard. *Ar't asleepe husband? A boulster lecture* (London: R. Bishop, 1640).

_____ *The English Gentleman* (London: John Haviland, 1630).

Bright, Timothy. *A treatise of melancholie Containing the causes thereof, & reasons of the strange effects it worketh in our minds and bodies* (London: Thomas Vautrollier, 1586).

Brome, Alexander. *The cunning lovers a comedy* (London: William Sheares, 1654).

Brome, Richard. *A Joviall Crew* (London: J.Y., 1652).

_____ *Five new playes, viz. The English moor, or the mock-marriage. The love-sick court, or the ambitious politique: Covent Garden weeded. The new academy, or the new exchange. The queen and concubine* (London: A. Crook, 1659).

_____ (ed.). *Lachrymae musarum The tears of the muses: exprest in elegies* (London: Thomas Newcomb, 1649).

_____ *The antipodes a comedie* (London: I. Okes, 1640).

_____ *The damoiselle, or, The new ordinary* (London: T.R., 1653).

_____ *The English Moore, or, The Mock-Mariage*, ed. Sarah Jayne Steen (Columbia: University of Missouri Press, 1983).

_____ *The northern lasse a comoedie* (London: Aug. Mathewes, 1632).

_____ *The sparagus garden a comedie* (London: I. Okes, 1640).

Brooke, Nicholas. *Horrid Laughter in Jacobean Tragedy* (London: Open Books, 1979).

Browne, Thomas. *Religio Medici* ([London]: Andrew Crooke, 1642).

Brownrigg, Ralph. *Twenty five sermons* (London: Thomas Roycroft, 1664).

Brucher, Richard J. "'Tragedy, Laugh On': Comic Violence in *Titus Andronicus*", *Renaissance Drama*, 10 (1979): 71–91.

C., J. *A pleasant comedie, called the two merry milke-maids* (London: Bernard Alsop, 1620).

Carlell, Lodowick. *The passionate lovers, a tragi-comedy. The first and second parts* (London: Humphrey Moseley, 1655).

Carlin, Claire L. (ed.). *Imaging Contagion in Early Modern Europe* (London: Palgrave, 2005).

Cathcart, Charles. "*Lust's Dominion: or, the Lascivious Queen*: Authorship, Date, and Revision", *Review of English Studies*, 52 (2001): 360–75.

_____ "'You Will Crown Him King That Slew Your King': *Lust's Dominion* and Oliver Cromwell", *Medieval and Renaissance Drama in England*, 11 (1999): 264–74.

Cave, Richard, Elizabeth Schafer and Brian Woolland (eds) *Ben Jonson and Theatre: Performance, Practice, and Theory* (London: Routledge, 1999).

Chamberlain, Robert. *The Swaggering Damsell* (London: Thomas Cotes, 1640).

Chapman, George. *Monsieur D'Oliue A comedie* (London: T.C., 1606).

_____ *The conspiracie, and tragedie of Charles Duke of Byron, Marshall of France* (London: G. Eld, 1608).

Chettle, Henry. *The tragedy of Hoffman or A reuenge for a father* (London: I[ohn] N[orton], 1631).

Cooke, John. *Greenes Tu quoque, or, The cittie gallant* (London: Iohn Trundle, 1614).

_____ *Greene's Tu quoque, or, The cittie gallant*, ed. Alan J. Berman (New York: Garland, 1984).

Cope, Jackson I. *The Theater and the Dream: From Metaphor to Form in Renaissance Drama* (Baltimore: Johns Hopkins University Press, 1973).

Cornwallis, William. *Essayes. By Sr William Corne-Waleys the younger, Knight* (London: Edmund Mattes, 1600–1601).

D., J. *The knave in graine, new vampt A witty comedy* (London: J.O., 1640).

Daborne, Robert. *A Christian turn'd Turke: or, The tragicall liues and deaths of the two famous pyrates, Ward and Dansiker* (London: William Barrenger, 1612).

Daniel, Samuel. *Hymens triumph A pastorall tragicomaedie* (London: Francis Constable, 1615).

Davenant, Sir William. *The triumphs of the Prince d'Amour A masque presented by His Highnesse at his pallace in the Middle Temple, the 24th of Februarie 1635* (London: Richard Meighen, 1635).

_____ *The vnfortvnate lovers a tragedie* (London: R.H., 1643).

_____ *The works of Sr. William Davenant, Kt.* (London: T.N., 1673).

Davis, Lloyd. "Embodied Masculinity in Shakespeare's *Julius Caesar*", *EnterText*, 3:1 (2003): 161–82, at http://people.brunel.ac.uk/~acsrrrm/entertext/3_1_pdfs/davis.pdf

Dawson, Anthony, and Paul Yachnin. *The Culture of Playgoing in Shakespeare's England: A Collaborative Debate* (Cambridge: Cambridge University Press, 2001).

Debax, Jean-Paul. "*Oh, oh, oh, Ah, ah, ah*: The Meanings of Laughter in the Interludes", in Roberta Mullini (ed.), *Tudor Theatre: For laughs (?)/Pour rire: Puzzling Laughter in Plays of the Tudor Age/Rires et problèmes dans le théâtre des Tudors* (Bern: Peter Lang, 2002), 81–93.

Dekker, Thomas. *If it be not good, the Diuel is in it* (London: I.T., 1612).

_____ *Satiro–mastix. Or The vntrussing of the humorous poet* (London: Edward White, 1602).

_____ *The Dramatic Works of Thomas Dekker*, ed. Fredson Bowers, 4 vols (Cambridge: Cambridge University Press, 1953–61).

_____ *The guls horne-booke* (London: R.S., 1609).

_____ *The pleasant comedie of old Fortunatus* (London: William Aspley, 1600).

_____ *The pleasant comodie of patient Grisill* (London: Henry Rocket, 1603).

Della Casa, Giovanni. *Galateo of Maister Iohn Della Casa, Archebishop of Beneuenta*, trans. Robert Petersen (London: Raufe Newbery, 1576).

Dessen, Alan C. *Recovering Shakespeare's Theatrical Vocabulary* (Cambridge: Cambridge University Press, 1995).

_____, and Leslie Thomson. *A Dictionary of Stage Directions in English Drama 1580–1642* (Cambridge: Cambridge University Press, 1999).

Dick, A.L. *Paideia Through Laughter: Jonson's Aristophanic Appeal to Human Intelligence* (The Hague: Mouton, 1974).

Digby, Kenelm. *A late discourse made in a solemne assembly of nobles and learned men at Montpellier in France touching the cure of wounds by the powder of sympathy* (London: R. Lownes, 1658).

Döring, Tobias. *"How to do things with tears*: Trauer spielen auf der Shakespeare-Bühne", *Poetica*, 33:3/4 (2001): 355–89.

Dryden, John. *Of dramatick poesie, an essay* (London: Henry Herringman, 1668).

Dutton, Richard. "The Lone Wolf: Jonson's Epistle to *Volpone*", in Julie Sanders, Kate Chedgzoy and Susan Wiseman (eds), *Refashioning Ben Jonson: Gender, Politics and the Jonsonian Canon* (London: Macmillan, 1999), 114–33.

Evans, Robert C. "'This Art Will Live': Social and Literary Responses to Ben Jonson's *The New Inn*", in Claude J. Summers and Ted-Larry Pebworth (eds), *Literary Circles and Cultural Communities in Renaissance England* (Missouri: University of Missouri Press, 2001), 75–91.

Farley-Hills, David. *The Comic in Renaissance Comedy* (London: Macmillan, 1981).

Farquhar, George. *Love and a bottle a comedy* (London: Richard Standfast, 1699).

Field, Nathan. *A woman is a weather-cocke A new comedy* (London: John Budge, 1612).

Fletcher, Angus. "Jonson's Satiric-Comedy and the Unsnarling of the Satyr from the Satirist", *Ben Jonson Journal*, 6 (1999): 247–69.

Fletcher, John. *The night-walker, or The little theife A comedy* (London: Thomas Cotes, 1640).

Folkerth, Wes. *The Sound of Shakespeare* (London: Routledge, 2002).

Ford, John. *The chronicle historie of Perkin Warbeck A strange truth* (London: Hugh Beeston, 1634).

_____ *'Tis pitty shee's a whore* (London: Nicholas Okes, 1633).

Fudge, Erica, Susan Wiseman and Ruth Gilbert (eds). *At the Borders of the Human: Beasts, Bodies and Natural Philosophy in the Early Modern Period* (London: Palgrave, 2002).

Fulwell, Ulpian. *A pleasant enterlude, intituled, Like will to like quoth the Deuill to the collier* (London: Edward Allde, 1587).

Galbraith, David. "Theories of comedy", in Alexander Leggatt (ed.), *The Cambridge Companion to Shakespearean Comedy* (Cambridge: Cambridge University Press, 2002), 3–17.

Gascoigne, George. *The glasse of gouernement A tragicall comedie* (London: C. Barker, [1575]).

Gayton, Edmund. *Pleasant Notes Upon Don Quixote* (London: William Hunt, 1654).

George, David. "Early Cast Lists for Two Beaumont and Fletcher Plays", *Theatre Notebook*, 38 (1974): 9–11.

Ghose, Indira. "Laughter and Blasphemy in the Shakespearean Theater", *Medieval and Renaissance Drama in England*, 16 (2003): 228–39.

_____ "Licence to Laugh: Festive Laughter in *Twelfth Night*" in Manfred Pfister (ed.), *A History of English Laughter: Laughter from "Beowulf" to Beckett and Beyond* (Amsterdam: Rodopi, 2002), 35–46.

Goffe, Thomas. *The careles shepherdess a tragi-comedy* (London: Richard Rogers and William Ley, 1656).

Goldberg, Jonathan. "Making Sense", in Levin, Richard A. *Looking for an Argument: Critical Encounters with the New Approaches to the Criticism of Shakespeare and his Contemporaries* (London: Associated University Presses, 2003), 94–100.

Gomersall, Robert. *The Tragedie of Lodouick Sforza* (London: n.p., 1628).

Gosson, Stephen. *Playes confuted in fiue actions* (London: Thomas Gosson, [1582]).

Greene, Robert. *The Historie of Orlando Furioso* (London: John Danter, 1594).

_____ (attr. T.G.) *The tragedy of Selimus Emperour of the Turkes. Written T.G.* (London: Iohn Crooke and Richard Serger, 1638).

Greg, W.W. *Dramatic Documents from the Elizabethan Playhouses*, 2 vols (Oxford: Clarendon Press, 1931).

Gum, Coburn S. *The Aristophanic Comedies of Ben Jonson* (The Hague: Mouton, 1972).

Gurr, Andrew. *Playgoing in Shakespeare's London* (Cambridge: Cambridge University Press, 1987; 3rd edn, 2004).

_____ *The Shakespearean Stage, 1574–1642*, 3rd edn (Cambridge: Cambridge University Press, 1992).

_____, and Mariko Ichikawa. *Staging in Shakespeare's Theatres* (Oxford: Oxford University Press, 2002).

H., I. *This Worlds Folly Or A warning-peece discharged vpon the wickednesse thereof* (London: William Jaggard, 1615).

Haarberg, Jon. *Parody and the Praise of Folly* (Oslo: Scandinavian University Press, 1998).

Habington, William. *The Queene of Arragon A tragi-comedie* (London: Thomas Cotes, 1640).

Hagen, Tanya. "An English Renaissance Understanding of the Word 'Tragedy'" *Early Modern Literary Studies*, Special Issue 1 (1997): 5.1–30, at http://purl.oclc.org/emls/si-01/si-01hagen.html

Hall, Joseph. *Virgidemiarum sixe bookes. First three bookes, of tooth-lesse satyrs* (London: Thomas Creede, 1597).

_____ *Virgidemiarum sixe bookes. The three last bookes* (London: Richard Bradocke, 1598).

Happé, Peter. "Jonson's On-stage Audiences: *Spectaret populum ludis attentius ipsis*", *Ben Jonson Journal*, 10 (2003): 23–41.

Hara, Eiichi. "The Absurd Vision of Elizabethan Crime Drama: *A Warning for Fair Women, Two Lamentable Tragedies*, and *Arden of Faversham*", *Shiron*, 38 (1999): 1–36.

Harvey, Gabriel. *A New Letter of Notable Contents* (London: John Wolfe, 1593).

Hausted, Peter. *The rivall friends A comoedie.* (London: Humphrey Robinson, 1632).

Hawkes, Terence (ed.). *Alternative Shakespeares Volume 2* (London: Routledge, 1996).

Helgerson, Richard. *Forms of Nationhood: The Elizabethan Writing of England* (Chicago: Chicago University Press, 1992).

Heminges, William. *The fatal contract, a French tragedy* (London: J.M., 1653).

Herrick, Marvin T. *Comic Theory in the Sixteenth Century* (1950; Urbana: University of Illinois Press, 1964).

Heywood, Thomas. *A woman kilde with kindnesse* (London: William Iaggard, 1607).

_____ *Loves maistresse: or, The Queens masque* (London: Robert Raworth, 1636).

_____ *The English traueller As it hath beene publikely acted at the Cock-pit in Drury-lane* (London: Robert Raworth, 1633).

_____ *The first and second partes of King Edward the Fourth* (London: F.K., 1600).

_____ *The second part of, If you know not me, you know no bodie* (London: Nathaniell Butter, 1606).

_____ *The siluer age* (London: Nicholas Okes, 1613).

_____ *The wise-woman of Hogsdon A comedie* (London: Henry Shephard, 1638).

Hooley, Daniel. "Horace's Rud(e)-imentary Muse: *Sat.* 1.2", *Electronic Antiquity*, 5:2 (October, 1999), at http://scholar.lib.vt.edu/ejournals/ElAnt/V5N2/hooley.html

Hoy, Cyrus. *Introductions, Notes and Commentaries to Texts in 'The Dramatic Works of Thomas Dekker'*, 4 vols (Cambridge: Cambridge University Press, 1980).

Ichikawa, Mariko. *Shakespearean Entrances* (Basingstoke: Palgrave Macmillan, 2002).

Ingelend, Thomas. *A pretie and mery new enterlude: called the Disobedient child* (London: Thomas Crolwell, [?1570]).

Jonson, Ben. *Ben Jonson*, ed. C.H. Herford, Percy Simpson and Evelyn Simpson, 11 vols (Oxford: Clarendon Press, 1925–52).

_____ *Epicene*, ed. Richard Dutton (Manchester: Manchester University Press, 2004).

_____ *Every Man In his Humour*, ed. Robert Miola (Manchester: Manchester University Press, 2000).

_____ *Four Comedies*, ed. Helen Ostovich (London: Longman, 1996).

Jordan, Thomas. *The walks of Islington and Hogsdon, with the humours of Woodstreet-compter* (London: Thomas Wilson, 1657).

Joseph, B.L. *Elizabethan Acting*, 2nd edn (Oxford: Oxford University Press, 1964).

Joubert, Laurent. *Treatise on Laughter*, trans. Gregory David de Rocher (Alabama: Alabama University Press, 1980).

Kay, Dennis. *Melodious Tears: The English Funeral Elegy from Spenser to Milton* (Oxford: Clarendon Press, 1990).

Killigrew, Thomas. *The prisoners and Claracilla two tragae-comedies* (London: T. Cotes, 1641).

_____ *Thomaso*, in *Comedies and Tragedies written by Thomas Killigrew* (London: Henry Herringman, 1664).

Kinney, Arthur. *Markets of Bawdry: The Dramatic Criticism of Stephen Gosson* (Salzburg: Universität Salzburg, 1974).

Kirke, John. *The seven champions of Christendome* (London: I. Okes, 1638).

Knowles, Ronald (ed.). *Shakespeare and Carnival: After Bakhtin* (Basingstoke: Palgrave, 2001).

Knutson, Roslyn L. "Filling Fare: The Appetite for Current Issues and Traditional Forms in the Repertory of the Chamberlain's Men", *Medieval and Renaissance Drama in England*, 15 (2002): 57–76.

Kyd, Thomas. *The Spanish tragedie containing the lamentable end of Don Horatio, and Bel-imperia* (London: Edward Allde, 1592).

Lange, Marjory E. *Telling Tears in the English Renaissance* (Leiden: Brill, 1996).

Laroque, Francois. "Shakespeare's Festive Comedies", in Richard Dutton and Jean E. Howard (eds), *A Companion to Shakespeare's Works: The Comedies* (Oxford: Blackwell, 2003), 23–46.

Leggatt, Alexander. *Jacobean Public Theatre* (London: Routledge, 1992).

Leishman, J.B. (ed.). *The Three Parnassus Plays (1598–1601)* (London: Ivor Nicholson & Watson Ltd, 1949).

Levin, Kate D. "Playing with Lyly: Theatrical Criticism and Non-Shakespearean drama", *Research Opportunities in Renaissance Drama*, 40 (2001): 25–54

Levin, Richard A. *Looking for an Argument: Critical Encounters with the New Approaches to the Criticism of Shakespeare and his Contemporaries* (London: Associated University Presses, 2003).

_____ "The Proof of the Parody", *Essays in Criticism*, 24 (1974): 312–16.

_____ "The Relation of External Evidence to the Allegorical and Thematic Interpretation of Shakespeare", *Shakespeare Studies*, 13 (1980): 1–30.

Lodge, Thomas, and Robert Greene. *A looking glasse for London and England* (London: Thomas Creede, 1594).

Lopez, Jeremy. *Theatrical Convention and Audience Response in Early Modern Drama* (Cambridge: Cambridge University Press, 2003).

Lower, William. *The Phaenix in her flames* (London: Thomas Harper, 1639).

Lyly, John. *Campaspe: Sappho and Phao*, eds David Bevington and G.K. Hunter (Manchester: Manchester University Press, 1999).

_____ *Sappho and Phao played beefore the Queenes Maiestie on Shroue-tewsday by Her Maiesties children and the boyes of Paules* (London: Thomas Cadman, 1584).

McJannet, Linda. *The Voice of Stage Directions: The Evolution of a Theatrical Code* (Newark: University of Delaware Press, 1999).

Mann, David. *The Elizabethan Player: Contemporary Stage Representation* (London: Routledge, 1991).

Manning, John. "Whitney's *Choice of Emblems*: A Reassessment", *Renaissance Studies*, 4 (1990): 155–200.

Manuche, Cosmo. *The Bastard: A Tragedy* (London: M. M., 1652).

Markham, Gervase, and William Sampson. *The true tragedy of Herod and Antipater with the death of faire Marriam* (London: G. Eld, 1622).

Marlowe, Christopher. *The troublesome raigne and lamentable death of Edward the second* (London: William Jones, 1594).

Marston, John. *Antonios reuenge. The second part* (London: Thomas Fisher, 1602).
_____ *Iacke Drums entertainment: or The comedie of Pasquill and Katherine* (London: Richard Olive, 1601).
_____ *What You Will* (London: G. Eld, 1601).
Massinger, Philip. *The Roman actor A tragaedie.* (London: B.A. and T.F., 1629).
May, Thomas. *The Heire* (London: B.A., 1622).
Middleton, Thomas. *A mad world, my masters.* (London: Walter Burre, 1608).
_____ "In the just worth of that well deserver, Mr John Webster, and upon this Masterpiece of tragedy", in John Webster, *The tragedy of the Dutchesse of Malfy* (1623).
_____ *The Mayor of Quinborough* (London: Henry Herringman, 1661).
_____ *The widdow a comedie* (London: Humphrey Moseley, 1652).
_____ *Women Beware Women*, in *Two New Playes* (London: Humphrey Moseley, 1657).
_____, and Thomas Dekker. *The roaring girle. Or Moll Cut-Purse* (London: Thomas Archer, 1611).
_____, and William Rowley. *The changeling.* (London: Humphrey Moseley, 1653).
Milhous, Judith, and Robert D. Hume. "New Light on English Acting Companies in 1646, 1648, and 1660", *Review of English Studies*, 42 (1991): 487–509.
Milton, John. *Paradise Lost*, ed. Alistair Fowler, 2nd edn (London: Longman, 1998).
Moisan, Thomas. "'The King's Second Coming': Theater, Politics, and Textualizing the 'Times' in the Dedicatory Poems to the 1647 Folio of Beaumont and Fletcher", in Moisan and Douglas Bruster (eds), *In the Company of Shakespeare: Essays in English Renaissance Literature in Honour of G. Blakemore Evans* (Madison: Farleigh Dickinson University Press, 2002), 270–91.
Montaigne, Michel de. *Essays written in French by Michael Lord of Montaigne*, trans. John Florio, 3 vols (London: Melch. Bradwood, 1613).
Mullini, Roberta (ed.). *Tudor Theatre: For laughs (?)/Pour rire (?): Puzzling Laughter in Plays of the Tudor Age/Rires et problèmes dans le théâtre des Tudors* (Bern: Peter Lang, 2002).
Munday, Anthony, and Robert Chettle. *The death of Robert, Earle of Huntington* (London: William Leake, 1601).
Munro, Lucy. "A Neglected Allusion to *Pericles* and *Hengist King of Kent* in Performance", *Notes and Queries*, 249 (2004): 307–10.
_____ *Children of the Queen's Revels: A Jacobean Theatre Repertory* (Cambridge: Cambridge University Press, 2005).
Nabbes, Thomas. *Totenham Court A pleasant comedie* (London: Richard Ovlton, 1638).
Nashe, Thomas. *The Works of Thomas Nashe*, ed. Ronald B. McKerrow, rev. F.P. Wilson, 5 vols (Oxford: Clarendon Press, 1958).
Neill, Michael. "'Amphitheatres in the Body': Playing with Hands on the Shakespearean Stage", in *Putting History to the Question: Power, Politics, and Society in English Renaissance Drama* (New York: Columbia University Press, 2000), 167–203.
Nungezer, Edwin. *A Dictionary of Actors and of Other Persons Associated with the Public Representation of Plays in England before 1642* (1929; New York: AMS Press, 1971).

Oxford Dictionary of National Biography, at http://www.oxforddnb.com

Oxford English Dictionary, at http://www.oed.com

Paster, Gail Kern. "Leaky Vessels: The Incontinent Women of Jacobean City Comedy", *Renaissance Drama*, n.s., 18 (1987): 71–86.

_____ "Melancholy Cats, Lugged Bears, and Early Modern Cosmology: Reading Shakespeare's Psychological Materialism across the Species Barrier", in Paster, Katherine Rowe and Mary Floyd-Wilson (eds), *Reading the Early Modern Passions: Essays in the Cultural History of Emotion* (Philadelphia: University of Pennsylvania Press, 2004), 113–29.

_____, Katherine Rowe and Mary Floyd-Wilson (eds). *Reading the Early Modern Passions: Essays in the Cultural History of Emotion* (Philadelphia: University of Pennsylvania Press, 2004).

Patrides, C.A. "Shakespeare: The Comedy Beyond Comedy", in Claude J. Summers and Ted-Larry Pebworth (eds), *Figures in a Renaissance Context* (Ann Arbor: University of Michigan Press, 1989), 47–73.

Pfister, Manfred (ed.) *A History of English Laughter: Laughter from "Beowulf" to Beckett and Beyond* (Amsterdam: Rodopi, 2002).

Pikli, Natália. "The Crossing Point of Tears and Laughter, A Tragic Farce: Shakespeare's *Titus Andronicus*", *AnaChronist* (2000): 51–69.

Playfere, Thomas. *The whole sermons of that eloquent diuine, of famous memory; Thomas Playfere* (London: T.S., 1623).

Pollard, Tanya. *Drugs and Theater in Early Modern England* (Cambridge: Cambridge University Press, 2004).

Prescott, Anne Lake. "The Ambivalent Heart: Thomas More's Merry Tales", *Criticism*, 45:4 (2003): 417–33.

Preston, Thomas. *A lamentable tragedy mixed ful of pleasant mirth, conteyning the life of Cambises king of Percia* [London: Iohn Allde, 1570?].

Prynne, William. *Histrio-mastix, The Player's Scourge, or actors tragaedie* (London: Michael Sparke, 1633).

Quarles, Francis. *Diuine Poems* (London: M.F., 1633).

R[owley], S[amuel]. *The Noble Spanish Souldier* (London: Nicholas Vavasour, 1634).

Rainoldes, John. *Th'overthrow of stage-playes, by the way of controversie betwixt D. Gager and D. Rainoldes* ([Middleburg]: [Richard Schilders], 1599).

Randolph, Thomas. *Aristippus, or, The Ioviall philosopher presented in a priuate shew: to which is added, The conceited pedler* (London: Robert Allot, 1630).

_____ *Poems with the Muses looking-glasse: and Amyntas* (Oxford: Leonard Lichfield, 1638).

Reiss, Timothy J. "Renaissance Theatre and the Theory of Tragedy", in Glyn P. Norton (ed.), *The Cambridge History of Literary Criticism: The Renaissance* (Cambridge: Cambridge University Press, 1999), 229–47.

Richman, David. *Laughter, Pain, and Wonder: Shakespeare's Comedies and the Audience in the Theatre* (Newark: University of Delaware Press, 1990).

Roston, Murray. "*Volpone*: Comedy or Mordant Satire?", *Ben Jonson Journal*, 10 (2003): 1–22.

Ruggles, George. *Ignoramus a comedy as it was several times acted with extraordinary applause before the Majesty of King James*, trans. R[obert] Codrington (London: W. Gilbertson, 1662).

Rupp, Suzanne. "Milton's Laughing God", in Manfred Pfister (ed.), *A History of English Laughter: Laughter from "Beowulf" to Beckett and Beyond* (Amsterdam: Rodopi, 2002), 47–56.

Rutter, Carol Chillington. "Looking Like a Child – or – *Titus*: The Comedy", *Shakespeare Survey*, 56 (2003): 1–27.

Rymer, Thomas. *A Short View of Tragedy* (London: Richard Baldwin, 1693).

_____ *The tragedies of the last age consider'd and examin'd by the practice of the ancients and by the common sense of all ages* (London: Richard Tonson, 1678).

Salgādo, Gāmini (ed.). *Eyewitnesses of Shakespeare* (London: Sussex University Press, 1975).

Sanders, Julie. "Beggars' Commonwealths and the Pre-Civil War Stage: Suckling's *The Goblins*, Richard Brome's *A Jovial Crew*, and James Shirley's *The Sisters*", *Modern Language Review*, 97 (2002): 1–14.

Screech, M.A. *Laughter at the Foot of the Cross* (Harmondsworth: Penguin, 1999).

Shakespeare, William. *Cymbeline*, ed. Roger Warren (Oxford: Clarendon Press, 1998).

_____ *Hamlet*, ed. Harold Jenkins (London: Arden, 1996).

_____ *King Lear*, ed. R.A. Foakes (London: Arden, 1997).

_____ *The Complete Works of Shakespeare*, 5th edn, ed. David Bevington (New York: Pearson, 2004).

_____ *Troilus and Cressida,* ed. Kenneth Muir (1982; Oxford: Oxford University Press, 1994).

_____, and John Fletcher. *Henry VIII*, ed. John Margeson (Cambridge: Cambridge University Press, 1990).

Sharpham, Edward. *Cupids whirligig As it hath bene sundry times acted by the Children of the Kings Majesties Reuels*. (London: E. Allde, 1607).

Sheridan, Richard Brinsley. *The Critic*, in Lewis Gibbs (ed.), *Sheridan's Plays* (1906; London: Dent, 1960).

Shirley, James. *The ball A comedy* (London: Tho. Cotes, 1639).

Sidnell, M.J. (ed.). *Sources of Dramatic Theory* (Cambridge: Cambridge University Press, 1991).

Sidney, Sir Philip. *The Defence of Poesy*, in Katherine Duncan-Jones (ed.), *Sir Philip Sidney* (Oxford: Clarendon Press, 1989).

Skinner, Quentin. "Hobbes and the Classical Theory of Laughter", in Tom Sorell and Luc Foisneau (eds), *Leviathan after 350 Years* (Oxford: Clarendon Press, 2004), 139–66.

Smith, Bruce R. *The Acoustic World of Early Modern England: Attending to the O-factor* (Chicago: University of Chicago Press, 1999).

Somerset, J. Alan B. *Records of Early English Drama: Shropshire*, 2 vols (Toronto: Toronto University Press, 1994).

Steggle, Matthew. "*Greenes* Baboone: Thomas Greene, Baboon Impersonator?", *Theatre Notebook*, 60 (2006): 72–5.

_____ (ed.). *Listening to the Early Modern, Early Modern Literary Studies*, 7:1 / Special Issue 8 (2001), at http://purl.org/emls/07-1/07-1toc.htm

_____ *Richard Brome: Place and Politics on the Caroline Stage* (Manchester: Manchester University Press, 2004).

Stephens, John. *Essayes and characters, ironicall, and instructiue* (London: E. Allde, 1615).

Stern, Tiffany. "'A small-beer health to his second day': Playwrights, Prologues, and First Performances in the Early Modern Theater", *Studies in Philology*, 101:2 (2004): 172–99.

_____ *Making Shakespeare: From Stage to Page* (London: Routledge, 2005).

_____ *Rehearsal from Shakespeare to Sheridan* (Oxford: Clarendon Press, 2000).

Stern, Virginia F. *Gabriel Harvey: His Life, Marginalia and Library* (Oxford: Clarendon Press, 1979).

Strode, William. *The floating island a tragi-comedy, acted before his Majesty at Oxford, Aug. 29. 1636. by the students of Christ-Church* (London: H. Twiford, 1655).

Suckling, Sir John. *Aglaura.* (London: John Haviland, 1638).

Swiss, Margo, and David A. Kent (eds). *Speaking Grief in English Literary Culture: Shakespeare to Milton* (Pittsburgh: Duquesne University Press, 2003).

Tatham, John. *Knavery in all trades, or, The coffee-house a comedy* (London: J.B., 1664).

Teague, Frances N. (ed.). *Acting Funny: Comic Theory and Practice in Shakespeare's Plays* (Cranbury, NJ: Associated University Presses, 1994).

Thomas, Keith. "The Place of Laughter in Tudor and Stuart England", *Times Literary Supplement* (21 January 21): 77–81.

Thomson, Peter. "Richard Tarlton and his Legend", in Edward J. Esche (ed.), *Shakespeare and his Contemporaries in Performance* (Aldershot: Ashgate, 2000), 191–210.

Tomkis, Thomas. *Albumazar A comedy presented before the Kings Maiestie at Cambridge, the ninth of March. 1614* (London: Nicholas Okes, 1615).

_____ *Lingua: or The combat of the tongue, and the fiue senses for superiority* (London: G. Eld, 1607).

Vaught, Jennifer C. "Men Who Weep and Wail: Masculinity and Emotion in Sidney's *New Arcadia*", *Literature Compass*, 3 (2005) n.p., online at http://www.Literature-compass.com/viewpoint.asp?section=2&ref=460

Wager, W. *A comedy or enterlude intituled, Inough is as good as a feast* (London: John Allde, 1570).

Wanley, Nathaniel. *The Wonders of the Little World* (London: T. Basset, 1673).

Weever, John. *The mirror of martyrs, or The life and death of that thrice valiant capitaine, and most godly martyre Sir Iohn Old-castle knight Lord Cobham* ([London]: William Wood, 1601).

Whetstone, George. *The right excellent and famous historye, of Promos and Cassandra* [London: Richarde Ihones, 1578].

White, Martin. *Renaissance Drama in Action: An Introduction to Aspects of Theatre Practice and Performance* (London: Routledge, 1998).

Whitney, Charles. *Early Responses to Renaissance Drama* (Cambridge: Cambridge University Press, 2006).

Wiles, David. *Shakespeare's Clown: Actor and Text in the Elizabethan Playhouse* (Cambridge: Cambridge University Press, 1987).

Woolland, Brian (ed.). *Jonsonians* (Aldershot: Ashgate, 2003).

Wright, Thomas. *The passions of the minde in generall. Corrected, enlarged, and with sundry new discourses augmented* (London: Valentine Simmes, 1604).

Yarington, Robert. *Two Lamentable Tragedies* (London: Matthew Law, 1601).

Index